Reading
EXPLORER 5

Nancy Douglas • Helen Huntley
Bruce Rogers

HEINLE
CENGAGE Learning™

Australia • Brazil • Japan • Korea • Mexico • Singapore • Spain • United Kingdom • United States

HEINLE
CENGAGE Learning™

Reading Explorer 5
Nancy Douglas, Helen Huntley, and Bruce Rogers

VP and Director of Operations: Vincent Grosso
Publisher: Andrew Robinson
Executive Editor: Sean Bermingham
Senior Development Editor: Derek Mackrell
Assistant Editor: Claire Tan
Senior Technology Development Manager: Debie Mirtle
Associate Technology Project Manager: Melissa Skepko
Director of Global Marketing: Ian Martin
Director of US Marketing: Jim McDonough
Content Project Manager: Tan Jin Hock
Senior Print Buyer: Mary Beth Hennebury
National Geographic Coordinator: Leila Hishmeh
Cover/Text Designer: Page 2, LLC
Compositor: Page 2, LLC
Cover Images: (Top: London Eye) Richard Nowitz/National Geographic Image Collection, (bottom: Sri Lankan fishermen) Steve McCurry/National Geographic Image Collection

Credits appear on page 256, which constitutes a continuation of the copyright page.

Acknowledgments
The Author and Publishers would like to thank the following teaching professionals for their valuable feedback during the development of this series.

Jamie Ahn, English Coach, Seoul; **Heidi Bundschoks**, ITESM, Sinaloa México; **José Olavo de Amorim**, Colégio Bandeirantes, São Paulo; **Marina Gonzalez**, Instituto Universitario de Lenguas Modernas Pte., Buenos Aires; **Tsung-Yuan Hsiao**, National Taiwan Ocean University, Keelung; **Michael Johnson**, Muroran Institute of Technology; **Thays Ladosky**, Colégio Damas, Recife; **Ahmed Mohamed Motala**, University of Sharjah; **Mae-Ran Park**, Pukyong National University, Busan; **David Persey**, British Council, Bangkok; **David Schneer**, ACS International, Singapore; **Atsuko Takase**, Kinki University, Osaka; **Deborah E. Wilson**, American University of Sharjah

Additional thanks to Rachel Love, Jim McClelland, and Jim Burch at National Geographic Society.

This series is dedicated to the memory of Joe Dougherty, who was a constant inspiration throughout its development.

For permission to use material from this text or product, submit all requests online at **www.cengage.com/permissions**
Further permissions questions can be emailed to
permissionrequest@cengage.com

Student Book ISBN-13: 978-1-111-35602-6
Student Book ISBN-10: 1-111-35602-5
Student Book + Student CD-ROM ISBN-13: 978-1-111-35600-2
Student Book + Student CD-ROM ISBN-10: 1-111-35600-9
Student Book (US edition) ISBN-13: 978-1-111-82796-0
Student Book (US edition) ISBN-10: 1-111-82796-6

Heinle
20 Channel Center Street
Boston, Massachusetts 02210
USA

Cengage Learning is a leading provider of customized learning solutions with office locations around the globe, including Singapore, the United Kingdom, Australia, Mexico, Brazil, and Japan. Locate your local office at: **international.cengage.com/region**

Cengage Learning products are represented in Canada by Nelson Education, Ltd.

Visit Heinle online at **elt.heinle.com**
Visit our corporate website at **www.cengage.com**

Printed in the United States of America
1 2 3 4 5 6 7 – 15 14 13 12 11

Contents

Get ready to Explore Your World!

A woman from **Tennessee** can control a robotic arm directly from her brain. How does she do it? **p. 129**

The glaciers on the **Canada-U.S.** border are disappearing. Will Glacier Park soon have to change its name? **p. 112**

Over 50% of people in the **U.S.** suffer from some form of allergy. Why are allergies so widespread? **p. 50**

In February 2009, a U.S. jet crashed after taking off from **Newark**. Was lack of sleep responsible? **p. 191**

NORTH AMERICA

In 2004, archaeologist Christina Conlee made a grim discovery in southern **Peru**. What did she find? **p. 11**

SOUTH AMERICA

Astronomers are using a telescope in **Chile** to answer the mysteries of the universe. What do they hope to find? **p. 27**

Ants from **Argentina** are helping a U.S. distribution company improve its productivity. How? **p. 139**

Germany is a world leader in alternative energy. What is the secret of its success? **p. 88**

In Lovozero, **Russia**, children are deliberately exposed to ultraviolet light. Why? **p. 104**

The ancient city of Babylon in **Iraq** was one of the Seven Wonders of the World. Is anything left of it today? **p. 174**

EUROPE

AFRICA

ASIA

Phonetic written symbols reached **Japan** and **Korea** in the ninth and fifteenth centuries. How did they get there? **p. 165**

One of the most powerful leaders in history ruled from **Constantinople** (modern-day Istanbul). Who was he? **p. 201**

In **Sumbawa, Indonesia**, a volcano has been turned into a giant pit. Why? **p. 230**

AUSTRALIA

An island off the coast of **South Africa** is known as the "Island of Exiles." Why? **p. 240**

Tutankhamun's tomb is world famous. But which tomb in Egypt's **Valley of the Kings** was the greatest? **p. 58**

Millions of people head each year to a town in **Yunnan province**, China. What are they searching for? **p. 72**

ANTARCTICA

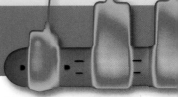

Scope and Sequence

Unit	Theme	Lesson	Strategy Focus	Vocabulary Building	Video
1	Collapse	**A:** Lost Civilizations: *Spirits in the Sand* **B:** An Empire's Fall: *The Collapse of Angkor*	Description and Visualization Matching Ideas and Sources	Word Partnership: *intrinsic* Word Partnership: *promote*	**Temples in the Jungle**
2	Beyond Earth	**A:** Seeing Further: *Cosmic Vision* **B:** Planet Hunters: *Are We Alone?*	Understanding Sequences Understanding Cause/Effect Relationships	Word Link: *trans-* Word Link: *in-*	**Comet Watchers**
3	Health and Genes	**A:** Human Heart: *Mending Broken Hearts* **B:** Tiny Invaders: *The War on Allergies*	Scanning for Details Using Concept Maps	Usage: *exacerbate* vs. *compound* Thesaurus: *release*	**Fighting Malaria**
Reading Extension	Valley of the Kings	**World Heritage Spotlight:** Ancient Thebes with Its Necropolis – Egypt	**A Global View:** Health and Mortality	Word Link: *trans-* Definitions: *volume*	
4	Tradition and Change	**A:** City Under Seige: *Vanishing Venice* **B:** Lost Horizons: *Searching for Shangri-La*	Understanding Figurative Language Understanding Chronological Sequence	Usage: *complement* vs. *compliment* Word Partnership: *negotiate*	**The High Road to Shangri-La**
5	Eco-Living	**A:** Carbon Footprint: *It Starts at Home* **B:** Renewable Energy: *Plugging Into the Sun*	Distinguishing Main Ideas and Supporting Information Classifying Ideas	Word Partnership: *obstacle* Word Link: *sub-*	**Our Stormy Star**
6	Light	**A:** From Light to Sight: *What is Light?* **B:** Laser Technology: *Light Engineering*	Connecting People and Accomplishments Creating a Mental Map of a Text	Usage: *conscious* Usage: *medium*	**Lighting the Dark**
Reading Extension	Glacier Park	**World Heritage Spotlight:** Waterton-Glacier International Peace Park – USA/Canada	**A Global View:** Environmental Sustainability	Word Link: *circ/circum* Word Forms: noun/verb Word Partnership (review) Definitions: *conscious*	

Welcome to Reading Explorer!

A lost city in a remote jungle, a newly-discovered star that dwarfs our sun, a man with bionic legs who climbs mountains—these are just some of the fascinating worlds and remarkable people you'll encounter in *Reading Explorer 5*.

Each Unit in *Reading Explorer 5* contains two main reading passages based on authentic *National Geographic* articles, as well as a range of academic reading tasks. As you work through the passages and tasks, you'll develop strategies for previewing a text, tactics for decoding vocabulary (such as using context and identifying word parts), and essential reading and critical thinking skills such as identifying referencing and cohesion (how the parts of a text link together) and understanding rhetorical purpose (how an author achieves his or her meaning). You'll also expand your knowledge of academic vocabulary (a complete list is included at the end of this book).

The four *Reading Extension* sections provide additional reading and vocabulary practice in the context of important global issues and heritage sites. These require you to use visual and textual literacy skills to interpret information presented in a variety of formats—just as you would when you're reading an academic journal or web site.

Finally, you can explore the topics further—and continue to practice your reading, vocabulary, and viewing skills—using the interactive tasks on the Student CD-ROM.

We hope you will enjoy using *Reading Explorer 5*.

Now you're ready to **explore your world!**

UNIT 1
Collapse

Discuss these questions with a partner.

1. Can you name any societies or civilizations that were once powerful but no longer exist today?

2. Why do you think some societies and civilizations have not lasted?

3. What do you think are the main pressures affecting societies today?

▲ A carved face lies half-buried in vegetation at the site of the ancient city of Angkor, in present-day Cambodia.

9

1A

Nasca Lines

Lost Civilizations

▲ In the desert of southern Peru, thousands of giant figures are etched, or drawn, on the land—a spider (above), a monkey, and more. Known as the Nasca lines, many are hundreds of meters long and have inspired wonder since the first air travelers noticed them in the 1920s. Researchers have reconstructed how the lines were made (above right): By removing dark stones on the ground and exposing the lighter sand beneath, the Nasca created markings that lasted for centuries in the desert's arid climate.

Before You Read

A. Matching. The following water-related words and phrases appear in the reading about the Nasca on pages 11–13. Match each one with its definition.

arid	drainage system	drought	evaporation
irrigation	precipitation	water table	well

1. _____ an area, or basin, from which rainwater flows downhill into a river, sea, etc.
2. _____ supplying an area of land with water in order to help crops grow
3. _____ the change from a liquid to a gas usually caused by rising temperatures
4. _____ extremely dry, so that very few plants can grow
5. _____ a long period of time during which no rain falls
6. _____ a hole in the ground from which water is taken
7. _____ the upper limit in the ground that is saturated (filled) with water
8. _____ rain, snow, or hail

B. Skim and Predict. Skim the passage on pages 11–13, looking especially at the title, headings, photos, and the first sentence of each paragraph. Try to answer the question below. Then read the passage to check your ideas.

What was the main purpose of the Nasca lines?

Spirits in the Sand

Recent findings shed light on the lives—and mysterious disappearance—of the ancient Nasca.

▲ A Nasca geoglyph seen from the ground. Some of these giant lines carved into the desert sand were meant to be walked upon during religious ceremonies.

1   SINCE THEIR MYSTERIOUS DESERT drawings became widely known in the late 1920s, the people known as the Nasca have puzzled archaeologists, anthropologists,[1] and anyone else who is fascinated
5   by ancient cultures. Their elaborate lines and figures, called geoglyphs, are found distributed, seemingly at random, across the desert outside Nasca and the nearby town of Palpa. Waves of scientists—and amateurs—have come up with various interpretations
10   for the designs. At one time or another, they have been explained as Inca roads, irrigation plans, even, controversially, landing strips for alien spacecraft.

Since 1997, an ongoing Peruvian-German research collaboration called the Nasca-Palpa Project has been
15   putting these theories to the test. The leaders of the project are Johny Isla and Markus Reindel of the German Archaeological Institute. As well as studying where and how the Nasca lived, the researchers have investigated why they disappeared and the meaning
20   of the strange, abstract designs they left behind. If Isla and his colleagues are right, the story of Nasca begins, and ends, with water.

Living on the Edge

The coastal region of southern Peru and northern
25   Chile is one of the driest places on Earth. In the small, protected basin where the Nasca culture arose, ten rivers descend from the Andes. Most of these rivers are dry at least part of the year. Surrounded by a thousand shades of brown, these ten ribbons of
30   green offered a fertile spot for the emergence of an early civilization. "It was the perfect place for human settlement, because it had water," says geographer Bernhard Eitel, a member of the Nasca-Palpa Project. "But it was a very high-risk environment."

35   According to Eitel and his colleague Bertil Machtle, the micro-climate in the Nasca region has undergone considerable variation over the past 5,000 years. When a high-pressure system over central South America called the Bolivian High moves to the
40   north, more rain falls on the western slopes of the Andes. When the high shifts southward, precipitation decreases. This causes the rivers in the Nasca valleys to run dry.

Despite the risky conditions, the Nasca lived in the
45   area for eight centuries following their appearance in about 300 B.C. As the rainfall cycle continued, people moved east or west along the river valleys. In the arid southern valleys, early Nasca engineers devised practical ways of coping with the scarcity of water.
50   An ingenious system of horizontal wells tapped into the inclined water table as it descended from the Andean foothills. These irrigation systems, or puquios, allowed the Nasca to bring subterranean[2] water to the surface.

[1] An **anthropologist** is someone who studies people, society, and culture.
[2] If something is said to be **subterranean**, it is under the ground.

◀ A head jar found in a tomb beside a decapitated body at La Tiza. It would have been used in the Nasca's ritual sacrifices.

The Nasca brought ▶ *Spondylus* shells and other offerings to stone platforms in the desert, praying for water.

55 The Nasca people were in fact remarkably "green," perhaps because of the environmental challenges they faced. The creation of the puquios displayed a sophisticated sense of water conservation, since the underground aqueducts[3] minimized evaporation.
60 The farmers planted seeds by making a single hole in the ground rather than plowing, thereby preserving the substructure of the soil. The Nasca also recycled their garbage as building material. "It's a society that managed its resources very
65 well," says Isla. "This is what Nasca is all about."

Praying for Water

For centuries, Andean people have worshipped the gods of mountains that feed the Nasca drainage system. According to National Geographic explorer
70 Johan Reinhard, the Nasca have traditionally associated these mountains—mythologically, if not geologically—with water. Evidence for Reinhard's thesis came in 1986, when he found the
75 ruins of a ceremonial stone circle at the summit of Illakata, one of the region's tallest mountains.
80 Reinhard believes the Nasca lines were most likely related to worship of mountain gods, because of their connection to water.

Further evidence connecting Nasca rituals to water worship was revealed by the Nasca-Palpa Project
85 researchers in 2000. On a plateau[4] near the village of Yunama, Markus Reindel made an important discovery. As he was excavating a mound, he uncovered several broken pots and other relics that clearly represented ritual offerings. Then he came
90 upon pieces of a large seashell. It was of a genus[5] called *Spondylus*.

"The *Spondylus* shell is one of the few items of Andean archaeology that has been well studied," Reindel says. "It's a very important religious
95 symbol for water and fertility . . . It was brought from far away and is found in specific contexts, such as funerary objects and on these platforms. It was connected in certain activities to praying for water. And it's clear in this area, water was the
100 key issue."

In 2004, archaeologist Christina Conlee made a much grimmer discovery. Conlee was working at a site near a dry river valley in the southern Nasca region. While excavating a Nasca tomb, she
105 unearthed a skeleton. However, the first part to emerge from the dirt was not the skull, but the neck bones. "We could see the vertebrae[6] sitting on top," Conlee says. "The person was seated, with arms crossed and legs crossed, and no head."

The first part of the skeleton to emerge was not the skull, but the neck bones. "The person was seated, with arms crossed and legs crossed, and no head."

110 Cut marks on the neck bones indicate the head had probably been severed by a sharp knife. A ceramic pot known as a head jar rested against the elbow of the skeleton. An illustration on the jar showed a decapitated[7] "trophy head." Out of the head grew
115 a strange tree trunk with eyes.

[3] An **aqueduct** is a structure, often a bridge, that carries water.
[4] A **plateau** is a large area of high and fairly flat land.
[5] A **genus** is a class of similar things, especially a group of animals or plants that includes several closely related species.
[6] **Vertebrae** are the small circular bones that form the spine of a human being or animal.
[7] If someone is **decapitated**, their head is cut off.

Everything about the burial—the head jar, the placement and position of the body—suggests the body was disposed of in a careful manner. Conlee suspects the skeleton represents a ritual sacrifice.

120 "Although we find trophy heads spread throughout the Nasca period," she said, "there are some indications that they became more common in the middle and late period, and also at times of great environmental stress, perhaps drought. If this was a
125 sacrifice, it was made to appease[8] the gods, perhaps because of a drought or crop failure."

Beginning of the End

Despite their offerings, the Nasca's prayers would ultimately go unanswered. Water—or more precisely,
130 its absence—was increasingly critical in the Nasca's final years, between about A.D. 500 and 600.

In the Palpa area, scientists have traced the movement of the eastern margin of the desert about 19 kilometers (12 miles) up the valleys between
135 200 B.C. and A.D. 600. At one point, the desert reached an altitude of over 1,900 meters (6,500 feet). Similarly, the population centers around Palpa moved farther up the valleys, as if they were trying to outrun the arid conditions. "At the end of the sixth
140 century A.D.," Eitel and Mächtle conclude in a recent paper, "the aridity culminated[9] and the Nasca society collapsed."

Nevertheless, environmental stresses were not the only vital factor. "It wasn't just climate conditions
145 that caused the collapse of Nasca culture," emphasizes Johny Isla. "A state of crisis was provoked[10] because water was more prevalent in some valleys than in others, and the leaders of different valleys may have been in conflict."
150 By about A.D. 650, the more militaristic Wari (Huari) Empire had emerged from the central highlands and displaced the Nasca as the predominant culture in the southern desert region.

Almost 1,500 years later, the legacy of the Nasca lives
155 on. You can see it in the artifacts[11] of their ancient rituals, in the remains of their irrigation systems, and—most famously—in the lines of their mysterious desert designs. The lines surely provided a ritualistic reminder to the Nasca people that their fate was
160 intrinsically tied to their environment. In particular, the lines represent a bond with the Nasca's most precious resource, water. You can still read their

▲ Recent discoveries, such as these mummified remains of a parrot, monkey, and infant child, help us gain a clearer understanding of the lives of the Nasca people.

reverence for nature, in times of plenty and in times of desperate want, in every line and curve
165 they scratched onto the desert floor. And when your feet inhabit their sacred space, even for a brief and humbling moment, you can *feel* it.

[8] If you try to **appease** someone, you try to stop them from being angry at you by giving them what they want.
[9] If you say that an activity or process **culminates** in or with a particular event, you mean that the event happens at the end of it.
[10] If you **provoke** someone, you deliberately annoy them and try to make them behave aggressively. If something **provokes** a reaction, it causes the reaction.
[11] An **artifact** is an ornament, tool, or other object that is made by a human being, especially one that is historically or culturally interesting.

Reading Comprehension

A. Multiple Choice. Choose the best answer for each question.

1. The phrase *come up with* (line 9) is closest in meaning to _____.
  a. modified   b. thought of   c. looked over   d. rejected

2. What is true about the Nasca-Palpa project?
  a. It was the first group to discover the Nasca lines.
  b. It involves experts from more than one country.
  c. It has been researching the Nasca site since the 1920s.
  d. It consists of both professionals and amateurs.

3. Which of the following is most similar to the place where the Nasca lived?
  a. an area of farmland surrounded by a desert
  b. a single mountain standing on a flat plain
  c. an island circled by stormy seas
  d. a city surrounded by agricultural lands

4. The main purpose of paragraph 4 (lines 35–43) is to _____.
  a. provide support for the theory of Bernhard Eitel
  b. show why the Bolivian High sometimes moves north
  c. explain why the rivers in the Nasca region have run dry
  d. challenge the conclusions of the Nasca-Palpa research

5. The idea that the Nasca lines were related to the worship of gods living in the mountains was first supported by the discovery of _____.
  a. the pieces of a large seashell   c. a stone circle on Illakata
  b. broken pots near Yunama   d. a skeleton near a dry valley

6. Which of the following statements about the "head jar" first mentioned in paragraph 11 (from line 110) is definitely known to be true?
  a. When discovered, it contained the skull belonging to the skeleton.
  b. The people who buried the skeleton placed a small tree inside the jar.
  c. There was an image on the jar of an unusual tree growing from a head.
  d. It had been placed where the head of the skeleton had once been.

7. Which of the following is closest in meaning to this sentence from lines 150–153?
  By about A.D. 650, the more militaristic Wari (Huari) Empire had emerged from the central highlands and displaced the Nasca as the predominant culture in the southern desert region.
  a. By A.D. 650, the Wari (also known as the Huari) had become more aggressive than the Nasca and were able to invade the central highlands from the south.
  b. The warlike Wari (or Huari) Empire pushed out of its homeland in the central highlands and replaced the Nasca as the leading power in the south by around A.D. 650.
  c. Around A.D. 650, the hostile Wari (Huari) Empire took over the central highlands in much the same way that the Nasca had occupied the southern desert region centuries before.
  d. After the fall of the Nasca in A.D. 650, the Wari (also spelled Huari) came to power in the central highlands, which had previously been controlled by the Nasca.

8. Which of these statements would the author probably agree with?
  a. In many ways, the Nasca were responsible for their own decline.
  b. It is still possible to feel the presence of the Nasca in the land where they lived.
  c. After years of research, all the mysteries of the Nasca lines have finally been solved.
  d. Water was not as important to the culture of the Nasca as was once believed.

Descriptive writing is writing that appeals to the senses. It allows you to hear, smell, taste, feel, and especially see what the author is describing. One way to help you visualize something the author describes is to draw a simple diagram or sketch of the object.

B. Visualizing. Use the description below (adapted from information in paragraph 5) to draw a simple diagram of a *puquio*. Use arrows to point out important features of your drawing: the foothill, the water table, the well, and the flow of the water into the valley.

An ingenious system of horizontal wells, tapping into the sloping water table as it descends from the Andean foothills, allowed settlements to bring subterranean water to the surface. Known as *puquios*, these irrigation systems still water the southern valleys.

The author provides several other visual descriptions in the article. Find and sketch another object or situation that the author describes.

C. Critical Thinking. Discuss these questions with a partner.

1. The author says that the Nasca people seem to have been "remarkably 'green.'" What is meant by that? What evidence does the author provide that the Nasca were "green"?

2. Look again at the photo of the Nasca lines on page 10. What do you think is the best explanation for the purpose of these lines? Has reading this article changed your opinion?

3. Johny Isla talks about a "state of crisis" (line 146) caused by conflict over resources. Can you think of any recent situations that have similarities to the Nasca example?

Vocabulary Practice

A. Completion. Complete the information by circling the most appropriate word in each pair.

Climate Change Killed off Maya Civilization, Study Says

With their **1.** ingenious / prevalent architectural techniques and **2.** marginal / sophisticated concepts of astronomy and mathematics, the Maya were among the greatest of all ancient civilizations. At their peak, around A.D. 800, the Maya totaled 15 million people ranging from present-day Mexico to Honduras. Then, suddenly, their society collapsed, leaving cities deserted and immense pyramids in ruins. What caused the collapse of the Maya civilization?

Researchers now **3.** nevertheless / suspect that climate change is the answer. According to one study, a long period of dry climate, with three intense droughts, led to the Maya's end. These droughts matched downturns in the Maya culture, such as abandonment of cities and

▲ The Temple of the Great Jaguar in Tikal, Guatemala, once held the tomb of a Mayan king. The pyramid still stands today, but the civilization that built it disappeared centuries ago.

decreased stonecarving and building activity. According to this **4.** margin / thesis, the Maya were particularly at risk because 95 percent of their population depended wholly on lakes, ponds, and rivers that provided just 18 months supply of water for drinking and agriculture.

5. Ingeniously / Nevertheless, this drought theory is still controversial. Some archeologists believe the Maya's fall can only be understood in the **6.** context / institute of the social and political conditions **7.** intrinsic / prevalent at the time. A weak economic base and a period of political instability, they argue, made the Maya's collapse more likely.

B. Definitions. Match a word in red from **A** with each definition. Two words are extra.

1. _____ advanced or complex

2. _____ common or widespread

3. _____ on the other hand; however

4. _____ the edge of a place or area

5. _____ a research or teaching organization

6. _____ (to) believe something is probably true

7. _____ the general situation around or relating to something

8. _____ basic and essential; not dependent on external factors

Word Partnership	Use *intrinsic* with: (*n.*) intrinsic **value**, intrinsic **motivation**, intrinsic **factor**. You can also say something is ***intrinsic to*** something else, e.g. *storytelling is **intrinsic to** human society*.

1B An Empire's Fall

▲ The temple of Angkor Wat, pictured here as it looked when it was built in the 12th century, remains a symbol of classic Khmer (Cambodian) architecture. Originally built in honor of a Hindu god, it later became a Buddhist temple, and stands today as the world's largest religious monument.

Rise and Fall of Angkor

A.D. 802–850	889–900	1200s	Early 1300s	1400s	Modern day
Jayavarman II unifies rival groups and becomes the first king of the Khmer Empire.	Angkor is established as the empire's capital city.	The height of the Khmer kingdom: the empire controls land throughout Southeast Asia.	Theravada Buddhism becomes the empire's official religion.	Armies from neighboring kingdoms— Champa (in today's Vietnam) and Ayutthaya (now Thailand)—win land from the Khmer, marking the beginning of the end of Angkor.	

☐ Before You Read

A. Notes Completion. Use the information on this page to complete the notes about the Khmer Empire.

The Khmer Empire

Empire founded by:

Capital city:

Religion(s):

Name of famous landmark:

Start of empire's decline:

What we don't know for sure:

▲ Temple-wall inscriptions reveal the everyday lives of the Khmer. One thing the carvings do not explain: what caused the collapse of Angkor?

▲ Today, scattered ruins of Angkor's temples remain, together with the remains of vast waterworks, including reservoirs (man-made lakes), dams, and canals.

B. Skim and Predict. Skim the first page of the article (page 18). Read the title, captions, and the first sentence of each paragraph. Predict what you think the reading is mainly about. Read the rest of the article to check your ideas.

THE COLLAPSE OF ANGKOR

After rising to sublime[1] heights, the sacred city may have engineered its own downfall.

◄ At the edge of the Srah Srang reservoir in Angkor, Cambodia, stone lions stand guard over the ruins of the Khmer empire.

1 ALMOST HIDDEN AMIDST the forests of northern Cambodia is the scene of one of the greatest vanishing acts of all time. This was once the heart of the Khmer kingdom, which lasted from the
5 ninth to the 15th centuries. At its height, the Khmer empire dominated much of Southeast Asia, from Myanmar (Burma) in the west to Vietnam in the east. As many as 750,000 people lived in Angkor, its magnificent capital. The most extensive
10 urban complex of the preindustrial world, Angkor stretched across an area the size of New York City. Its greatest temple, Angkor Wat, is the world's largest religious monument even today.

Yet when the first European missionaries arrived in
15 Angkor in the late 16th century, they found a city that was already dying.

Scholars have come up with a long list of suspected causes for Angkor's decline. These include foreign invaders, a religious change of heart, and a shift to
20 maritime trade. But it's mostly guesswork: roughly 1,300 inscriptions survive on temple doors and monuments, but the people of Angkor left not a single word explaining their kingdom's collapse.

SOME SCHOLARS ASSUME that Angkor died the way
25 it lived: by the sword. The historical records of Ayutthaya, a neighboring state, claim that warriors from that kingdom "took" Angkor in 1431. If so, their motive is not difficult to guess. No doubt Angkor would have been a rich prize: inscriptions
30 boast that its temple towers were covered with gold. After its rediscovery by Western travelers just over a century ago, historians deduced from Angkor's ruins that the city had been looted[2] by invaders from Ayutthaya.

35 Roland Fletcher, co-director of a research effort called the Greater Angkor Project, is not convinced. Some early scholars, he says, viewed Angkor according to the sieges[3] and conquests of European history. "The ruler of Ayutthaya,
40 indeed, says he took Angkor, and he may have taken some formal regalia[4] back to Ayutthaya with him," says Fletcher. But after Angkor was captured, Ayutthaya's ruler placed his son on the throne. "He's not likely to have smashed the place up
45 before giving it to his son."

A RELIGIOUS SHIFT may also have contributed to the city's decline, by diminishing royal authority. Angkor was a regal-ritual city; its kings claimed to be the world emperors of Hindu mythology and
50 erected temples to themselves. But in the 13th and 14th centuries, Theravada Buddhism gradually took over from Hinduism. Its principles of social equality may have threatened Angkor's elite. "It was very subversive,[5] just like Christianity was
55 subversive to the Roman Empire," says Fletcher.

[1] If you say something is **sublime**, you mean it has a wonderful quality.
[2] If a store or house is **looted**, people have stolen things from it, for example, during a war or riot.
[3] A **siege** is a military or police operation in which soldiers or police surround a place in order to force the people there to come out.
[4] **Regalia** are the ceremonial jewelry, objects, or clothes that symbolize royalty or high office.
[5] Something that is **subversive** is intended to weaken or destroy a political system or government.

The regal-ritual city operated on a moneyless economy, relying on tribute[6] and taxation. The kingdom's main currency was rice, the staple food of the laborers who built the temples and the
60 thousands who ran them. At one temple complex, Ta Prohm, more than 66,000 farmers produced nearly 3,000 tons of rice a year. This was then used to feed the temple's priests, dancers, and workers. Scholars estimate that farm laborers comprised
65 nearly half of Greater Angkor's population. A new religion that promoted ideas of social equality might have led to rebellion.

Or maybe the royal court simply turned its back on Angkor. Angkor's rulers often erected new temple
70 complexes and let older ones decay. This may have doomed the city when sea trade began to develop between Southeast Asia and China. Maybe it was simple economic
75 opportunism that, by the 16th century, had caused the Khmer center of power to shift: the move to a location closer to the Mekong River, near Cambodia's present-day capital, Phnom Penh,
80 allowed it easier access to the South China Sea.

ECONOMIC AND RELIGIOUS changes may have contributed to Angkor's downfall, but its rulers faced another foe. Angkor was powerful largely thanks to an advanced system of canals and
85 reservoirs. These enabled the city to keep scarce water in dry months and disperse excess water during the rainy season. But forces beyond Angkor's control would eventually bring an end to this carefully constructed, rational system.

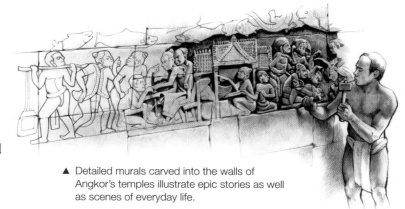

▲ Detailed murals carved into the walls of Angkor's temples illustrate epic stories as well as scenes of everyday life.

90 Few ancient sites in southern Asia could compare to Angkor in its ability to guarantee a steady water supply. That reliability required massive feats of engineering. The first scholar to appreciate the scale of Angkor's waterworks was French archaeologist

Roughly 1,300 inscriptions survive, but the people of Angkor left not a single word explaining their kingdom's collapse.

95 Bernard-Philippe Groslier. In 1979, he argued that the great reservoirs, or *barays*, served two purposes: to symbolize the Hindu cosmos[7] and to irrigate the rice fields. Unfortunately, Groslier could not pursue his ideas further. Cambodia's civil war,[8] the brutal
100 regime of the Khmer Rouge,[9] and the subsequent arrival of Vietnamese forces in 1979 turned Angkor into a no-go zone for two decades.

Then, in 2000, Roland Fletcher and his colleague Damian Evans saw some NASA radar images
105 of Angkor. The researchers marveled at the sophistication of Angkor's infrastructure. "We realized that the entire landscape of Greater Angkor is artificial," Fletcher says. Teams of laborers constructed hundreds of kilometers of
110 canals and dikes[10] that diverted water from the rivers to the barays. Overflow channels bled off excess water that accumulated during the summer monsoon months. After the monsoon, irrigation channels dispensed the stored water. "It was an
115 incredibly clever system," says Fletcher.

6 A **tribute** is something you give, say, do, or make to show that you admire and respect someone.
7 The **cosmos** is the universe.
8 A **civil war** is a war fought between different groups of people who live in the same country.
9 The **Khmer Rouge** was a radical communist movement that ruled Cambodia from 1975 to 1979 after winning power through a guerrilla war.
10 A **dike** is a wall built to prevent flooding.

▼ Pilgrims to Angkor Wat traditionally offer lotus flowers to the temple's gods.

▲ A monk stands beneath forest roots that have covered the ruins at Ta Prohm, as the surrounding jungle reclaims the land.

Fletcher was therefore baffled when his team made a surprising discovery. An extraordinary piece of Angkorian workmanship—a vast structure in the waterworks—had been destroyed, apparently 120 by Angkor's own engineers. "The most logical explanation is that the dam failed," Fletcher says. The river may have begun to erode the dam, or perhaps it was washed away by an unusually heavy flood. The Khmer broke apart the remaining 125 stonework and modified the blocks for other purposes.

ANY WEAKENING OF THE WATERWORKS would have left the city vulnerable to a natural phenomenon that none of Angkor's engineers could have predicted. 130 Starting in the 1300s, it appears that Southeast Asia experienced a period of extreme climate change which also affected other parts of the world. In Europe, which endured centuries of harsh winters and cool summers, it was known as the Little 135 Ice Age.

To an already weakened kingdom, extreme weather would have been the final blow. Decades earlier, Angkor's waterworks were already struggling. "We don't know why the water system was operating 140 below capacity," says Daniel Penny, co-director of the Greater Angkor Project. "But what it means is that Angkor . . . was more exposed to the threat of drought than at any other time in its history."

If inhabitants of parts of Angkor were starving 145 while other parts of the city were hoarding a finite quantity of rice, the most likely result was social instability. "When populations in tropical countries exceed the carrying capacity of the land, real trouble begins," says Yale University anthropologist 150 Michael Coe. "This inevitably leads to cultural collapse." A hungry army weakened by internal problems would have exposed the city to attack. Indeed, Ayutthaya's invasion happened near the end of a long period of drought.

155 Add to the climate chaos the political and religious changes already affecting the kingdom, and Angkor's prospects were bleak, says Fletcher. "The world around 160 Angkor was changing. Society was moving on. It would have been a surprise if Angkor persisted."

The Khmer Empire was not the first civilization brought down by climate 165 catastrophe. Centuries earlier, loss of environmental stability likewise brought down another powerful kingdom halfway around the world. Many scholars now believe that the 170 fall of the Maya city-states in Mexico and Central America followed a series of droughts in the ninth century. "Essentially, the same thing happened to Angkor," says Coe, 175 who in the 1950s was the first to detect similarities between the Khmer and Maya civilizations.

In the end, the tale of Angkor is a sobering[11] lesson in the limits 180 of human ingenuity. "Angkor's hydraulic[12] system was an amazing machine, a wonderful mechanism for regulating the world," Fletcher says. Its engineers managed to keep the 185 civilization's achievement running for six centuries—until a greater force overwhelmed them.

[11] A situation that is **sobering** is one that seems serious and makes you become serious and thoughtful.
[12] **Hydraulic** equipment or machinery involves or is operated by a fluid that is under pressure, such as water or oil.

Finely carved heads of both Buddhist and Hindu deities ▲ are evidence of the shifting of power and faith in Angkorian civilization.

Reading Comprehension

A. Multiple Choice. Choose the best answer for each question.

Purpose

1. What was the author's main purpose in writing this article?
   a. to offer various explanations for the fall of Angkor
   b. to trace the history of Angkor from the 9th to the 15th century
   c. to explain the inscriptions left in the temples by the people of Angkor
   d. to describe the irrigation system that allowed Angkor to flourish

Negative Detail

2. According to the information in the first and second paragraphs, which of the following is NOT true about Angkor?
   a. It once ruled a large part of Southeast Asia.
   b. It was at one time the largest urban center in the world.
   c. It once held as many people as New York City does today.
   d. It was in decline when Europeans arrived in the 16th century.

Vocabulary

3. The phrase *by the sword* (line 25) is closest in meaning to _____.
   a. suddenly   c. violently
   b. unexpectedly   d. secretively

Reference

4. The word *it* in line 45 refer to _____.
   a. the kingdom of Ayutthaya
   b. the destruction of Angkor
   c. the formal regalia
   d. the city of Angkor

Inference

5. We can infer from information in paragraph 7 (lines 56–67) that the greatest number of people in Angkor worked as _____.
   a. construction workers   c. priests
   b. dancers   d. agricultural workers

Inference

6. What does the author imply in paragraph 8 (lines 68–80) about the city of Phnom Penh?
   a. It is located on the South China Sea.
   b. Before the rise of Angkor, it was the center of Khmer power.
   c. It is closer to the Mekong River than Angkor.
   d. It was founded about the same time as Angkor.

Rhetorical Purpose

7. Why does the author mention the Little Ice Age in paragraph 13 (lines 127–135)?
   a. to show that climate change caused more cultures to fail in Europe than in Asia
   b. to emphasize the extent and significance of climate change in the 1300s
   c. to explain why European civilizations were not as advanced as Angkor
   d. to show how Angkor's climate in the 1300s was similar to Europe's

Detail

8. How did the climate in Angkor change in the 1300s?
   a. Winters became too cool to grow rice.
   b. There were terrible storms and constant flooding.
   c. The climate became dryer than it had previously been.
   d. Rising temperatures caused great discomfort.

Strategy Focus: Matching Ideas and Sources

Writers often cite sources—for example, experts on a subject—to support their own point of view, or to put forward ideas that give their readers a more balanced view of a topic. There are two methods to present experts' ideas: direct quotation and indirect quotation. Direct quotation uses quotation marks ("_____") to indicate this is exactly what the author said or wrote. Indirect quotation is given in the authors' own words, without quotation marks.

B. Matching. Match the ideas (**A–I**) with the sources of those ideas (**1–5**). More than one idea can be matched with some of the sources.

_____ **1.** historians of a century ago

_____ **2.** Roland Fletcher

_____ **3.** Bernard–Philippe Groslier

_____ **4.** Daniel Penny

_____ **5.** Michael Coe

A. When a population outgrows its food supply, that culture will probably fail.

B. Theravada Buddhism may have weakened the power of Angkor's rulers.

C. The king of Ayutthaya probably did not badly damage Angkor because his son was going to become the next ruler of the city.

D. Like Angkor, the Mayan city states were weakened by climate changes.

E. Foreign invaders conquered and stole material from Angkor.

F. Photographs taken from space show that Angkor's irrigation system was more complex than previously thought.

G. Angkor's irrigation system served a symbolic purpose as well as a practical one.

H. During the period of extreme weather in the 1300s, Angkor was very vulnerable to drought.

I. It would have been amazing if Angkor had managed to survive all the threats that it faced.

C. Critical Thinking. Discuss these questions with a partner.

1. According to the article, what kinds of challenges did the kingdom of Angkor face? Which of these continue to threaten modern civilizations?

2. This article and the previous article ("Spirits in the Sand") both tell the story of an ancient culture. In what ways were these cultures similar? In what ways were they different?

3. Angkor Wat today is an important symbol of the modern nation of Cambodia. What place or monument in your country do you think best symbolizes your country? Why?

Vocabulary Practice

A. Completion. Complete the information with the correct form of the words in the box. Two words are extra.

channel	currency	disperse	internal
logical	mechanism	persistent	promote
regime	vulnerable		

California's Pipedream in Crisis?

During the past century California has spent a lot of hard **1.** _____ building some of the most sophisticated **2.** _____ for delivering water on the planet. Thousands of kilometers of pipes and **3.** _____ cross the state, providing water for farms, factories, and houses. However, the state's water resources are now severely stretched. Some experts argue that California is **4.** _____ to the same fate of ancient civilizations, such as the Khmer and the Maya, that collapsed when water resources became insufficient.

Some reasons for the crisis are environmental. A **5.** _____, three-year drought has drained most of the state's reservoirs to low levels. California's largest **6.** _____ storehouse of surface water—the Sierra Nevada mountain range—has less snow due to warming temperatures, leaving the state more reliant on external sources.

Recently, laws have been introduced to **7.** _____ water conservation in major cities. These aim to cut water use 20 percent by 2020. The most **8.** _____ solution to the crisis, say water experts, is for Californians to learn to live within the water resources of a dry landscape.

▲ Californian communities like Salton City survive on water pumped in from the Colorado River.

▲ Overuse of freshwater rivers and lakes also threatens the species that depend on them, such as this adult male kingfisher.

B. Definitions. Use the correct form of words in the box in **A** to complete the definitions.

1. A system of government that is severe or harsh is called a _____.
2. A _____ is a passage along which water flows.
3. If something _____, it continues to exist or happen for a long period.
4. Being _____ means being easily affected by something bad.
5. If you encourage something to happen, you _____ it.
6. The money used in a particular country is its _____.
7. If you _____ something, you spread it over a wide area.
8. A _____ is a machine, or a system for doing something.

Word Partnership

Use **promote** with:
(n.) promote **democracy**, promote **development**, promote **growth**, promote **health**, promote peace, promote **stability**, promote **trade**, promote **a product**.

▲ A modern-day visitor explores the ruins of Angkor.

EXPLORE MORE

Temples in the Jungle

A. Preview. This unit's video is about the fall and rediscovery of Angkor. Read these extracts from the video, and match each phrase in blue with a definition.

1. . . . a French naturalist named Henri Mouhot came across the ruins.

2. . . . historians have pieced together the story.

3. . . . invaders attacked and set fire to the city.

4. . . . the Khmer's story came to a close not long afterward.

5. . . . a climactic battle around 1431 brought about the end.

a. _____ resulted in   **b.** _____ finished   **c.** _____ burned

d. _____ reconstructed   **e.** _____ discovered

B. Summarize. Watch the video, *Temples in the Jungle*. Then complete the summary below using the correct form of words in the box. Two words are extra.

channel	disperse	ingenuity	institute	internal
nevertheless	sophisticated	suspect	thesis	vulnerable

For hundreds of years, the once-powerful capital of the Khmer empire—Angkor—was little more than a myth. Few people in the outside world
1. _____ that it might actually still exist.
2. _____, when a French naturalist named Henri Mouhot rediscovered the site of the ancient capital in the mid-19th century, he was amazed by the ruins that still survived. Among these were
3. _____ examples of Khmer temple architecture, including the greatest of all Angkor's temples, Angkor Wat.

Mouhot's discovery drew the attention of the world. But one great question remained: what had happened to Angkor? Over the years, archeologists and historians began to solve the mystery. Angkor rose to power largely thanks to the
4. _____ of its engineers, whose elaborate system of irrigation wells and **5.** _____ allowed the city to store and
6. _____ fresh water. However, the city was hit by a series of droughts that caused rice harvests to fail. These, together with other
7. _____ factors—such as social and religious changes and political instability—left the empire **8.** _____ to attack from foreign invaders. Angkor was then reclaimed by the jungle, until its rediscovery centuries later.

C. Think About It.

1. What additional information do we learn from the video that is not mentioned in the passage on pages 18–20?

2. Does the information in the video contradict (conflict with) any of the information in the passage?

To learn more about lost civilizations, visit elt.heinle.com/explorer

UNIT 2
Beyond Earth

Discuss these questions with a partner.

1. Do you think life might exist on planets other than Earth?

2. How has astronomy helped human societies? How might it help us in the future?

3. The astronomer Galileo Galilei (1564–1642) said, "Doubt is the father of invention." What do you think he meant?

▲ An artist's vision of newly discovered Gliese 581e, a rocky planet about 20 light-years from Earth.

25

2A Seeing Further

A In **1609**, Galileo gave birth to modern astronomy when he used the world's first telescope, a simple wooden tool with a 3.8 cm (1.5 inch) lens. He was able to view Earth's moon, spots on the sun, and planets in our solar system.

B By **1845**, reflecting telescopes such as Lord Rosse's "Leviathan of Parsonstown" in Ireland allowed astronomers to see beyond our own galaxy, the Milky Way.

C Since its launch in **1990**, the Hubble space telescope has sent back information about the life and death of stars and the origins of our universe.

D First used in **2005**, the Large Binocular Telescope (LBT) in Arizona delivers images ten times sharper than Hubble's. The LBT belongs to a new generation of telescopes that may help us solve the universe's remaining mysteries.

Before You Read

A. Match and Discuss. Match each description (**A–D**) with a picture. Then answer the questions.

1. How have telescopes changed over the years?
2. Using telescopes, what have we been able to see and learn?
3. Astronomers hope that telescopes like the LBT will help solve the universe's remaining mysteries. What questions do you think scientists are trying to answer?

B. Scan. Quickly scan the article on pages 27–29. Which of the astronomers and telescopes above are mentioned in the article? Which other astronomers and telescopes can you find? Circle them as you scan the article.

Cosmic Vision

A new generation of giant telescopes will carry the eye to the edge of the universe.

▲ An astronomer works inside a dome at the Mount Wilson Observatory.

1 WHEN PEOPLE START STARGAZING with a telescope, they are typically first astonished by the view. Saturn's golden rings appear in fine detail, star clusters glitter like jewelry on black velvet, galaxies
5 glow with gentle starlight older than the human species. The view brings home the realization that we and our world are an integral part of a gigantic system. That's the initial reaction. The next is a desire for a bigger telescope.

10 The first person to point a telescope at the night sky was Galileo, roughly 400 years ago. With his telescope, Galileo was able to chart four bright satellites as they moved around Jupiter—like planets in a miniature solar system—something
15 that contemporary critics had dismissed as physically impossible.

Galileo's telescope also revealed thousands of previously invisible stars. When he tried to map all of them in just one constellation, Orion, he gave up,
20 confessing that he was "overwhelmed by the vast quantity of stars." Evidently the Earth was a small part of a big universe, not a big part of a small one.

Some six decades later, Isaac Newton pioneered a new kind of telescope—the reflecting telescope. This
25 made it possible to obtain a much clearer view of the universe. Mirrors required that only one surface be used to reflect starlight to a focal point. Since the mirror was supported from behind, it could be quite large without sagging under its own weight,
30 as large lenses tended to do.

It was with such a reflecting telescope that William Herschel discovered the planet Uranus in 1781. Six decades later, Lord Rosse built a massive reflecting telescope called Leviathan on his estate in Ireland.
35 This allowed Rosse to become the first person to observe spiral-armed galaxies beyond the Milky Way.

Today's largest telescopes have mirrors up to some ten meters (33 feet) in diameter, more than five times the size of Leviathan. Some are as large as
40 office buildings, and highly automated. They can clean dust off their optics,[1] open their dome, carry out observations throughout the night, and shut down in the event of threatening weather, all with little or no human intervention.

[1] The **optics** of a telescope are its lenses.

◀ Released on Hubble's 20th anniversary, this image shows a mountain of dust and gas rising in the Carina Nebula.

▲ Lasers beam from telescopes at the Starfire Optical Range in New Mexico. Such adaptive optics (AO) systems allow astronomers to create clearer images of stars.

45 Three of today's largest telescopes—Gemini North, Subaru, and Keck—stand within a short distance of one another atop Hawaii's Mauna Kea, an inactive volcano. Surprisingly, Subaru is one of the few giant telescopes that anybody has ever actually
50 looked through (most astronomers choose to view a telescope's findings via a computer screen). For its inauguration[2] in 1999, an eyepiece was attached so that Princess Sayako of Japan could look through the telescope. For several nights afterward, eager Subaru
55 staffers did the same. "Everything you can see in the Hubble Space Telescope photos—the colors, the clouds—I could see with my own eyes, in stunning Technicolor," one recalled.

In addition to their light-gathering power, today's
60 big telescopes benefit from their adaptive optics (AO) systems, which compensate for atmospheric turbulence (the reason why stars glitter). Starting in 1995, astronomer Andrea Ghez has been able to use Keck's AO system to make a motion picture of seven
65 bright stars spinning around the invisible black hole at the center of our galaxy. Ghez used simulations of the dynamic movement of stars in the grip of the black hole to calculate that it has a mass of four million suns. That's enough gravitational force to
70 throw passing stars right out of our galaxy.

WHAT'S NEXT? Enhanced, even bigger telescopes, of course, with the capability to shoot cosmic pictures faster, wider, and in even greater detail.

Particularly innovative is the Large Synoptic Survey
75 Telescope, or LSST. The LSST will have a field of view covering an area the size of 50 full moons. From its site in the Chilean Andes, it will be able to capture sequences of events at distances of over ten billion light-years, 70 percent of the way across the
80 observable universe. "Since we'll have a big field of view, we can take a whole lot of short exposures and—*bang, bang, bang, bang*—cover the entire visible sky every several nights, and then repeat," says LSST Director Tony Tyson. "If you keep doing that
85 for ten years, you have a movie—the first movie of the universe."

The LSST's fast, wide-angle imaging could help answer two of the biggest questions confronting astronomers today: the nature of dark matter and
90 of dark energy. Dark matter makes its presence known by its gravitational attraction—it explains the rotation speed of galaxies. But it gives out no light, and its constitution is unknown. Dark energy is the name given to the mysterious phenomenon that, for
95 the past five billion years, has been accelerating the rate at which the universe expands. "It's a little bit scary," says Tyson, "as if you were flying an airplane and suddenly something unknown took over the controls."

100 Orbiting space telescopes are opening up another dimension. NASA's Kepler satellite, which launched in March 2009, is methodically imaging the constellation Cygnus. Its mission is to look for the slight dimming of light caused when planets—some
105 perhaps Earth-like—transit in front of their stars. Astronomers will then use Keck to analyze the stars identified by Kepler. They hope this will confirm the existence of planets.

In the future, pairs of orbiting mirrors linked by
110 laser-ranging systems could attain the power of telescopes measuring thousands of meters across. One day, observatories may sit in craters on the far side of the moon, probing the universe from surroundings ideally quiet, dark, and cold.

[2] The **inauguration** of something is a celebration of its opening or first public use.

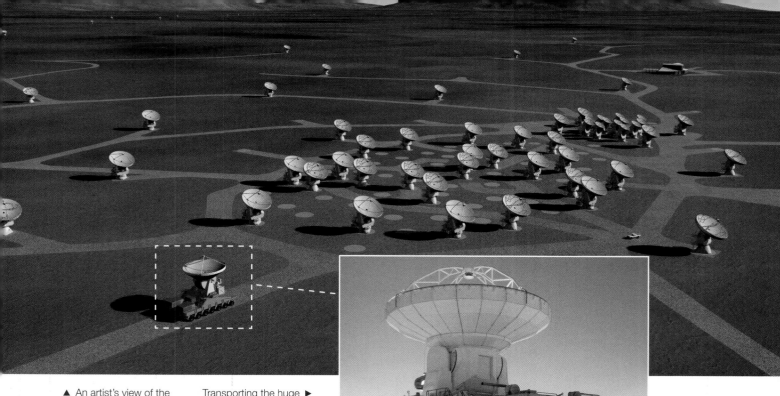

▲ An artist's view of the Atacama array, which will be one of the largest astronomical projects in existence.

Transporting the huge ▶ antennas to the site requires the use of custom-made 28-wheel heavy haulers.

115 FILM DIRECTORS LIKE to say that each movie is really two movies—the one you make, and the one you say you're going to make while raising the money. The point is that nobody can accurately predict the outcome of any genuinely creative venture.

120 The same is true of most scientific discoveries. Scientists can explain what they expect to accomplish with bigger and better telescopes, but such predictions are mostly just extrapolations³ from the past.

125 "If you're going to Washington to seek funding for a new telescope and you make a list of what you'll see through this new window on the universe, you know that the most interesting thing it will

130 discover is probably not on your list," says Tyson. "It's likely to be something totally new, some out-of-the-box⁴ physics that's going to blow our minds."

The marvelous model of the big-bang universe

135 pieced together in the 20th century arose largely from just such unanticipated discoveries. Edwin Hubble discovered the expansion of the universe accidentally, at the telescope. Cosmic expansion had been implied by Einstein's general theory

140 of relativity, but Hubble knew nothing of the prediction, and not even Einstein had taken it seriously. Dark matter was discovered accidentally; so was dark energy.

One day, observatories may sit in craters on the far side of the moon, probing the universe from surroundings ideally quiet, dark, and cold.

A telescope doesn't just show you what's out there;

145 it impresses upon you how little you know. As Galileo said, "the spyglass is very truthful." It has the power to give us new insights and to open our imagination to wonders as big as all outdoors.

³ **Extrapolations** are inferences about the future, or about some hypothetical situation, based on known facts and observations.
⁴ If we say something, usually an idea, is **out of the box**, we mean that it is different, original, and creative.

Reading Comprehension

A. Multiple Choice. Choose the best answer for each question.

Gist **1.** The main point of this reading is to _____.
  a. explain an important new development of astronomy
  b. contrast ground-based telescopes and space-based telescopes
  c. trace the development of telescopes through the past, present, and future
  d. discuss Galileo's and Newton's contributions to the field of astronomy

Vocabulary **2.** The use of the phrase *gave up* in line 19 indicates that Galileo was _____.
  a. upset   b. discouraged   c. successful   d. curious

Inference **3.** What can be inferred about the *contemporary critics* mentioned in line 15?
  a. They tried to prevent Galileo from publishing his research findings.
  b. They were surprised by Galileo's discovery of the satellite moons of Jupiter.
  c. They attacked the idea that the Earth was "a small part of a big universe."
  d. They did not believe that Jupiter could travel around the Sun.

Detail **4.** What does the author say about reflecting telescopes?
  a. They can be much larger than telescopes that use only lenses.
  b. They can be focused on only one object in the sky at a time.
  c. They are all highly automated and can clean dust from their optics.
  d. They can employ much larger lenses than earlier telescopes.

Detail **5.** According to the information in paragraph 7 (from line 45), the Subaru telescope is unusual because _____.
  a. it is the largest and most advanced reflecting telescope ever to be built
  b. it enabled viewers to see objects in color rather than in black and white
  c. it is the only telescope ever to be located on top of an extinct volcano
  d. it was once used to see objects directly rather than view them on a computer

Rhetorical Purpose **6.** The author explains the concept of *dark energy* in paragraph 11 (from line 87) by _____.
  a. discussing how it is formed and how it has spread throughout the universe
  b. providing a detailed description of what it actually looks like
  c. contrasting it in several ways with dark matter
  d. quoting an expert who compares it to a situation readers can understand

Rhetorical Purpose **7.** Why does the author mention *film directors* in paragraph 14 (from line 115)?
  a. Like astronomers, directors don't know what the final result of their creative efforts will be.
  b. Directors have been able to portray the discoveries of scientists in an exciting way.
  c. Like astronomers, directors need to use more and more advanced technology in their work.
  d. Directors, like astronomers, now have to raise a lot of money to complete their projects.

Detail **8.** Which of the following is NOT given as an example of one of the "unanticipated discoveries" that the author discusses?
  a. dark matter
  b. Earth-like planets
  c. cosmic expansion
  d. dark energy

B. Sequencing. Use the information in the article to put these events in the correct sequence. Number the events **1–9**. Then underline some words or phrases that the author uses to indicate sequence in this article.

_____ Newton invents the reflecting telescope.

_____ The LSST sees events that take place 10 billion light-years away.

_____ Lord Rosse uses Leviathan to discover galaxies outside the Milky Way.

_____ Telescopes on the far side of the Moon observe the universe.

_____ The telescope Subaru is first used.

_____ The Kepler satellite studies stars in the Cygnus constellation.

_____ Ghez begins to chart stars moving around a black hole in the middle of our galaxy.

_____ Galileo first examines the sky with a telescope.

_____ Hershel discovers Uranus.

C. Critical Thinking. Discuss these questions with a partner.

1. Building telescopes and sponsoring astronomical projects is very expensive. Some people believe that governments should spend this money for more practical purposes. With a partner or in a small group, list three reasons for and three reasons against spending money on astronomical research. Then give your own opinion about the issue.

2. How do you think the author of this article feels about funding astronomical research? Find specific words and sentences from the article that support your conclusion.

3. What point do you think the author is trying to make by his discussion of "unanticipated discoveries" (paragraphs 16–17)?

Vocabulary Practice

A. Completion. Complete the information with the correct form of the words in the box. Two words are extra.

attain	contemporary	dynamic	survey
chart	compensate	outcome	transit

Massive Star Discovered— Shatters Record

In early 2010, astronomers **1.** _____ a new star in a nearby galaxy that shattered the record as the most massive stellar monster ever seen. Weighing in at 265 times the mass of our sun, the giant may actually be slimmer than it was shortly after its birth, when it likely **2.** _____ a weight of 320 times the sun's mass.

Astronomers believe the discovery could rewrite the laws of **3.** _____ stellar physics. "Until now the astronomical community has assumed that the upper size limit for stars would be around 150 times the mass of the sun," says Richard Parker, an astronomer at the University of Sheffield in the U.K. The **4.** _____ of this discovery, he argues, could be a revolution in "the way we think about how stars form and die."

Parker's team carried out their **5.** _____ of the star, known as R136a1, using images taken with the European Southern Observatory's Very Large Telescope in Chile. The superstar burns its hydrogen fuel at such a(n) **6.** _____ rate that it is already considered middle-aged at just a million years old. By contrast, our sun is about five billion years old and still has another five billion years to go.

▲ Supernova 1987A, the bright star near the center of this picture, was photographed on February 23, 1987, as it self-destructed in the Large Magellanic Cloud, a nearby galaxy. More recently, R136a1, an even more massive star, was discovered in the same galaxy. It, too, will eventually die in a huge explosion.

B. Words in Context. Complete each sentence with the best answer.

1. Some powerful telescopes have been built on country _____, since they require large amounts of land.
   a. surveys   b. estates

2. Today's telescopes can _____ for atmospheric conditions.
   a. compensate   b. intervene

3. When planets _____ in front of their stars, the light reaching Earth is slightly reduced.
   a. attain   b. transit

4. Scientists are often unable to predict the _____ of their discoveries.
   a. outcome   b. compensation

5. Little human intervention is needed to operate _____ telescopes.
   a. dynamic   b. contemporary

6. Galileo was the first to _____ the satellites that move around Jupiter.
   a. chart   b. intervene

Word Link

Trans has the meaning of *across*, e.g., **trans**act, **trans**fer, **trans**form, **trans**it, **trans**ition, **trans**late, **trans**mit, **trans**parent, **trans**plant, **trans**port.

Earth

Saturn 95 Earths

CT Cha b 5,403 Earths

Jupiter 318 Earths

Planet Hunters

2B

▲ Saturn and Jupiter may be large relative to our home planet, but they're small compared to CT Cha b, one of the 370 plus *exoplanets*—planets circling stars outside our own solar system—that astronomers have so far discovered. With more than twice Jupiter's diameter and 17 times its mass, CT Cha b is the largest exoplanet for which a diameter has been measured. It orbits a young star more than 500 light-years away.

☐ Before You Read

A. Discussion. Look at the information above and answer the questions.

1. What do astronomers know about CT Cha b? Why is it unusual?

2. What is an exoplanet? Why do you think astronomers are hunting for them? What do you think the main challenges are?

B. Skim and Predict. Read the title, captions, and section headings and skim the rest of the passage on pages 34–36. Then answer the questions.

1. Circle the two main questions you think the passage is going to answer.
   a. How do astronomers locate and identify other Earth-like planets?
   b. Why is finding other Earth-like planets important?
   c. Will other Earth-like planets be similar to our own?

2. What do you think are possible answers to the questions you circled? Read the article to check your ideas. Underline key information in the passage to help you recall it.

ARE WE ALONE?

Throughout history, only one Earth has been known to exist in the universe. Soon there may be another. And another. And another.

▲ Monitors help researchers visualize huge amounts of data from the latest telescopes.

1 It took humans thousands of years to explore our own planet, and centuries to comprehend our neighboring planets. Nowadays, new worlds are being discovered every week.

5 To date, astronomers have identified more than 370 "exoplanets"—worlds orbiting stars other than the sun. There's a "hot Saturn" 260 light-years from Earth that orbits its parent star so rapidly that a year there lasts less than three days. Circling
10 another star 150 light-years out is a scorched "hot Jupiter," whose upper atmosphere is being blasted off to form a gigantic, comet-like tail. Astronomers have found three planets orbiting a pulsar—the remains of a once mighty star shrunk into a
15 spinning atomic nucleus the size of a city. Some worlds have evidently fallen into their suns. Others have been thrown out of their systems to become "floaters" that wander in eternal darkness.

Among all these, scientists are eager to find a hint
20 of the familiar: planets resembling Earth. That is, planets orbiting their stars at just the right distance—neither too hot nor too cold—to support life as we know it. We have not yet found planets that are quite like our own, presumably because
25 they're inconspicuous. To see a planet as small and dim as ours amid the glare of its star is like trying to see a firefly in a fireworks display. Yet by pushing technology to the limits, astronomers are rapidly approaching the day when they can find another
30 Earth. And when they do, they can investigate it for signs of life.

IN SEARCH OF OTHER EARTHS

The most direct approach to finding a planet is to take a picture of it with a telescope. At the time
35 of writing, astronomers had detected only 11 exoplanets this way. All of them are big and bright and conveniently far away from their stars.

The most effective way to detect an exoplanet, though, is to use a method known as the Doppler
40 technique. This involves analyzing starlight for evidence that the star is being pulled by the gravitational pull of its planets. In recent years astronomers have refined the technique to a fine degree. Now they can tell when a planet is pulling
45 its star by only one meter a second—about human walking speed. That's sufficient to detect a giant planet in a big orbit, or a small one if it's close to its star. But the Earth tugs the sun around at only one-tenth walking speed, or about the rate that an infant
50 can crawl. So far, astronomers are not able to detect so tiny a signal.

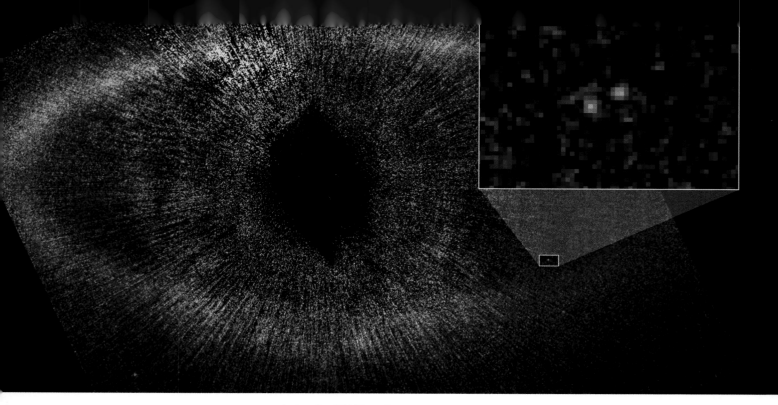

▲ A dust ring 25 billion miles across veils the planet Formalhaut b (inset). Captured by the Hubble telescope in 2004, this was one of the first images we have of a planet outside our solar system.

Another approach is to watch a star for a slight periodic dip in its brightness. This occurs when an orbiting planet passes in front of it and blocks a
55 fraction of its light. At most, a tenth of all planetary systems are oriented so that these mini-eclipses, called transits, are visible from Earth. So astronomers have
60 to monitor a lot of stars to capture just a few transits.

The dream of astronomers is to discover a rocky planet roughly the size of Earth orbiting in a
65 habitable zone. That is, not so close to a star that the planet's water has been baked away, nor so far out that it has frozen into ice. If they succeed, they will have found what biologists believe could be a promising abode[1] for life.

70 The best hunting grounds may be dwarf stars, smaller than the sun. Firstly, dwarf stars are plentiful (seven of the ten stars nearest to Earth are dwarf stars). They also provide a steady supply of sunlight to any life-bearing planets within their
75 habitable zone.

[1] An **abode** is a home.
[2] **Chlorophyll** is the green coloring matter in plants, which enables them to convert sunlight into energy.

Additionally, dwarf stars are dim, and so the habitable zone lies closer in. (Imagine dwarf stars as small campfires, where campers must sit close to be comfortable.) If the planet is closer to the
80 star, it's easier for astronomers to detect a transit

To see a planet as small and dim as ours amid the glare of its star is like trying to see a firefly in a fireworks display.

observation. A close-in planet also exerts a stronger pull on its star. That makes it easier to detect with the Doppler method. Indeed, the most promising planet yet found—the "super Earth" Gliese 581d—
85 orbits in the habitable zone of a red dwarf star only a third the mass of the sun.

LIFE—BUT NOT AS WE KNOW IT?

If an Earth-like planet is found within a star's habitable zone, a dedicated space telescope could
90 be used to look for signs of life. Most likely, scientists will examine the light coming from the planet for possible biosignatures such as atmospheric methane and oxygen. They might also look for the "red edge" produced when
95 chlorophyll[2]-containing plants reflect red light.

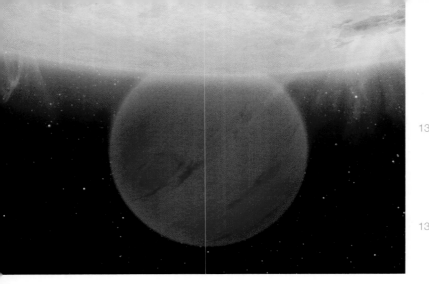

▲ Discovered by NASA's Spitzer Space Telescope, a hot, Neptune-sized planet orbits a star beyond our sun. The planet's lack of methane—an ingredient common to many planets in our own solar system—demonstrates the vast diversity of exoplanets still being discovered.

Directly detecting and analyzing the planet's own light will not be easy. Its light might be just one ten-billionth the light of the star's. But when a planet transits, starlight shining through the
100 atmosphere could reveal clues to its composition that a space telescope might be able to detect.

The challenge facing scientists is not just having to perform a chemical analysis of planets they cannot see. Scientists must also keep in mind that
105 extraterrestrial life may be very different from life here at home. The lack of the red edge from an exoplanet, for instance, does not exclude the possibility of life. Life thrived on Earth for billions of years before land plants appeared and populated
110 the continents.

The problem for scientists is that biological evolution is inherently unpredictable. It is possible that life originated on an Earth-like planet at the same time it did here. But life on that planet today
115 would almost certainly be very different from terrestrial[3] life. As the biologist Jacques Monod once commented, life evolves not only through necessity—the universal workings of natural law—but also through chance, the unpredictable
120 intervention of countless accidents.

Chance has played a role many times in our planet's history. The most dramatic examples are the mass extinctions that wiped out millions of species and created room for new life forms to evolve. Some
125 of these accidents appear to have been caused by

comets or asteroids colliding with Earth. An impact 65 million years ago, for instance, helped kill off the dinosaurs and opened up opportunities for the distant ancestors of human beings. Hence scientists
130 look not just for exoplanets identical to the modern Earth, but for planets resembling the Earth as it used to be or might have been.

It was not easy for earlier pioneers to undertake explorations of the ocean floors, map the far side of
135 the moon, or discern evidence of oceans beneath the frozen surfaces of Jupiter's moons. Neither will it be easy to find life on the planets of other stars. But we now have reason to believe that billions of such planets must exist. They hold the promise of
140 expanding not only the scope of human knowledge but also the richness of the human imagination.

³ When we say something is **terrestrial**, we mean it grows or lives on Earth.

▲ Reflecting America's fascination with extraterrestrials, an alien in a shop window sells alien T-shirts.

Reading Comprehension

A. Multiple Choice. Choose the best answer for each question.

Gist **1.** The best alternative title for this reading would be _____.
  a. Is There Intelligent Life on Other Planets?
  b. How Exoplanets Were First Discovered
  c. The Search for Earth-like Planets Around Other Stars
  d. The Story of Hot Saturn, Hot Jupiter, and Super Earth

Detail **2.** According to the author, a *floater* (line 18) is a planet that _____.
  a. is no longer circling a star   c. is the size of a city
  b. has fallen into its sun   d. is circling a pulsar star

Detail **3.** When this article was written, how many Earth-like exoplanets had been discovered?
  a. none   c. about 260
  b. about 150   d. over 370

Detail **4.** One reason it is difficult to detect Earth-like exoplanets is that _____.
  a. they move so slowly around their suns
  b. they are so far from their stars
  c. their gravitational pull is so slight
  d. their stars are very different to our sun

Vocabulary **5.** The use of the word *dedicated* (line 89) indicates that the space telescope mentioned in this sentence will _____.
  a. be extremely high-powered
  b. be used primarily for one purpose
  c. involve technology not now available
  d. require enthusiastic support

Detail **6.** The author indicates in paragraph 11 (from line 96) that observing and analyzing light from an exoplanet _____.
  a. has been accomplished several times
  b. will probably show signs of life
  c. will be difficult but not impossible
  d. can be done by telescopes on the ground

Inference **7.** The author implies that on some exoplanets, _____.
  a. life may have evolved without chlorophyll-bearing plants
  b. chlorophyll-bearing plants would not produce a "red edge"
  c. methane, ozone, and oxygen may produce a "red edge"
  d. life will be similar to that on Earth if it evolved at the same time

Cohesion **8.** Where would be the best place in paragraph 12 (lines 102–110) to insert this sentence?
  "The modern Earth may be the worst model we could use in searching for life elsewhere," notes Caleb Scharf, head of Columbia University's Astrobiology Center.
  a. before the first sentence   c. after the second sentence
  b. after the first sentence   d. after the third sentence

B. Matching. Match these effects given in the article (**1–8**) with the causes (**A–H**).

_____ **1.** A year on hot Saturn is only about three days long . . .

_____ **2.** So far, astronomers have not been able to locate any Earth-like exoplanets . . .

_____ **3.** Scientists have been able to observe 11 exoplanets by photographing them through a telescope . . .

_____ **4.** To observe transits, astronomers will have to observe many stars . . .

_____ **5.** When studying exoplanets, scientists look for oxygen and for the "red edge". . .

_____ **6.** Scientists know that there can be life on planets without chlorophyll-bearing plants . . .

_____ **7.** If an exoplanet does not show a "red edge," it doesn't necessarily mean it is lifeless . . .

_____ **8.** In the distant past, mass extinctions of plants and animals took place . . .

A. because only about 10 percent of these "mini-eclipses" can be seen from our planet.

B. because life on an exoplanet may be very different from life on present-day Earth.

C. because they are much smaller and less bright than the stars they circle.

D. because the Earth was struck by asteroids or comets.

E. because it orbits its star so quickly.

F. because these may be signs that life exists on these worlds.

G. because their size, brightness, and distance from their stars makes them relatively easy to observe.

H. because life existed on Earth for a very long time before land plants appeared.

C. Critical Thinking. Discuss these questions with a partner.

1. The author says that "the best hunting grounds [for Earth-like exoplanets] may be dwarf stars." What reasons does he give for this?

2. Do you think the author believes that Earth-like exoplanets will be found in the near future? Why or why not? Find words or sentences in the article to support your view.

3. Do you believe that life on exoplanets will be found? Why or why not? If yes, what do you think it will be like?

☐ Vocabulary Practice

A. Completion. Complete the information by circling the most appropriate word in each pair.

Alien Contact More Likely by "Mail" Than Radio, Study Says

A new study suggests it is more energy efficient to communicate across interstellar space by sending physical material—a sort of message in a bottle—than beams of electromagnetic radiation. Matter made of solid **1.** comment / composition—for **2.** instance / scope, organic or genetic material—can hold more information and journey farther than radio waves, which disperse as they travel.

▲ This gold aluminum cover protected Voyager's "Sounds of Earth" records during its long space flight. The records contain natural and man-made sounds from Earth, including samples of music from different cultures and eras. Voyager 1 now travels in deep space, having left our solar system years ago.

To date, the main focus among alien-hunters has been on radiation—radio and optical waves. But, so far, signs of alien life have been **3.** conspicuous / exerting only by their absence. That, however, does not mean that life is not **4.** oriented / thriving somewhere on a distant planet. Instead, the lack of signals could be because radio waves are diminished as they travel across space. **5.** Hence / Instance the great majority of their energy is wasted.

A more energy efficient way of communicating over great distances is to send a physical object with encoded information. The problem with this method is its slow speed. As astronomer Seth Shostak **6.** commented / exerted, "It's like the difference between sea post and airmail." Nevertheless, some astronomers argue we should be less concerned about trying to communicate within the **7.** nucleus / scope of our own lifetime. It may take tens of thousands of years for a message to reach and return from an alien civilization. Expecting to have a two-way conversation may be a mistake.

B. Definitions. Match the correct form of each word in red from **A** with its definition.

1. _____ the central part of an atom or cell
2. _____ the whole area or extent of something
3. _____ to face a particular direction
4. _____ to give an opinion or explanation
5. _____ use something in a strong way
6. _____ be healthy, successful, or strong
7. _____ particular example

8. _____ easy to see
9. _____ the way an item's parts are put together
10. _____ as a result; and so

Word Link

The prefix **in-** has the meaning of *not*, e,g., **in**conspicuous, **in**accurate, **in**adequate, **in**capable, **in**consistent, **in**definite.

Comet Watchers

A. Preview. Why do you think people go star-gazing? Have you ever looked at stars through a telescope? Have you ever been comet-watching? What did you see? Discuss with a partner.

B. Summarize. Watch the video, *Comet Watchers*. Then complete the summary below using the correct form of words in the box. Two words are extra.

chart	compensate	composition
context	instance	legislation
mechanism	nucleus	outcome
register		

For amateur astronomers, Halley's Comet may prove disappointing. Rather than the big bright object many expect, the comet is an inconspicuous spot of light, barely visible in the sky. However, professional astronomers working in Mauna Kea's observatories are able to view the comet in a very different **1.** _____.

▲ Appearing every 76 years, Halley's Comet has amazed and inspired mankind for centuries. But it was English astronomer Edmond Halley who, in 1705, uncovered the precise frequency of the comet's visits to Earth.

Among these astronomers is the University of Hawaii's comet specialist, Dale Cruikshank. The **2.** _____ of the telescope he is working with are not as advanced as other telescopes on Mauna Kea, but the telescope **3.** _____ for this by having a special camera, which allows Cruikshank to **4.** _____ changes in the comet's tail. Meanwhile, at NASA's infrared facility, scientists are making discoveries about the **5.** _____ of the comet, which includes elements like water, methane, carbon, and oxygen.

However, studies of Halley's Comet aren't always Earth-bound. Spacecraft flying close to the comet have also provided answers. For **6.** _____ , the Giotto probe—which flew within almost 560 kilometers (350 miles) of the comet's central **7.** _____—revealed jets of dust bursting from vents on the surface of the comet's solid core. The **8.** _____ of these studies is clear; we will learn more from this appearance of the comet, than in all previous observations combined.

C. Think About It.

1. Astronomer Dale Cruikshank says that stars help us "understand more about ourselves as well as the world we live in." What do you think he means? Do you agree?

2. Has the information in this unit changed your view of astronomy in any way? How?

To learn more about astronomy, visit elt.heinle.com/explorer

Health and Genes

Discuss these questions with a partner.

1. What are the most common illnesses affecting people in your country? Why do you think they are common?

2. Do you know anyone who suffers from allergies? What do you think causes them?

3. Do you think a person's health is largely due to their lifestyle and environment, or is it decided from the time they are born?

▲ A young cancer patient is comforted by his mother at a hospital in Barcelona, Spain.

3A

Human Heart

Tobacco smoking, physical inactivity, and poor diet are the main lifestyle-related factors leading to **cardiovascular** diseases (CVDs), which cause heart attacks and strokes. In America and Europe, CVDs have reached epidemic levels and are responsible for nearly half of all deaths. CVD-related **mortality** is also rising in the developing world, as more people become exposed to the risk factors.

A diet high in cholesterol, a substance prevalent in many fatty foods, is a leading cause of **coronary** heart disease. High levels of cholesterol can cause plaque to form in **arteries**, sometimes building up over many years (a process known as atherosclerosis). This eventually leads to arterial blockages, which restrict the flow of blood and cause heart attacks. As well as lifestyle factors, scientists are looking at how other factors, including **genetics**, may also contribute to the high incidence of CVDs.

Mortalities from cardiovascular diseases (per year)
- 500,000 to 1,231,373
- 175,000 to 499,999
- 80,000 to 174,999
- 35,000 to 79,999
- 360 to 34,999
- No data

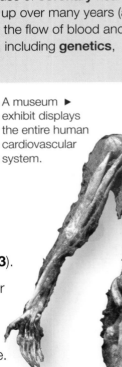

A museum ▶ exhibit displays the entire human cardiovascular system.

arteries tubes in the body that carry blood from the heart to other body parts
cardiovascular relating to the heart and blood vessels
coronary belonging or relating to the heart
genetics the study of how characteristics are passed on from one generation to another via genes
mortality (rate) (the number of) deaths in a particular place

☐ Before You Read

A. Discussion. Read the information above and answer the questions (**1–3**).

1. Where in the world is heart disease most common? Is your country or region highlighted? Is any of the information surprising?

2. What are the main factors affecting the health of the heart?

3. In your own words, explain the process that can lead to heart disease.

B. Skim and Predict. Read the title and first paragraph, and skim the rest of the passage on pages 43–45. Answer the question below. Then read the passage to check your ideas.

What do you think the passage is going to be mainly about?

a. concern about poor eating habits and the increase in heart disease
b. growing interest in the connection between heart disease and heredity
c. different methods used over the years to treat heart disease

Mending Broken Hearts

▲ Today, there are 3,500 heart transplants performed around the world every year. For every patient who gets a new heart, there are many who are not so lucky.

1　Cheeseburgers, smoking, stress: These are the prime suspects on the list of risk factors for heart disease, a global problem reaching epidemic proportions. Now discoveries about
5　genetic triggers may help us spot trouble before it starts.

Don Steffensen was putting duck-hunting decoys[1] out on a small lake one fall afternoon in southwestern Iowa when his heart attack hit.
10　The attack was massive and unexpected. It's likely that Steffensen survived only because a friend was carrying nitroglycerin tablets[2] and quickly slipped one under his tongue.

The Steffensen clan is enormous—more than 200
15　relatives spread over three generations. Although heart trouble is common in the family, it had never seemed unusual. The Steffensens were raised on the kind of farm food that the state is famous for—ham balls, meatloaf, pie, macaroni, and cheese.

20　But could the high incidence of heart trouble among the Steffensens be related to something else besides high-fat diets? Eleven years after Don's attack, his wife, Barbara, happened to overhear a doctor describing a study about the genetics of
25　heart attacks. Curious, Don and 20 of his relatives each submitted a sample of blood to the Cleveland Clinic, where the research was being conducted.

Eric Topol, a cardiologist[3] and genetics researcher at the clinic, spent a year studying their DNA.[4]
30　Each person's genome has millions of individual variations, but Topol was looking for something distinctive. The mutation he and his team finally spotted, in a gene called *MEF2A*, produced a faulty
35　protein. "We knew we had something," Topol says. "But the
40　question was: How does this sick protein,
45　present at birth, lead to heart attacks 50 years later
50　in life?"

▲ The human heart beats 100,000 times a day, pumping about six liters of blood through more than 95,000 kilometers of vessels.

[1] A **decoy** is a person or thing used to lure someone into danger. In hunting, it is an image of a bird or animal, used to lure game into a trap or within shooting range.
[2] **Nitroglycerin**, or glyceryl trinitrate, tablets can be used as heart medication and are often given to people suffering from a heart attack.
[3] A **cardiologist** is a doctor who specializes in dealing with the heart and its diseases.
[4] **DNA** stands for deoxyribonucleic acid, which is the primary chemical component of chromosomes and the material of which genes are made.

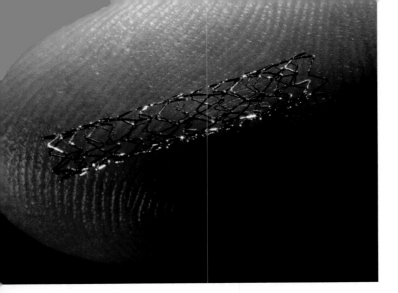

▲ This tiny metal stent could mean the difference between life and death. Inserted into a closed or blocked artery, stents like this help to restore the flow of blood to the heart.

Topol himself is lean and weathered in a cowboyish way. He talks slowly and eats minimally: salads for dinner and high-fiber cereal for breakfast. He doesn't eat lunch at all. "People have looked at
55 the cadavers[5] of men in their 20s who died in car accidents or as casualties of war, and nearly all had arterial cholesterol deposits," Topol says. "This disease starts much earlier than people realize."

Topol's study did find that although dysfunctional[6]
60 *MEF2A* is very rare, the chance of heart disease in those carrying it may approach 100 percent. Most other genetic variations identified thus far increase the risk by much less.

"Heart disease is not a one- or two-gene problem,"
65 says Steven Ellis, a Cleveland Clinic cardiologist. Ellis oversees a genetic study that collects DNA samples from patients who enter hospitals with atherosclerosis. Ellis, like most cardiac researchers, suspects that dozens of genes contribute to a
70 predisposition[7] to heart disease. Of the several dozen genes, each may contribute just one percent to a person's total risk—an amount that may be compounded, or offset, by outside factors like diet. As one doctor commented, any person's heart
75 attack risk is "50 percent genetic and 50 percent cheeseburger."

The point of tracking down all these small mutations, Ellis explains, is to create a comprehensive blood test—one that could calculate
80 a person's genetic susceptibility by adding up the number of risky (and, eventually, beneficial) variables. Combined with other important factors, such as smoking, weight, blood pressure, and cholesterol levels, doctors could decide which
85 patients need aggressive treatment, such as high-dose statins,[8] and which ones are likely to benefit from exercise or other lifestyle changes. Some genes can already predict whose cholesterol level will respond strongly to dietary changes, and
90 whose won't.

Assessing risk is crucial, Ellis says, because heart disease is often invisible. Fifty percent of men and 64 percent of women who die of heart disease die suddenly, without experiencing any
95 previous symptoms.

▲ As technology progresses, medical researchers are finding new ways to treat illnesses and save lives. For sufferers of heart diseases, artificial hearts like the one shown here may be cause for hope.

ALTHOUGH STANDARD TESTS can detect atherosclerosis, they aren't foolproof.[9] They may reveal plaques, but give no indication whether or not they are life-threatening. Tests like
100 angiography, for example, in which doctors inject a dye into the bloodstream and track it with X-rays, can show how much blood is flowing through an artery, but not discern the plaques embedded inside the artery wall—often the principal culprit in
105 a heart attack.

[5] A **cadaver** is a dead body, especially one intended for dissection.
[6] Something (in medical situations, an organ or body part) that is **dysfunctional** is not working or functioning normally.
[7] If something or someone has a **predisposition** to a disease or condition, they are more likely to get that disease, or suffer from that condition.
[8] **Statins** are a class of drug used to lower cholesterol levels.
[9] If something is **foolproof**, it is incapable of going wrong or failing to succeed.

Until there are tests, genetic or otherwise, that give a clearer measure of risk, everyone would be advised to exercise, watch their diet, and take statins for elevated cholesterol—the same advice doctors gave when the clogged-pipes model of heart disease was unchallenged (see below).

But statins, like any drug, carry the risk of side effects: muscle aches are a well-known effect, and periodic blood tests to check liver function are recommended. The fact is, many of us just like to eat cheeseburgers, lie back and watch TV, and get around in cars. And it's hard, says Leslie Cho, a director at the Cleveland Clinic, for a person to worry about a disease that hits ten years down the road—particularly since heart patients, unlike cancer patients, can't easily observe the progress of their disease. "You've done damage over years, and it will take years to undo that damage. That's a very hard thing to sell," she says. "We do what we can, but then people go home."

As one doctor told me, any person's heart attack risk is "50 percent genetic and 50 percent cheeseburger."

The good news is that genetic research continues to thrive. Should we want to, we will soon be able to know the state of our hearts—and our genes—in ever growing detail. That knowledge, and what we do with it, could make the difference between dying at 65 and living until 80. The choice, increasingly, will be ours.

Clogged Pipes and Ruptured Walls

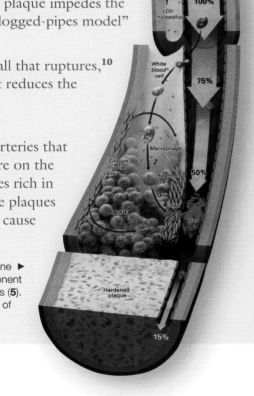

Worldwide, coronary heart disease kills 7.2 million people every year. Exacerbated by the export of Western lifestyle—motorized transport, abundant meat and cheese, workdays conducted from the comfort of a well-padded chair—incidence of the disease is soaring.

Until recently, cardiologists approached heart disease as a plumbing problem. Just as mineral deposits restrict the flow of water through a pipe, a build up of plaque impedes the flow of blood through an arterial channel. Doctors now dismiss this "clogged-pipes model" as an idea whose time has passed. It's just not that simple.

Most heart attacks are caused by plaque embedded within the artery wall that ruptures,[10] cracking the wall and triggering the formation of a blood clot. The clot reduces the volume of blood flowing to the heart muscle, which can die from lack of oxygen and nutrients. Suddenly, the pump stops pumping.

Contrary to the clogged pipes model, heart attacks generally occur in arteries that have minimal or moderate blockage, and their occurrence depends more on the kind of plaque than on the quantity. Findings suggest that softer plaques rich in cholesterol are more unstable and likely to rupture than the hard, dense plaques that extensively narrow the artery channel. But understanding the root cause of the disease will require much more research.

Buildup to a heart attack: Cholesterol in the blood enters the arterial wall (**1**). The body's immune ▶ system sends chemicals to consume the cholesterol (**2**); these grow to form foam cells, a component of plaque (**3**). Muscle cells on the wall create a cap (**4**), which may be weakened by the foam cells (**5**). If the cap cracks, plaque moves into the bloodstream (**6**). A clot may form, restricting the volume of blood, causing a heart attack.

[10] If something **ruptures**, it is breaking or being broken apart.

Reading Comprehension

A. Multiple Choice. Choose the best answer for each question.

Rhetorical Purpose **1.** The author probably begins the article with information about Don Steffensen because of _____.
- a. his age
- b. the size of his family
- c. his unhealthy diet
- d. his unusual genome

Detail **2.** According to the information in paragraph 6 (from line 51), most people do not realize that heart disease _____.
- a. can be predicted in most cases
- b. kills more people than wars or car accidents
- c. begins quite early in life
- d. can be prevented by eating salad and high fiber cereal

Detail **3.** What does the author say about dysfunctional *MEF2A*?
- a. It is not common, but it is very dangerous.
- b. It can cause problems other than heart disease.
- c. It cannot be detected with current technology.
- d. It is less dangerous than most genetic mutations.

Vocabulary **4.** The phrase *tracking down* in line 77 is closest in meaning to _____.
- a. taking apart
- b. classifying
- c. searching for
- d. isolating

Reference **5.** The word *ones* in line 86 refers to _____.
- a. doctors
- b. genes
- c. statins
- d. patients

Rhetorical Purpose **6.** The purpose of the statistics in paragraph 10 (from line 91) is to _____.
- a. prove that heart disease is more dangerous to women than to men
- b. show why risk assessment is vital for preventing heart disease
- c. warn readers not to ignore the signs of a heart disease
- d. explain how it is possible to misinterpret certain symptoms

Inference **7.** The author implies that the drugs known as statins _____.
- a. may cause liver damage
- b. are used to treat muscle pains
- c. will help patients lose weight
- d. produce results that are easily measured

Main Idea **8.** The main idea of the final section of the article (lines 140–157) is that _____.
- a. doctors are unsure exactly why plaque builds up inside artery walls
- b. the "clogged-pipes model" does not fully explain why heart attacks occur
- c. the export of Western lifestyle has caused a sudden increase in heart disease
- d. a diet high in cholesterol is the biggest single factor contributing to heart disease

We scan to find specific information that we need from an article, for example, key details like dates, names, amounts, or places. To scan, you must have a clear idea of the kind of information you are looking for. If possible, have one or two key words in mind. Then read through the material quickly looking for these words or related words. Don't try to read every word and don't worry about understanding every word that you read. When you find the relevant word(s), read the surrounding context to check how the information relates to the rest of the text.

B. Scanning. Quickly read the article again to find answers to these questions (**1–8**). Write the answers and note the line number(s) where you found the answers.

1. A single gene might contribute what percentage to a person's total risk of heart disease?

_____ line(s) _____

2. What would a comprehensive blood test for coronary risks show?

_____ line(s) _____

3. How did Don Steffensen first know about the genetics research?

_____ line(s) _____

4. What can an angiography test show?

_____ line(s) _____

5. Why do many people not worry about heart disease?

_____ line(s) _____

6. Where does Eric Topol work?

_____ line(s) _____

7. How did Don Steffensen survive his heart attack?

_____ line(s) _____

8. People with what condition would be advised to take statins?

_____ line(s) _____

C. Critical Thinking. Discuss these questions with a partner.

1. The author indicates that genetic factors can contribute to the possibility of heart disease. What evidence does he provide that this is true?

2. The author says that today, doctors no longer think of heart disease as a "plumbing problem." What model has replaced the "clogged-pipes" model?

3. Imagine that, in the future, there will be a medical test that can accurately predict your life expectancy. Would you want to know that information? Why or why not?

Vocabulary Practice

A. Completion. Complete the information using the correct word from each pair.

Gloria Stevens is lying on her back, staring at an image of her own beating heart. At this moment, she is **1.** exacerbating / submitting herself to a life-saving procedure. Her doctor is inserting a thin tube that will pass through a series of arteries to Gloria's heart. It eventually arrives at a spot where plaque has narrowed the arterial channel by 90 percent, severely **2.** compounding / impeding the blood passing through it. As Gloria watches on the monitor, the narrowing in her artery disappears, and suddenly a large **3.** stress / volume of blood starts flowing, like a river in flood.

The procedure is over. It has lasted only half an hour. In all likelihood, Gloria will be able to go home the next day. So will a few thousand other patients in the United States undergoing such routine procedures today—more than a million of them a year with a disease that has reached epidemic **4.** mutations / proportions. Genetic factors may account for some patients' heart disease, but in most cases it is **5.** compounded / submitted by a high fat diet and low levels of activity. Additionally, the **6.** proportion / stress of busy modern lifestyles is likely to **7.** exacerbate / impede cardiac symptoms.

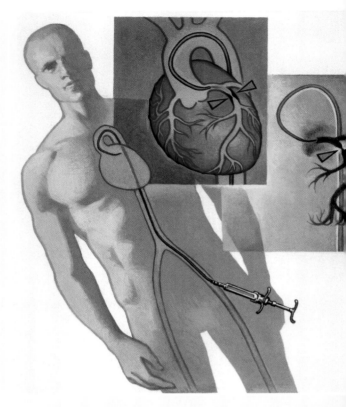

▲ Procedures such as angiography (illustrated) involve inserting a thin tube into an artery in the groin, and passing it through the body to the heart. The procedure allows doctors to identify and treat problems in a patient's coronary arteries.

The procedure has not fully cured Gloria of her coronary atherosclerosis, and she is still **8.** principal / susceptible to future blockages and coronary heart disease. But her quality of life will likely improve as a result of treatment. She'll breathe more easily and, maybe, she'll live longer, too.

B. Definitions. Match the correct form of each word in red in **A** to its definition. Two words are extra.

1. (to) make movement or development difficult _____

2. feeling of worry and tenseness _____

3. (to) develop different characteristics _____

4. amount of space something contains _____

5. a partial number compared to a total number _____

6. likely to be affected by something _____

7. first in order of importance _____

8. (to) allow something to be done _____

Usage

As verbs, **exacerbate** and **compound** have similar meanings. If something *exacerbates* a problem, it makes it worse. To *compound* a problem means to make it worse by adding to it. As a noun, **compound** has several usages: A *compound* is an enclosed area of land used for a particular purpose. In chemistry, a *compound* is a substance that consists of two or more elements. If something is a *compound* of different things, it is made of those things.

48 Unit 3 Health and Genes

3B

Tiny Invaders

▲ A magnified image of yellow pollen grains on a geranium plant, each of which can be measured in millionths of a meter.

A single grain of **pollen** may be only one-quarter the width of a human hair, but to a person with hay fever **allergies**, it's a dangerous invader. Particles of pollen from plants such as the ragweed enter the body through the nose, mouth, or skin and trigger an overactive response from the body's **immune system**. The result: People who are **allergic** to the pollen will suffer from repeated sneezing and watery, red eyes; often they will also have difficulty breathing. In recent decades, allergy rates have been on the rise worldwide. The question is: Why?

allergic being negatively affected by a substance because you have an allergy
allergy a condition that causes a person to become ill if they breathe, eat, or touch certain substances that normally do not make people sick
immune system the parts and processes of the body that fight illness and infection
pollen a fine powder produced by flowers which fertilizes flowers of the same species so they can produce seeds

☐ Before You Read

A. Discussion. Read the information above and use the glossary to help you understand the words in **blue**. Then answer these questions.

   1. What causes a hay fever allergy? What symptoms do people with hay fever usually suffer from?

   2. Do you know of other things, aside from plant pollen, that people can be allergic to? What happens if they eat, breathe, or touch these things?

   3. Allergy rates are on the rise worldwide. What do you think is causing this?

B. Scan and Predict. The passage on pages 50–52 has four main sections. Scan for where each section starts (look for words that are all capitalized), and write the line numbers below. Match each section with the topic you think it will be about (**a–e**). One topic is extra. Then read the article to check your ideas.

1 (from line 1) _____   **a.** how an allergy starts
2 (from line ____) _____   **b.** allergy symptoms and statistics
                               c. allergy prevention and treatment
3 (from line ____) _____   **d.** how allergies were first detected
4 (from line ____) _____   **e.** possible causes of rising allergy rates

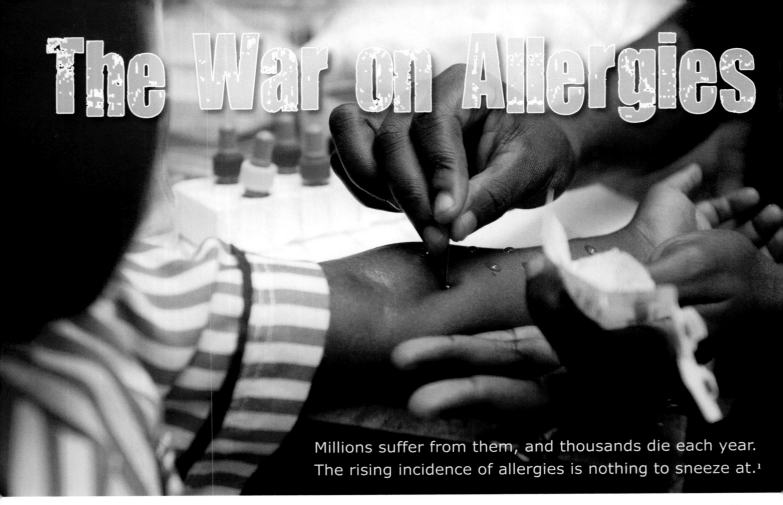

The War on Allergies

Millions suffer from them, and thousands die each year. The rising incidence of allergies is nothing to sneeze at.[1]

▲ Researchers perform allergy skin prick tests on school children in Accra, Ghana.

1 SUPPOSE THAT 54.3 PERCENT of your country's population had cancer. That figure might set off a nationwide panic—a search for something wrong with people's diet, the environment, activity
5 levels. In fact, that's the percentage of Americans who show a positive skin response to one or more allergens.

The manifestations[2] of allergy—sneezing, itching, rashes—are signs of an immune system running
10 amok,[3] attacking foreign invaders—allergens—that mean no harm. Allergens include pollen, dust mites, mold, food, drugs, stinging insects, or any other substance to which the body can choose to react, or overreact. Allergies rarely kill. They just
15 make the sufferer miserable—sometimes for brief periods, and sometimes for life.

Allergies are essentially an epidemic of modernity. As countries become more industrialized, the percentage of population affected by them tends
20 to grow higher. There are remote areas of South America or Africa where allergies are virtually nonexistent.

In contrast, six percent of young children in the U.S. today have food allergies. Federal legislation
25 requires manufacturers to clearly label whether major allergens—peanuts, soy, shellfish, eggs, wheat, milk, fish, and tree nuts—are ingredients in any product. Children sit at special tables at lunchtime; there are websites and support groups
30 for parents homeschooling their severely allergic children.

HERE'S HOW AN ALLERGY develops: One day, a body is exposed to a protein in something that seems perfectly harmless—the wheat flour, say, in a home-
35 baked muffin. But for some unclear reason, the body looks at the protein and sees trouble. There will be no symptoms at first, but the body is remembering—and planning.

[1] When we say something is "**nothing to sneeze at,**" we're saying it's actually important and deserves serious attention.
[2] **Manifestations** are clear and observable appearances, e. g. symptoms of a medical condition.
[3] If something is **running amok**, it has gone into a frenzy, acting in a wild or dangerous manner.

▲ Pollen from the ragweed plant can enter the body via nasal passages in the nose. The allergen releases proteins that cause an allergic reaction.

pollen

nose lining

pollen protein (Allergen)

Allergen binds with IgE

Mast cell

IgE

Irritating chemicals

That first exposure causes the immune system to produce an antibody called IgE (immunoglobulin E). Then IgE antibodies attach to certain cells, called mast cells, in tissue throughout the body. There they stay like wary soldiers waiting for war. With a second exposure, even months later, some of the allergen binds with the IgE on the mast cell. This time the mast cell releases a flood of irritating chemicals, which cause inflammation and itching.

A minor or isolated reaction can become more serious with repeated exposure to an allergen, or when other cells involved in the immune system, the T cells, come into play. Certain T cells remember the "insult" of the allergen and ensure that some part of the body keeps becoming inflamed. Often the allergen and the immune system become increasingly antagonistic,[4] and the reaction worsens.

THERE IS, UNQUESTIONABLY, a hereditary component to allergies. A child with one asthmatic[5] parent has a good chance of developing the condition. If both parents have asthma, the chance of occurrence increases.

Still, the rise in allergies is too rapid to be explained solely by genetics. "The genetic pool can't change that much in such a short time," says Donald Leung, director of an allergy-immunology program in the U.S. "There have to be environmental and behavioral factors as well." Dozens of theories have blamed everyone from urban landscapers for favoring male plants (the ones that produce pollen), to women who don't breastfeed.

Breastfeeding, the theory goes, confers greater protection against allergies.

Another probable factor: diet. "Reduced fresh fruit and vegetable intake, more processed food, fewer antioxidants,[6] and low intake of some minerals—these are all shown to be a risk," says professor of medicine Harold Nelson, considered one of the foremost experts on allergies in the U.S.

The use of antibiotics may also be an underlying cause of rising allergy rates. Certain bacteria in the intestine are associated with greater or lesser chances of having allergies. Researchers believe, as Donald Leung says, "Overuse of antibiotics may be disrupting certain gut flora that suppress allergy."

Another prime culprit: environmental pollutants. Exactly what pollutants and in what quantities are a source of heated debate. One of dozens of examples: Children who are raised near major highways and are exposed to diesel fumes from trucks register an increased sensitivity to allergens they already react to.

[4] If things or people are **antagonistic** toward each other, they oppose each other, behaving like enemies.
[5] Someone who is **asthmatic** suffers from asthma, which is a lung condition that causes difficulty in breathing.
[6] **Antioxidants** are molecules, often found in plants, that are known to prevent cell damage.

Ironically it's not just the pollutants
that are doing us in. It may be too
much cleanliness. A prevalent theory
among allergists is known as the
hygiene hypothesis. While it's true that
industrialization brings with it better
health care and fewer serious childhood
infections, it also brings an obsession with
cleanliness. We are not exposed to dirt at
a young enough age to give our immune
systems a good workout. Also, because of
the high cost of energy, more homes are
built with better insulation—insulation
that seals in mold and dust.

"The hygiene hypothesis has been on the
scene since people first started looking at
allergies," says associate professor Andrew
Liu. "John Bostock, the guy who first
identified hay fever, noted that it was a
condition of the educated. He couldn't report any
cases among poor people."

But if dirt is a good thing, why are allergies
and asthma so prevalent in poor, inner-city
neighborhoods? "It's not just a question of
exposure to dirt that reduces allergies—it has to
be the right kind of dirt," says Liu. "We're talking
about exposure to endotoxin
and good microbes in soil and
animal waste." Research supports
the hygiene hypothesis. "There
was a famous study," says Harold
Nelson, "where one of the
protective factors for asthma was
having a pig in the house."

SINCE MOST OF US are unable to room with a pig, we
have to come up with a plan. Can we avoid allergies
altogether? Can we get rid of allergies we already
have? Can we desensitize our immune systems?

"We still don't know exactly how to prevent
allergies," says Andrew Liu. "We know the immune
response is supposed to be a helpful one, that it's
not supposed to be the cause of disease. We know
that the immune system of someone with allergies
needs to be reeducated. But how? It's not
always clear."

Leung agrees, adding, "If you are exposed
to . . . microbial products early in life, it may
prevent allergies. But later in life the early exposure

▲ Studies have shown that children who are exposed to farm animals suffer less from allergies than their urban-living peers.

may actually make things worse." There are
those who argue that to prevent allergies, we
should reduce exposure to harmful allergens at
an early age. Others believe allergens should be
administered in large quantities at an early age.
Many believe it depends on the specific allergen.
And food allergies may work on an altogether
different principle. Confused? So are the allergists.

"There was a famous study where one of the
protective factors for asthma was having a
pig in the house."

But there is hope that allergy sufferers may one
day live in a world that's far more comfortable.
Suddenly there's a booming market for products
and services that were unimaginable 30 years
ago. Hotels offer allergy sufferers rooms with
special ventilation systems and linens washed
with nontoxic products. Scientists are finding
ways to get rid of the allergenic proteins in
common offenders. Researchers at the University
of Melbourne in Australia also claim to have
developed the first hypoallergenic rye grass;
it doesn't cause hay fever.

But the questions remain: Are allergies truly
preventable? How much genetic engineering is
feasible? And even if we can eliminate the allergens
we fight today, what will our immune systems
decide are the enemies tomorrow?

Reading Comprehension

A. **Multiple Choice.** Choose the best answer for each question.

Gist **1.** The best alternative title for the article would be _____.
   a. A New Theory on How Allergies Develop
   b. How Can We Prevent Allergies in Our Children?
   c. Medical Science's Latest Victory over Allergies
   d. What's Causing the Allergy Epidemic?

Inference **2.** In paragraph 1, the author implies that _____.
   a. more than half of all Americans will suffer from some form of cancer
   c. because more people are now affected by allergies, the nation has begun to panic
   b. a surprisingly high percentage of people have positive skin responses to allergens
   d. scientists are trying to find something wrong in our diet and activity levels

Inference **3.** Which of the following statements can be inferred from the information on page 50?
   a. People living in South American and African cities are seldom affected by allergies.
   b. More U.S. children are affected by allergies than children in most other countries.
   c. Children who are severely affected by allergies do not attend regular schools.
   d. People were more affected by allergies in the past than they are at present.

Detail **4.** Which of the following actually produces the chemicals that cause allergic reactions?
   a. T cells   c. mast cells
   b. allergens   d. IgE antibodies

Vocabulary **5.** The phrase *come into play* on line 51 is closest in meaning to _____.
   a. begin to have an effect   c. start to weaken
   b. form suddenly   d. move to another place

Negative Detail **6.** According to the author, scientists do NOT believe allergies are solely caused by heredity because _____.
   a. so many people have developed allergies so quickly
   b. there are so many new types of allergies today
   c. studies show that allergies can only be transmitted by one parent
   d. the symptoms of allergies are so much more severe today

Detail **7.** According to the information in paragraph 12 (from line 92), what do studies show about the effect of diesel fumes on children?
   a. They cause children to develop new allergies.
   b. They make existing allergies worse.
   c. They may help prevent further allergies.
   d. They can cause allergies when the children grow up.

Paraphrase **8.** Which of the following is closest in meaning to this sentence from lines 140–142:
   "We know that the immune system of someone with allergies needs to be reeducated."
   a. Certainly, people with allergies must be taught new ways of thinking about their problem.
   b. Scientists know that they must develop new ways of thinking about the immune system.
   c. Clearly, the immune systems of people with allergic responses must somehow be altered.
   d. As we know, people around the world must learn more about their own immune systems.

A major part of this article is a discussion of known causes and possible causes of allergies. One way to present visually the relationships in an article or part of an article—for example, the factors which contribute to something—is to create a concept map. The concept map below illustrates the causes and possible causes of allergies.

B. Completion. Look over pages 51–52 again, paying attention to factors that cause or may cause people to develop allergies. Complete the concept map using words from the article. Use up to three words for each blank.

Children with
(**1**) _____
parent(s) are more likely to
have the same condition.
But increase in allergies is
too (**2**) _____
to be solely due to heredity.

Greater consumption of (**4**) _____ food is a risk
factor. People take in fewer fruits, (**5**) _____,
_____, and _____.

Some (**6**) _____ in
the body are related to allergies.
(**7**) _____ of
antibiotics may affect these bacteria.

(**3**) _____

Heredity

ALLERGIES

Antibiotics

Environment

(**10**) _____ **Hypothesis**

One example: (**8**) _____
fumes may make allergies worse.
Scientists are debating exactly which
(**9**) _____ are culprits.

People are not exposed to enough
(**11**) _____ when young.
Houses have better (**12**) _____
which seals in (**13**) _____.

C. Critical Thinking. Discuss these questions with a partner.

1. The author indicates that allergies are more common in developed countries than in developing countries. Give reasons from the article and your own ideas to explain why this is true.

2. In your own words, explain what the author means by the "hygiene hypothesis" (paragraphs 13–15). What evidence does the author produce to support this hypothesis?

3. In the last paragraph of the article, the author asks a series of "rhetorical questions" (questions that he does not expect an answer to). What is the purpose of these questions?

Vocabulary Practice

A. Completion. Complete the information using the correct form of the words in the box. One word is extra.

component	confer	federal	legislation
positive	register	release	solely
suppress	virtually		

Seven-year-old Cameron Liflander frequently suffers from watery, swollen eyes, caused by the **1.** _____ of chemicals in response to his allergies. This makes him **2.** _____ no different from more than 50 million other Americans today. But his problem is not **3.** _____ the watery eyes or scratchy throat we associate with allergies. Cameron's body is at war with his environment. And his mother fears that one day the environment could win.

A boy is treated for asthma (a breathing problem usually caused by allergies) at a Chicago school.

Cameron was a sickly baby, but his growth rate was relatively normal. He drank breast milk, which is supposed to **4.** _____ some protection against allergies, for almost a year. One day his mother gave him a bite of tuna. Cameron turned red and started choking. Benadryl, a medicine to **5.** _____ allergies, helped him recover, but the next severe reaction sent him to the emergency room. It would be the first of many visits.

Cameron still requires a daily supply of drugs and skin creams to help counter his asthma and allergic skin conditions. Nevertheless, life is looking more **6.** _____ now for Cameron. For instance, his reaction to certain substances is decreasing with age. He now tolerates soy—a huge relief because soy is a **7.** _____ in a vast range of products. In addition, recent **8.** _____ by the U.S. **9.** _____ government on labeling major allergens in food products has allowed him and countless other allergy sufferers to avoid foods which trigger reactions.

B. Definitions. Use the correct form of words in the box in **A** to complete the definitions.

1. If something is _____ true, it is almost entirely true.

2. The _____ of something are the parts that it is made of.

3. If you _____ someone or something, you stop holding them.

4. If a natural function of your body is _____, it is stopped or prevented.

5. When something _____ on a scale of measurement, it shows on the scale.

6. To _____ something, such as power, on someone, means to give it to them.

7. If the result of a medical or scientific test is _____, it shows that something has happened or is present.

8. A _____ system of government is one where states or provinces of the country have the power to make their own laws and decisions.

Thesaurus   **release** Also look up: (*v.*) liberate, clear, excuse, let go; (*ant.*) detain, imprison; (*n.*) acquittal, liberation; (*ant.*) detention, imprisonment

Fighting Malaria

A. Preview. This video is about a very useful flower. Do you know any useful flowers or herbs? What are they used for?

B. Summarize. Watch the video, *Fighting Malaria*. Then complete the summary below using the correct form of words in the box. Two words are extra.

▲ A Kenyan child plays in fields of pyrethrum flowers. Pyrethrum is a natural insecticide.

component	compound	conspicuous	elevate
institute	principal	release	solely
susceptible	thrive		

The Anopheles mosquito may be far less **1.** _____ than some of the larger and more famous predators which **2.** _____ in Kenya, but it is just as deadly.

At a research center just outside the capital, researchers breed these insects in order to learn more about them. The insects raised here are bred **3.** _____ for research, and are harmless, but in the wild, they are responsible for spreading the killer disease, malaria. Here in Kenya, up to 40 percent of the population suffers from malaria in one year, including millions of children, who are more **4.** _____ to malaria than adults.

However, Kenya is also the home to a very effective mosquito killer. It's a flower, a type of chrysanthemum, called pyrethrum. Pyrethrum extract is a **5.** _____ of many **6.** _____ used as insecticides. When it is **7.** _____, it paralyzes the insect's nervous system, leaving the insect vulnerable. It also kills the insect very quickly.

The **8.** _____ benefits of using pyrethrum are that it's environmentally friendly, and the mosquitoes have no time to build resistance to this fast-acting disease-killer.

C. Think About It.

1. How does pyrethrum fight malaria? Describe what happens to a partner.

2. What surprised you most about the information in this unit? Share your answer with a partner.

To learn more about health and genes, visit elt.heinle.com/explorer

A. World Heritage Spotlight. Read the information on pages 58–59 and answer the questions (**1–3**).

1. Scanning. Match each person with a description (**a–f**).

___ Akhenaten	**a.** discovered the tomb of Seti I
___ Giovanni Belzoni	**b.** his tomb is still undiscovered
___ Howard Carter	**c.** probably the father of King Tut
___ Ramses II	**d.** his tomb was discovered in 1817
___ Ramses VIII	**e.** the greatest builder of monuments
___ Seti I	**f.** discovered the tomb of Tutankhamun

2. Vocabulary from Context. Find words or phrases in the text on page 58 to match the definitions (**a–f**).

a. a person's mind, thoughts, feelings _____

b. filled, or equipped (with objects) _____

c. more advanced techniques _____

d. mostly untouched _____

e. skillfully cut or sculpted _____

f. spectacular ornaments _____

3. Discussion. What do archaeologists think probably caused King Tut's death? What evidence supports this view?

B. A Global View. Read the text and graphics on pages 60–61 and discuss the following questions with a partner.

1. How many health-related MDGs are mentioned? Which goal has made the least progress so far?

2. Which part of the world has been most successful in reducing its number of undernourished children? By how much has the number been reduced?

3. By how much has global infant mortality been reduced? What reason is given for this decline?

4. Which part of the world suffers most from infant mortality, undernourishment, and communicable disease? What reasons are given for this? What other factors might be contributing?

5. Which parts of the world suffer from overnutrition? What health problems could result from this?

6. In which parts of the world are injuries the leading cause of unnatural death? What might explain this?

Valley of the Kings

Site: **Ancient Thebes with Its Necropolis**

Location: **Egypt**

Category: **Cultural**

Status: **World Heritage Site since 1979**

Egypt's New Kingdom

18th Dynasty	19th Dynasty	20th Dynasty

1539 B.C.

Akhenaten 1353–1336

Tutankhamun 1333–1323

Seti I 1290–1279

Ramses II 1279–1213

1078 B.C.

Ramses VIII 1129–1128

During Egypt's New Kingdom (1539–1078 B.C.), virtually all of its kings, or pharaohs, were buried in underground tombs on the Nile's west bank, in a place now called the Valley of the Kings. The valley was believed to be a transit place to the afterlife, and each pharaoh received elaborate preparations for his journey. Mummification preserved the king's body so it could be reunited with his eternal soul after death; the tombs were also stocked with all the material goods a ruler might need in the next world—furniture, clothes, and dazzling jewelry.

More than 60 tombs have been found dispersed throughout the valley. The majority were looted before modern times, but one burial place remained largely intact due to its inconspicuous location—the tomb of the young King Tutankhamun, reopened by British archaeologist Howard Carter in 1922. King Tut's is the best-preserved surviving tomb, but the grandest in the whole valley was probably the tomb of Seti I. Its maze of internal passages, decorated with elaborate paintings and drawings, led to a delicately carved sarcophagus, which the Italian adventurer Giovanni Belzoni discovered in 1817. We can never know what other treasures existed, however, as the tomb had been looted long ago.

Since Belzoni's time, archaeologists have surveyed the valley using increasingly sophisticated methods. Nevertheless, they suspect there are still discoveries to be made. In 1989, Kent R. Weeks of University of Chicago's Oriental Institute found the resting places of several sons of Ramses II (the son of Seti I) in the largest tomb complex yet discovered. And researchers still dream of locating the tomb of Ramses VIII, the sole pharaoh of the 20th Dynasty whose tomb has not been identified. It is possible that the Valley of the Kings has not yet revealed all of its secrets.

"I sought a resting-place, found one, and [attempted] to sit; but when my weight bore on the body of an Egyptian, it crushed it like a band-box. I naturally [used] my hands to sustain my weight, but they found no better support; so that I sunk altogether among the broken mummies, with a crash of bones, rags, and wooden cases, which raised such a dust as kept me motionless for a quarter of an hour . . ."

– Giovanni Belzoni, describing his passage through an Egyptian tomb in the early 19th century

▲ This picture illustrates the preparation of the tomb of Seti I, from initial carving of the rock wall (far left) to the entry of the king's sarcophagus (upper right).

Did Malaria Kill King Tut?

More than 5,000 artifacts were found inside the tomb of Tutankhamun when it was reopened in 1922. But despite the volume of riches, a mystery remained: why did the king die when he was just 19?

In 2005, CT scans of the king's mummy showed Tut did not die from a blow to the head, as many people suspected. A hole in the back of his head had instead been made during the mummification process. The study also showed Tut died soon after fracturing his left leg.

Three years later, samples from Tut's mummy (above right) were submitted for DNA analysis. The studies showed part of Tut's left foot was affected by a condition known as necrosis, or "tissue death." This would have impeded his ability to walk, which is probably why he is shown in contemporary drawings either sitting or walking with a cane. The analysis also revealed that Tut had suffered from malaria. The disease probably weakened his immune system, leaving him vulnerable to infection following his leg fracture.

One other factor may have contributed to Tut's early death: his mother and father were full brother and sister. DNA analysis proves that Tut was the son of a mysterious woman known today only as the Younger Lady. This woman was also sister to a man scientists believe was Tut's father—a badly preserved mummy thought to be Akhenaten, an earlier pharaoh. A married brother and sister is more likely to pass on twin copies of harmful genes. This may have left the young Tut more susceptible to genetic mutations, such as the disease in his foot, which probably contributed to his early death.

Ramses II

Tutankhamun

Akhenaten?

Seti I

▲ A painting depicts Ramses II (Ramses the Great) making offerings to the Egyptian god Amun. During his 66-year rule, Ramses expanded Egypt's borders and built more temples, monuments, and statues than any other pharaoh.

Egypt's Valley of the Kings contains over 60 royal tombs. Together they comprise, says archaeologist Kent R. Weeks, "the richest archaeological site on Earth."

Health and Mortality

A Global View

The Millennium Development Goals (MDGs) are eight international development goals that all 192 United Nations member states and several international organizations have agreed to achieve by the year 2015. Adopted at a meeting of world leaders at UN Headquarters in New York in September 2000, the MDGs comprise the largest ever effort to meet the needs of the world's poorest people.

Several MDG targets are health-related. So far, progress in most of these has been mixed. MDG 1, for instance, commits to halving the proportion of people suffering from hunger by 2015. In 2010, the percentage of underweight children stood at 16 percent, down from 25 percent in 1990. But that still leaves at least one hundred million children undernourished, most in sub-Saharan Africa. The goal to reduce infant mortality by two-thirds between 1990 and 2015 (MDG 4) has also made partial progress. Although annual global infant mortality fell by 30 percent in 1990–2008, in some low-income countries one out of every 10 children dies before reaching the age of five.

MDG 5 has seen the least encouraging progress so far. In 2005, more than half a million women died during pregnancy, childbirth, or in the six weeks after delivery. In sub-Saharan Africa, a woman's risk of dying from treatable or preventable complications of pregnancy and childbirth is 1 in 22, compared to 1 in 7,300 in developed regions. Similarly, sub-Saharan Africa is the region most at risk from HIV/AIDS, tuberculosis, malaria, and other diseases (MDG 6). According to the World Health Organization (WHO), 2.7 million people contracted the HIV virus in 2008, a decline of 16 percent since 2000—progress at least partly due to more widespread use of antiretroviral therapy (ART). However, by the end of 2008 there were still more than five million untreated HIV-positive people in low- and middle-income countries.

◀ Vunei Kasachi comforts her ten-month-old son, Nicholas, a malaria patient at Kalene Mission Hospital in Zambia. Use of treated bed nets such as this one has been shown to reduce transmission of malaria by about 90 percent.

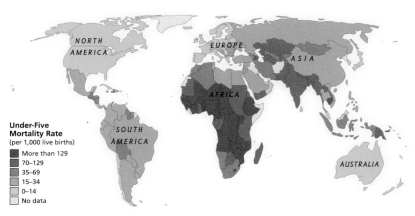

Under-Five Mortality Rate (per 1,000 live births)
- More than 129
- 70–129
- 35–69
- 15–34
- 0–14
- No data

Under-Five Mortality ▲

By 2010, infant mortality had fallen to 72 per 1,000 live births, but that represents less than half the UN's reduction target. Progress so far has largely been due to better disease prevention: the percentage of infants immunized against measles, for example, increased from 73 to 83 percent from 1990 to 2008.

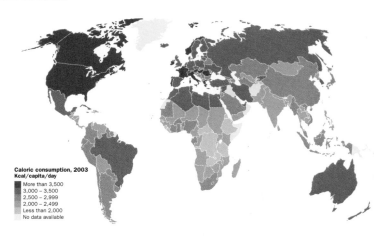

Caloric consumption, 2003 Kcal/capita/day
- More than 3,500
- 3,000 – 3,500
- 2,500 – 2,999
- 2,000 – 2,499
- Less than 2,000
- No data available

Caloric Intake ▲

Recommendations for adult caloric intake vary, depending on age, gender, body size, and daily activity, but most range from 2,000 to 3,000 calories per day. While millions, particularly in sub-Saharan Africa, suffer from a lack of available calories and are undernourished, an increasing percentage of the world, mainly in developed countries, is suffering from excessive consumption and, as a result, obesity.

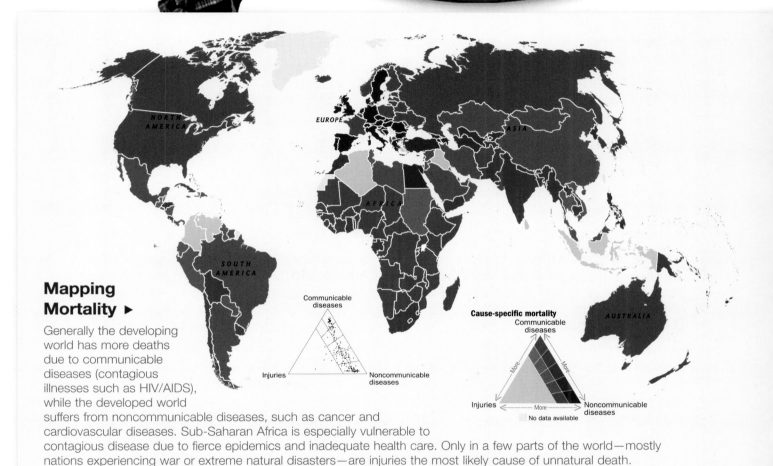

UN Millennium Development Goals

Goal 1: Eradicate extreme poverty and hunger
Goal 4: Reduce child mortality rate
Goal 5: Improve maternal health
Goal 6: Combat HIV/AIDS, malaria, and other diseases

Mapping Mortality ▶

Generally the developing world has more deaths due to communicable diseases (contagious illnesses such as HIV/AIDS), while the developed world suffers from noncommunicable diseases, such as cancer and cardiovascular diseases. Sub-Saharan Africa is especially vulnerable to contagious disease due to fierce epidemics and inadequate health care. Only in a few parts of the world—mostly nations experiencing war or extreme natural disasters—are injuries the most likely cause of unnatural death.

Communicable diseases

Injuries   Noncommunicable diseases

Cause-specific mortality

Communicable diseases

More   More

Injuries ◄——— More ———► Noncommunicable diseases

No data available

Charting the Undernourished ▶

While there has been progress—particularly in China—in reducing the percentage of the world's undernourished, there has been virtually no change in the total number. Sub-Saharan Africa continues to struggle with hunger and is the region most vulnerable to famine.

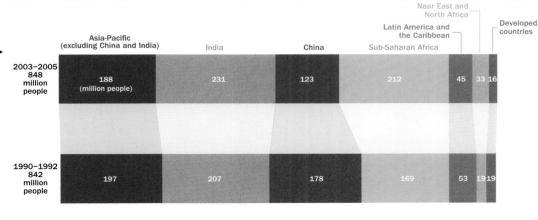

	Asia-Pacific (excluding China and India)	India	China	Sub-Saharan Africa	Latin America and the Caribbean	Near East and North Africa	Developed countries
2003–2005 848 million people	188 (million people)	231	123	212	45	33	16
1990–1992 842 million people	197	207	178	169	53	19	19

A. Word Link. Each of the verbs in the box contains **trans**, meaning *across*. Match each verb with its definition. One word is extra. Use your dictionary to help you. Then use the correct form of words from the box to complete the sentences (**1–4**).

transcribe	transfer	transfix	transform	transgress
translate	transmit	transplant	transport	

a. put into a different language _____

b. move to a different job _____

c. break a moral law or rule of behavior _____

d. move a body part from one person to another _____

e. take goods or people from one place to another in a vehicle _____

f. send something, e.g., a signal or disease, from one place to another _____

g. change from one thing or state into another, usually something better _____

h. write or type out text from notes or an audio recording _____

1. An ambulance is used to _____ a sick person to a hospital.

2. Illnesses such as typhoid are _____ through dirty water.

3. New medical procedures have _____ the lives of the elderly in developed countries.

4. Nowadays, it is possible to _____ various body parts, such as the heart and liver.

B. Choosing the Right Definition. Study the numbered definitions for *volume*. Then write the number of the definition (**1–6**) that relates to each sentence below. One definition is extra.

volume /vǫlyum/ (**volumes**) **1** N-COUNT The **volume of** something is the amount of it that there is. **2** N-COUNT The **volume** of an object is the amount of space that it contains or occupies. **3** N-COUNT A **volume** is one book in a series of books. **4** N-COUNT A **volume** is a collection of several issues of a magazine, such as all the issues for one year. **5** N-UNCOUNT The **volume** of a radio, television, or sound system is the loudness of the sound it produces. **6** PHRASE If something such as an action **speaks volumes about** a person or thing, it gives you a lot of information about them.

_____ **a.** Listening to music at a loud **volume** may cause long-term damage to hearing ability.

_____ **b.** The **volume** of email messages worldwide has increased greatly in recent years.

_____ **c.** Drought can cause the **volume** of water in a lake to decrease significantly.

_____ **d.** The amount of jewelry a person wears often speaks **volumes** about the person's wealth.

_____ **e.** The second **volume** of Nelson Mandela's autobiography covered the years 1962–1994.

Tradition and Change

Discuss these questions with a partner.

1. Are there traditional aspects of your country that are disappearing because of the pressures of modern life?

2. Where do people from your country go when they want to visit somewhere old or traditional? Why do people visit those places?

3. Which are the most visited cities or regions in your country? How has tourism affected those places?

▲ A donkey introduces a piece of the modern world to a household in Fez el Bali, a traditional neighborhood in Fez, Morocco, in 1984.

4A City Under Seige

▲ Every year, crowds of tourists travel to Venice, Italy. Highlights for many visitors are the chance to ride in a gondola along the famous Grand Canal, and to attend Carnevale, an elaborate costume party that is one of the city's biggest celebrations. ▶

Before You Read

A. Quiz. How much do you know about Venice? Answer the questions. Then check your answers below.

1. Every year, approximately how many people visit the city of Venice?

a. 20,000   b. 200,000   c. 2,000,000   d. 20,000,000

2. Venice is regularly threatened by *acqua alta* (high tides) and has been sinking into the water for years. Over the last century, how much has the city sunk?

a. 13 cm (5 inches)   b. 18 cm (7 inches)   c. 25 cm (10 inches)   d. 38 cm (15 inches)

3. What did the city of Venice recently prohibit people from doing in the Piazza San Marco (the city's main square)?

a. feeding birds   b. selling T-shirts   c. riding skateboards   d. eating gelato (ice cream)

B. Skim for Gist. Look quickly at the article on pages 65–67. Which problem facing Venice do you think the article is mainly about? Circle one option below. Then read through the passage to check your ideas.

a. dangers caused by rising tides   c. problems caused by tourism
b. the city's declining birthrate   d. rising levels of pollution

Vanishing Venice

The city Thomas Mann[1] called "half fairy tale and half tourist trap" finds itself threatened by more than just the rising tide. Cathy Newman investigates the trouble with Venice.

1 NOWHERE IN ITALY is there a crisis more beautifully framed than in Venice. Neither land nor water, the city lifts like a mirage from a lagoon[2] at the head of the Adriatic. For centuries it has threatened to vanish
5 beneath the waves of the *acqua alta*, the relentlessly regular flooding caused by rising tides and sinking foundations. But that is the least of its problems.

Just ask Mayor Massimo Cacciari, professor of philosophy, fluent in German, Latin, Ancient Greek;
10 a man who raises the level of political intellect to just short of the stratosphere.[3] Ask about the acqua alta and Venice sinking, and he says, "So go get boots."

Boots are fine for water, but useless against the flood that causes more concern for Venetians than any
15 lagoon spillover: the flood of tourism. Number of Venetian residents in 2007: 60,000. Number of visitors in 2007: 21 million.

In May 2008, for example, on a holiday weekend, 80,000 tourists descended on the city. Public parking
20 lots in Mestre, where people board a bus or train to the historic center, filled with floodwater and were closed. Those who managed to get to Venice surged through the streets like schools of bluefish, snapping up pizza and gelato, leaving paper and plastic bottles in
25 their wake.[4]

"Beauty is difficult," says Mayor Cacciari, sounding as if he were addressing a graduate seminar in aesthetics[5] rather than answering a question about municipal[6] policy. The black of Cacciari's dark hair and luxuriant
30 beard complement his current mood. The preceding day, heavy rains had flooded Mestre again. Rain caused the flood, not acqua alta, Cacciari says. "High tide is not a problem for me. It's a problem for you foreigners." End of discussion on flooding.

[1] **Thomas Mann** (1875–1955) was the author of the 1912 novella *Death in Venice*.
[2] A **lagoon** is a body of water cut off from the open sea by coral reefs or sand bars.
[3] The **stratosphere** is the atmospheric layer between about 15 and 50 km (10 and 30 miles) above the Earth.
[4] Something that is left in someone's **wake** remains behind after the person has left.
[5] **Aesthetics** is a branch of philosophy dealing with the nature of beauty.
[6] Something that is **municipal** is controlled or owned by the government of a city or town.

"Now, Venice gets giant cruise ships. You can't understand Venice from ten stories up. You might as well be in a helicopter."

35 No, he stresses, the problems lie elsewhere. The cost of maintaining Venice: "There is not enough money from the state to cover it all—the cleaning of canals, restoration of buildings, raising of foundations. Very expensive." The cost of
40 living: "It's three times as costly to live here as in Mogliano, 20 kilometers away. It's affordable only for the rich or elderly who already own houses because they have been passed down. The young? They can't afford it."

45 Finally, there is tourism. Of that, Cacciari says: "Venice is not a sentimental place of honeymoon. It's a strong, contradictory, overpowering place. It is not a city for tourists. It cannot be reduced to a postcard."

50 IF YOU ARE A VENETIAN who lives in a fifth-floor walk-up apartment—someone who gets up, goes to work, goes home—Venice is a different place altogether. The abnormal is normal. A flood is routine. The alarm sounds, protective steel doors
55 come down. Boots, essential to any Venetian wardrobe, are pulled on. The four kilometers (two and a half miles) of *passerelle*—an elevated boardwalk supported on metal legs—are set up. Life goes on.

60 When Silvia Zanon goes to Campo San Provolo, where she teaches middle school, she knows it will take 23 minutes to walk there from her apartment on the Calle delle Carrozze. On the way she crosses the Piazza San Marco, blissfully[7] empty in early
65 morning. "I step on the paving stones and fall in love with the city all over again," she says.

Gherardo Ortalli, a professor of medieval history, finds his path less poetic. "When I go out in the *campo* with my friends, I have to stop because
70 someone is taking a photograph of us as if we are aboriginals,"[8] he says. "Perhaps one day we will be. You will go and see a sign on a cage: 'Feed the Venetians.' When I arrived 30 years ago, the population was 120,000. Now it is less
75 than 60,000."

The decline seems inexorable.[9] Ortalli thinks Venice will end up as simply a theme park for the rich, who will jet in to spend a day or two in their palazzo, then leave. It is 10 a.m., and he is headed
80 toward a kiosk to buy a newspaper before going to his office, though you can hardly find the papers for all the tourist kitsch: miniature masks, gondola pins, jester[10] caps. "Everything is for sale," he sighs. "Even Venice."

85 THE OFFICIAL IN CHARGE of managing the impact of tourism in Venice is Augusto Salvadori. Love is an inadequate word to describe how Salvadori feels about Venice. He is not just the city's director of tourism and promoter of tradition; he is
90 its defender.

[7] Somewhere that is **blissful** is a place that is happy and peaceful.
[8] **Aboriginals** are the original and native people of a country or region.
[9] Something that is **inexorable** cannot be prevented from continuing or progressing.
[10] A **jester** is a professional clown employed by the nobility during the Middle Ages. Their hats are known for being colorful and pointy-tipped.

"The city is consumed by tourism," says Salvadori, seated in his office in a 16th-century palazzo. "What do Venetians get in exchange? During part of the year Venetians cannot elbow their way onto public transportation. The cost of garbage collection increases; so does the price of living."

"Perhaps to help," Salvadori says, "we put a city tax on hotels and restaurants. [Now] they say tourists will not come—but I say, tourists won't come for a few euros?" He glares. "I cannot be worried about hotels. I have to think of the Venetians. My battle is for the city. Because Venice is my heart."

Tourism has been part of the Venetian landscape since the 14th century, when pilgrims stopped en route to the Holy Land. So, what's so different about tourism now? I ask Ortalli. "Now, Venice gets giant cruise ships. The ship is ten stories high. You can't understand Venice from ten stories up. You might as well be in a helicopter. But it's not important. You arrive in Venice, write a postcard, and remember what a wonderful evening you had."

"THERE GOES ANOTHER PIECE of Venice," Silvia Zanon, the teacher, said sadly when La Camiceria San Marco, a 60-year-old clothing store, had to move to a smaller, less prime spot because the rent had tripled. Susanna Cestari worked there for 32 years. "It's like leaving the house where you were born," she said while packing boxes for the move.

Since December 2007, at least ten hardware stores have gone out of business. In the Rialto market, souvenir sellers have replaced vendors who sold sausages, bread, or vegetables. Tourists will not notice. They do not visit Venice to buy an eggplant.

Tourism in Venice generates $2 billion a year in revenue, probably an underestimate because so much business is done off the books. It is, reports the University of Venice's International Center of Studies on the Tourist Economy, "the heart and soul of the Venetian economy—good and bad." Some people suggest that Venice's wounds are self-inflicted. "They don't want tourists," observes a former resident, "but they want their money."

There is talk about implementing new policies to limit the number of tourists, imposing additional taxes, and urging visitors to avoid the high seasons of Easter and Carnival. But tourism—together with the loss of resident population, and combined with the interests of hotel owners, gondoliers, and water taxi drivers who all have an interest in maximizing the influx of visitors—defies simple solutions.

"It is not a city for tourists," says Venice's mayor. "It cannot be reduced to a postcard."

"Let me remind you, the loss of population . . . is not only a problem in Venice but in all historical towns, not only Italy," cautioned Mayor Cacciari. "The so-called exodus, which dates back very far in time, is deep rooted in the lodging[11] issue." For some, a solution to Venice's troubles already seems out of reach. "It is too late," Gherardo Ortalli, the historian, says. "The stones will remain. The people won't."

But for now there is still life as well as death in Venice. Silvia Zanon, on her way to school, still crosses San Marco only to fall in love with the city again. And, assuming it is in season, you can still manage to buy an eggplant. The city's beauty, difficult and bruised, somehow survives.

▲ Elevated boardwalks known as *passerelle* allow visitors to appreciate Venice's waterways without getting their feet wet.

[11] A **lodging** is a temporary, often rented, place to stay or live.

Reading Comprehension

A. Multiple Choice. Choose the best answer for each question.

Main Idea **1.** What is the main idea of this article?
- a. Besides flooding, Venice faces several other serious environmental problems.
- b. The flooding problem in Venice is caused mainly by rain, not by the *acqua alta*.
- c. The most difficult problem facing Venice is the large number of tourists it receives.
- d. Because tides are rising and foundations are sinking, Venice is disappearing into the sea.

Rhetorical Purpose **2.** Why does the author present the statistics in paragraph 3 (lines 13–17)?
- a. to indicate that more tourists are coming to Venice than before
- b. to emphasize the decline of population of Venice
- c. to contrast the number of tourists with the number of residents
- d. to point out the dangers of serious flooding

Detail **3.** What does Mayor Cacciari say about the young people of Venice in paragraph 6 (from line 35)?
- a. Most of them have moved to the nearby town of Mogliano.
- b. They find it is too expensive to live in Venice these days.
- c. They are involved in cleaning canals, restoring buildings, and raising foundations.
- d. Many of them live in houses that have been passed down from their parents.

Detail **4.** Which of the following is given as an example of an ordinary resident of Venice?
- a. Massimo Cacciari
- c. Gherardo Ortalli
- b. Silvia Zanon
- d. Augusto Salvadori

Inference **5.** What can be inferred about the holiday weekend in May 2008, mentioned in the article?
- a. There were more tourists than residents in the city that weekend.
- b. Many residents left the city that weekend because of the floods.
- c. All of the city's parking lots were full of cars that weekend.
- d. Vendors ran out of snacks for tourists such as pizza and gelato.

Rhetorical Purpose **6.** Why does the author mention "an eggplant" in paragraphs 17 (from line 122) and 21 (from line 154)?
- a. to give an example of an ordinary product that is becoming harder to find in Venice
- b. to indicate that eggplants are a favorite food of visitors to Venice
- c. to show that eating habits in Venice have changed over time
- d. to demonstrate that prices for food in Venice have climbed in recent years

Vocabulary **7.** The phrase *off the books* (line 130) indicates that much of the tourist business in Venice is done _____.
- a. unofficially
- c. unwillingly
- b. carelessly
- d. rapidly

Reference **8.** The word *they* in line 135 refers to the _____.
- a. people who live in Venice
- b. International Center of Studies on the Tourist Economy
- c. people who say that Venice's wounds are self-inflicted
- d. tourists who visit Venice

Understanding Figurative Language

Some words in this article have a figurative meaning instead of a literal meaning.
Read these two sentences.

The farmers *plowed* their fields. (literal)

The ship *plowed* the sea. (figurative)

In the first sentence, farmers use real plows (agricultural tools) to prepare their land for planting. In the second sentence, the ship moves through the sea *like* a plow.
There is no real plow.

B. Classification. Find these words or phrases in the article. Mark them **F** if they are used figuratively and **L** if used literally.

_____ **1.** flooding (paragraph 1)

_____ **2.** stratosphere (paragraph 2)

_____ **3.** flood (paragraph 3)

_____ **4.** foundations (paragraph 6)

_____ **5.** elevated (paragraph 8)

_____ **6.** poetic (paragraph 10)

_____ **7.** theme park (paragraph 11)

_____ **8.** consumed (paragraph 13)

_____ **9.** garbage collection (paragraph 13)

_____ **10.** pilgrims (paragraph 15)

_____ **11.** wounds (paragraph 18)

_____ **12.** bruised (paragraph 21)

C. Critical Thinking. Discuss these questions with a partner.

1. Look again at your answer to task A, question 1. Do you think that the author offers enough evidence to support her idea? Why or why not?

2. "[Tourism] is the heart and soul of the Venetian economy—good and bad" (line 132–133). What effects (good and bad) does the author mention in the passage? What other positive and negative effects can tourism have on a city or a region?

3. Write a list of some of the major problems that your own hometown or country faces. Which do you think are the most serious? Are any similar to the ones that affect Venice?

Vocabulary Practice

A. Completion. Complete the information by circling the most appropriate word in each pair.

The Alps Under Pressure

A popular image of the European Alps consists of cow bells, cheese-making, and quiet villages **1.** framed / imposed against a background of snow-capped mountains. But a less **2.** sentimental / complementary picture must also include the twelve million trucks and about fifty million cars which cross the mountains each year.

The movement of 77 million tons of goods annually through the mountains **3.** inflicts / frames significant environmental damage on the Alpine environment. Carbon dioxide (CO_2) from vehicle fumes becomes trapped in the narrow valleys beneath an upper layer of warmer air. The steep valley walls also **4.** maximize / implement the sounds generated by the traffic. The **5.** elevated / inadequate levels of noise and pollution **6.** impose / complement serious problems on the health of Alpine residents.

▲ The famous location for *The Sound of Music* is now struggling to deal with the noise of traffic.

Laws have been **7.** elevated / implemented to reduce the number of vehicles in residential areas, but they have so far proved largely **8.** inadequate / maximized for reducing the overall volume of traffic. There are hopeful signs, however: October 2010 saw the completion of the first of two single track tunnels comprising the Gotthard Base Tunnel—the **9.** sentimental / so-called "GBT"—which at 57 km (35 miles) is the world's longest rail tunnel. It is hoped that, when it opens for traffic in 2017, the rail tunnel will help reduce the environmental strain on one of the world's most famous landscapes.

B. Definitions. Match the correct form of words in red from above with their correct definition.

1. _____ (to) damage, make suffer
2. _____ (to) make larger in amount or importance
3. _____ not enough
4. _____ surrounded or outlined
5. _____ nostalgic for things in the past
6. _____ (to) differ, but go well together
7. _____ raised up higher
8. _____ carry out, fulfill
9. _____ generally named
10. _____ (to) force something on someone

Usage

Complement and **compliment** sound alike, but have different meanings.

Complement means that things may be different, but they combine well together, e.g. (v.) The tie **complemented** his suit. (n.) The tie is a good **complement** to his suit.

Compliment means to say something nice to or about someone, e.g., (n.) My daughter made a nice **compliment** about my new dress. (v.) My daughter **complimented** me on my new dress.

4B Lost Horizons

Shangri-La: For many people, the word evokes a faraway place of great beauty where people live in harmony and peace. The name comes from James Hilton's 1933 novel, *Lost Horizon*, a tale of plane-crash survivors who discover a monastery called Shangri-La hidden in a remote part of Tibet—a secret paradise where there is no war or suffering.

Hilton's story, and the 1937 movie based on it, was likely inspired by the writings of explorer Joseph Rock, whose travels to remote parts of China and Tibet in search of exotic plants and unknown cultures appeared in *National Geographic Magazine* from 1922 to 1935. Unlike semi-mythical places such as Timbuktu or Machu Picchu, however, there never actually was a place called Shangri-La. But that changed in 2001, when a modern-day Shangri-La was born . . .

▲ Photos like these, taken in the 1920s and '30s by Joseph Rock of a Tibetan monastery (above) and of Lugu Lake in Yunnan Province, China (top), may have inspired the story of Shangri-La. The "skeleton dancers" are young monks performing in a ceremony during Cham-ngy on-wa, a religious festival.

☐ Before You Read

A. Discussion. Read the information above. Then discuss the questions with a partner.

1. What is Shangri-La? What probably inspired the myth?

2. Why do you think Hilton called his novel *Lost Horizon*? What did he mean by "horizon"?

B. Skim for Main Idea. Skim the first main section of the article (to line 79), and answer the questions below. Then read the whole article to check your ideas.

1. How is the modern-day Shangri-La similar to and different from the mythical one?

2. Why do you think the author goes in search of a "truer Shangri-La" (line 79)?

SEARCHING FOR SHANGRI-LA

Writer Mark Jenkins goes in search of a mythical paradise—while those who live there dream of a different life.

WELCOME TO SHANGRI-LA.

A decade ago, this was an obscure, one-horse village on the edge of the Tibetan Plateau, a virtual ghost town of derelict buildings and deserted dirt roads. Most residents had moved out of their traditional homes into more modern structures with running water and septic[1] systems. The historic quarter they left behind seemed doomed.

Today, this town is one of the hottest tourist destinations in China, gateway city to the Three Parallel Rivers World Heritage site in northwestern Yunnan Province. Tourism saved the place. The Tibetan farmhouses were rediscovered as unique, endemic[2] architecture that could turn a profit. Redevelopment began immediately. Water and sewer lines, electricity, and the Internet were brought in. The old homes were rebuilt and turned into fancy shops. New shops were constructed with carved dragons and tigers to attract Chinese tourists. Which they did: In a recent year more than three million tourists, almost 90 percent of them Chinese, visited the new Shangri-La.

IN ITS PREVIOUS INCARNATION,[3] Shangri-La was Zhongdian, a 2,500-meter-high (1.5-mile high) trade-route town located just east of some of the deepest and most dramatic gorges in the world. 30 This was the remote region that eccentric botanist Joseph Rock explored in the 1920s and '30s. Rock's expeditions in search of exotic plants and unknown cultures later inspired *Lost Horizon*, James Hilton's novel about a remote mountain 35 paradise. Hilton named his vision Shangri-La,

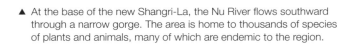

▲ At the base of the new Shangri-La, the Nu River flows southward through a narrow gorge. The area is home to thousands of species of plants and animals, many of which are endemic to the region.

which sounds like—and almost certainly is—a thin disguise for Shambhala, the earthly paradise in Tibetan Buddhism where there is no war and no suffering.

40 But much has changed since then. Large-scale commercial logging began in the 1950s, and by the mid-1990s more than 80 percent of the area's income came from timber operations. In 1998, due in part to overlogging, the Jinsha river flooded. 45 Nearly 4,000 people died, and millions lost their homes. In response, the Chinese government banned all commercial logging in the Three Rivers region.

[1] A **septic** system is a sewage system in which waste is decomposed by the action of bacteria in "septic tanks."
[2] Something that is **endemic** to a place is unique and can only be found in that place.
[3] An **incarnation** of something, usually a quality or idea, is a person or a thing that typifies that quality or idea.

▲ The Songzanlin Monastery is a 300-year-old Tibetan Buddhist complex located just outside the town of Shangri-La (formerly Zhongdian).

Forced to recreate its economy, Zhongdian
50 turned to tourism, capitalizing on[4] its distinctive architecture and proximity to the gorges. An airport was built in 1999, and the first major road to Kunming was finished a year later. By 2001, revenues from the tourism industry had already
55 surpassed the previous income from logging.

That same year, local officials were authorized to rename their town and county Shangri-La. The
60 crowning tourist-catching achievement came in 2003 when the United Nations officially acknowledged the remarkable biodiversity of the river gorges and designated the region the Three Parallel Rivers World Heritage
65 site. Instantly, Shangri-La became the new hot spot for Chinese travelers willing to pull on hiking boots and experience the frontier firsthand.

Although the nearest gorge is within easy reach of the tourist hotels in Shangri-La, almost none
70 of the biological diversity of the Three Parallel Rivers region can be found near the city. Nor does the town possess the seclusion and serenity that the name Shangri-La suggests. So if another Shangri-La exists—a place more closely resembling
75 the myth of our collective imagination—it must lie someplace else, somewhere further out in the remote mountains where Joseph Rock discovered his version of paradise. That's where I went looking for a truer Shangri-La.

80 THE TRAIL NEAR MOUNT KAWAGEBO, the highest mountain in Three Parallel Rivers, becomes so steep it starts to switchback every four or five meters. Snow gives way to trees, then to dense forest. At a ridge, I look down into what seems to
85 be another world. Wedged in a valley beside a steep forest is a tiny square of brilliant green—another vision of Shangri-La.

It takes hours, descending hundreds of switchbacks, to reach the enchanted[5] place. A man
90 with a load of wood on his back is waiting. He leads the way beneath a giant walnut tree, past pigs and goats, over a stone fence, along a barley field, to a whitewashed Tibetan home. Up a dirt ramp, we pull the leather thong,[6] a little door opens, and
95 we step into the 15th century. A shrunken woman in a red head wrap greets us with both hands, pours two cups of boiling yak butter tea, then disappears.

Grandparents, parents, kids, and an uncle all share the farmhouse. All have their tasks: the uncle
100 carrying sacks of corn and sorting horseshoes; the young mother, baby on back, tending the stove and preparing dinner; the patriarch[7] slowly writing something in a ledger[8] in shaky Tibetan script.

"Up a dirt ramp, we pull the leather thong, a little door opens, and we step into the 15th century."

Dinner is served. Rice with assorted dishes—pork
105 fat in garlic sauce, yak meat with peppers, fried vegetables, glasses of homemade, hot barley wine, apples for dessert. And then the patriarch opens a carved cabinet door and clicks the remote. There's a soccer match on TV he doesn't want to miss.

110 The young mother pours us more yak butter tea. She is 17 and her name is Snaw. She says her dream is to leave this place—the Shangri-La of my imagination—and go to the new town of Shangri-La. She's heard that women her age go to school
115 there and on Saturday they go shopping, walking arm in arm along the mall.

[4] **Capitalizing on** something, like an opportunity or resource, is taking advantage of it, usually to make money.
[5] Something **enchanted** seems to be magical, and is delightful and fascinating.
[6] A **thong** is a thin strip of leather or other material.
[7] A **patriarch** is the male head of a family.
[8] A **ledger** is a book in which records, usually financial and commercial, are kept.

◄ In the village of Nguluko, Yunnan Province, a woman has her teeth pulled using tools left by explorer Joseph Rock, who visited the area in the 1930s.

SOME YOUNG WOMEN'S DREAMS have already come true. Yang Jifang, a tall, striking 22-year-old Naxi woman, graduated from the Eastern Tibet Training
120 Institute (ETTI) in downtown Shangri-La. There she learned English and computer skills; she now works as a guide at a local adventure-travel firm. She goes back to her rural village every month, bringing money and medicine to her parents.
125 "Life for my parents in the village is very hard," she says. "There is no business, just farming."

The training institute was founded in 2004 by Ben Hillman, a professor at the Australian National University who specializes in development in
130 western China. The institute hosts an intensive 16-week vocational school with the objective of helping students from rural areas bridge the gap to urban job opportunities.

"Culture is something that's constantly evolving,"
135 says Hillman, who warns me not to apply a Western sense of authenticity to the modern Shangri-La. "Economic development can rekindle[9] interest in cultural heritage, which is inevitably reinterpreted," Hillman says. "I don't think we can judge that
140 without reverting to some kind of elitism,[10] where wealthy and fortunate people who can travel to remote parts of this planet want to keep things locked in a cultural zoo."

The real challenge for Shangri-La's ethnic
145 minorities, Hillman says, is to develop skills for the modern world. "They are traditionally agropastoralists, experts at subsistence[11] farming —growing barley, raising yaks and pigs. But these aren't the skills that most youth need today."

150 His students are from disparate ethnicities, but most come from dirt-poor farming households. None intend to return to a hard farm life. The training institute is perhaps the kind of place Snaw dreams about while she milks yaks in a freezing
155 snowstorm.

Late in the afternoon, several graduates of the institute gather in the teachers' lounge, excited to tell their stories. The last to speak is a vibrant 21-year-old student named Tashi Tsering. A
160 Tibetan, he too learned English and service industry skills at ETTI and now works as a guide, taking tourists to Tibetan towns and villages as far away as Lhasa. He wishes his friends back in the village could have the same opportunity he has
165 enjoyed. "Now I can play an important role in the future!" he says.

Tsering looks out the window at bustling Shangri-La, his eyes following a plane descending into the Shangri-La airport. We can't see it from here, but
170 near the airport stands a large white stupa, a sacred Tibetan monument that Buddhists walk around clockwise, the same direction a prayer wheel spins. But cars negotiating the intersection must circle the stupa counterclockwise. Consequently, women
175 heading home to feed their pigs, and men herding yaks as they have for centuries, face directly into the paths of oncoming busloads of tourists. There have been collisions, but somehow it's working.

▲ In the newly named Shangri-La, locals gather for a Tibetan folk dance, which resembles the movement of spinning prayer wheels.

[9] To **rekindle** an interest is to revive or renew it, to make it begin again.
[10] **Elitism** is a belief that certain people, classes, or cultures are superior to others.
[11] **Subsistence farming** is a type of farming in which most of the produce is eaten or used by the farmer and his family.

Reading Comprehension

A. Multiple Choice. Choose the best answer for each question.

Yunnan Province, China

Negative Detail

1. Which of the following is NOT mentioned as one of the attractions for tourists to Shangri-La?
   a. its location near spectacular natural wonders
   b. the distinctive architecture of the Tibetan farmhouses
   c. the sites of several important historical events nearby
   d. shops with carved dragon and tiger statues

Reference

2. What does *the place* refer to in line 15?
   a. China
   b. Shangri-La/Zhongdian
   c. Three Parallel Rivers
   d. Yunnan

Cohesion

3. Where would be the best place to insert this sentence in paragraph 3 (lines 26–39)?
   Hilton also drew from another source, one much older than the writings of Joseph Rock.
   a. after the first sentence
   b. after the second sentence
   c. after the third sentence
   d. after the fourth sentence

Detail

4. What type of disaster helped change the course of Shangri-La's future?
   a. a forest fire
   b. a logging accident
   c. a flood
   d. an earthquake

Rhetorical Purpose

5. In paragraph 7 (from line 68), the author explains why _____.
   a. the town of Shangri-La is similar to the fictional Shangri-La
   b. he travels outside of Shangri-La to look for another Shangri-La
   c. there is so much biodiversity in the Three Parallel Rivers area
   d. the town of Shangri-La is not really secluded or quiet anymore

Inference

6. What does the author imply in paragraphs 9–11 (lines 88–116) about the agricultural area that he visits?
   a. There is no electricity or television available there.
   b. Several new shops have opened in the area.
   c. There is no school for older teenagers to attend there.
   d. Tourism is becoming more and more important there

Detail

7. What is the main goal of the ETTI?
   a. to help young people from rural villages find employment in the city
   b. to improve the living conditions of people living in rural villages
   c. to build infrastructure, such as roads and bridges, in rural areas
   d. to enable the exchange of students between China and Australia

Detail

8. What do the two students that the author mentions (Yang Jifang and Tashi Tsering) have in common?
   a. They both come from the same village.
   b. They both studied computer science.
   c. They both want to return to their hometowns.
   d. They both work as tourist guides.

B. Sequencing. Match the decades and years (**a–i**) with the events (**1–9**).

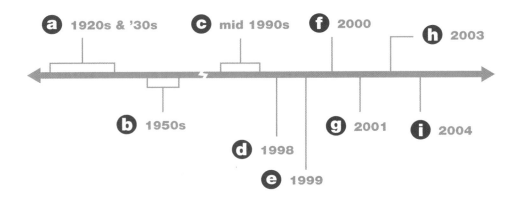

a 1920s & '30s   **c** mid 1990s   **f** 2000   **h** 2003

b 1950s   **g** 2001   **i** 2004

d 1998

e 1999

_____ **1.** Commercial logging begins in Zhongdian.

_____ **2.** Three Parallel Rivers is named a World Heritage site.

_____ **3.** Joseph Rock explores the Three Rivers region.

_____ **4.** Logging accounts for 80 percent of the area's economy.

_____ **5.** A major road to Kunming is completed.

_____ **6.** Logging is forbidden after the Jinsha River flood.

_____ **7.** The ETTI is established.

_____ **8.** The airport is opened.

_____ **9.** Zhongdian is officially renamed Shangri-La.

C. Critical Thinking. Discuss these questions with a partner.

1. According to Ben Hillman (line 141–143), "wealthy and fortunate people who can travel to remote parts of this planet want to keep things locked in a cultural zoo." What do you think he means?

2. Why does the author conclude the article by describing an intersection?

3. How are the attitudes towards tourism expressed in this article different from the ones expressed in the previous article, "Vanishing Venice"?

Vocabulary Practice

A. Completion. Complete the information below using the correct form of the words in the box. Two words are extra.

disparate	graduate	minority	negotiate
obscure	parallel	proximity	revert
serene	tend		

Timbuktu

Preserving Timbuktu

Timbuktu, like Shangri-La, once held a special place in people's imaginations. At its height during the 15th century, the almost mythical city was so famous for its wealth that Europeans thought its roads must be paved with gold. Since then, however, Timbuku has **1.** _____ to being a small, **2.** _____ town on the wind-blown edges of the Sahara desert, largely forgotten by the outside world.

Located in present-day Mali, West Africa, Timbuktu rose to power largely due to its position near trading routes crossing the Sahara as well as its **3.** _____ to market towns along the Niger River. **4.** _____ to its emergence as a trading center was its rise as a center for Islamic education. Salt traders who **5.** _____ the hazardous desert paths to Timbuktu were accompanied by Islamic scholars who brought with them hundreds of thousands of manuscripts. These covered a wide range of **6.** _____ subjects: astronomy, medicine, mathematics, chemistry, law, and government.

The scholars' teachings led to the foundation of the University of Timbuktu, which at its peak had over 25,000 students. **7.** _____ of the university helped set up schools in nearby towns, which in turn served as models of peaceful governance for the various tribal groups and **8.** _____ peoples scattered throughout the region. Timbuktu's influence declined after the 1600s, but 700,000 of its historic manuscripts survive and are being studied by researchers today.

▲ A researcher studies manuscripts in the Imam Ben Essayouti library, Timbuktu. According to Issa Mohammed, president of the Timbuktu Heritage Institute, by preserving Timbuktu's documents, "not only we are preserving the heritage of Timbuktu, of the Islamic world, and of Africa, but we are preserving a message of love, peace, and living together in a multicultural world."

B. Definitions. Use the correct form of words in the box in **A** to complete the definitions.

1. People who _____ their animals look after them well.
2. Things that are _____ are clearly different from each other.
3. A person who is _____ is calm and quiet.
4. A place that is _____ is unknown or known only by a few people.
5. When something _____ to a previous state, it goes back to it.
6. _____ means nearness to a place or person.
7. People who _____ a region or obstacle are able to cross it successfully.
8. People who have a different race, culture, or religion than the majority population are called a _____ group.

Word Partnership

Negotiate can also mean to discuss a problem or arrangement: (*v.*) **agree to** negotiate, **fail** to negotiate, **refuse to** negotiate, **try to** negotiate (*n.*) negotiate **an agreement**, negotiate **a contract**, negotiate the **terms of a deal**.
If an arrangement or deal is being discussed, it is said to be **under negotiation**.

The High Road to Shangri-La

A. Preview. You will hear these phrases in the video. What do you think they mean? Match each phrase to its meaning.

1. But this paradise has its roots in reality, here in a far corner of western China . . .

2. Unless I can work in the unexplored regions, I would have no incentive to live.

3. These outlaws are no respecters of person and would just as likely kill us as they would a sheep or yak.

4. . . . the land of the Konkaling outlaws is again closed and their mountains remain guarded as of yore . . .

▲ Joseph Rock (left) and fellow explorer W. I. Hagen (right) are dwarfed by the giant King of Muli, who became a friend of Rock's during his explorations. "The king of Muli [rules] over 22,000 subjects . . . ," Rock wrote in 1928. "His power is absolute."

a. _____ (to) be unmotivated, or unwilling

b. _____ like before, or like it was a long time ago

c. _____ contains elements that are true or real

d. _____ people who are not influenced by someone else's rank or wealth

B. Summarize. Watch the video, *The High Road to Shangri-La*. Then complete the summary below using the correct form of words in the box. Two words are extra.

contemporary	exert	frame	impede	intervene
obscure	parallel	proximity	revert	serenity

The word *Shangri-La* brings to mind a place of perfect **1.** _____, a fictional paradise. But for some, Shangri-La is a very real place, one of harsh terrain and tough challenges.

Here in the Duron Valley of western China, hidden among **2.** _____ mountain villages, is a region that may have inspired the myth of Shangri-La. It was first visited in the 1920s by explorer Joseph Rock, who called it the "land of [his] dreams." During his travels, Rock encountered bandits determined to rob him. A local ruler, the King of Muli, fortunately **3.** _____ and ordered the bandits not to attack Rock, but to protect him. Hence, those bandits became Rock's bodyguards.

Today, a team of **4.** _____ explorers have journeyed here to follow in Rock's footsteps, determined to reach parts of the Konkaling mountain range that not even Rock has explored. The team manages to get to a high mountain ridge, but a fierce snow storm **5.** _____ their progress. Finally, the team has **6.** _____ all their strength, and they have to stop climbing. Despite their **7.** _____ to the summit, they will not get the view of Shangri-La they were hoping for.

Joseph Rock eventually lost the paradise he had discovered. After twenty years, the King of Muli could no longer protect him. The danger became too great for Rock to stay on in the region, which **8.** _____ to the way it was before, guarded and hidden. However, Rock did stay in China for another 20 years—collecting plants, writing stories, and taking photos of a land now lost in time.

C. Think About It.

1. Is there somewhere you've been, which you consider your Shangri-La? Why?

2. If you could travel in the footsteps of an explorer, whose journey would you retrace and why?

 To learn more about traditional societies, visit elt.heinle.com/explorer

UNIT 5
Eco-Living

◄ Mirrors at a solar
thermal plant in
California catch the
sun's rays and turn
them into usable
solar energy.

WARM UP

Discuss these questions with a partner.

1. What are the world's main sources of energy? Which are the most important in your country?

2. What are some advantages and disadvantages of each of these types of energy?

3. In what ways could people in your country reduce their energy consumption?

5A

Carbon Footprint

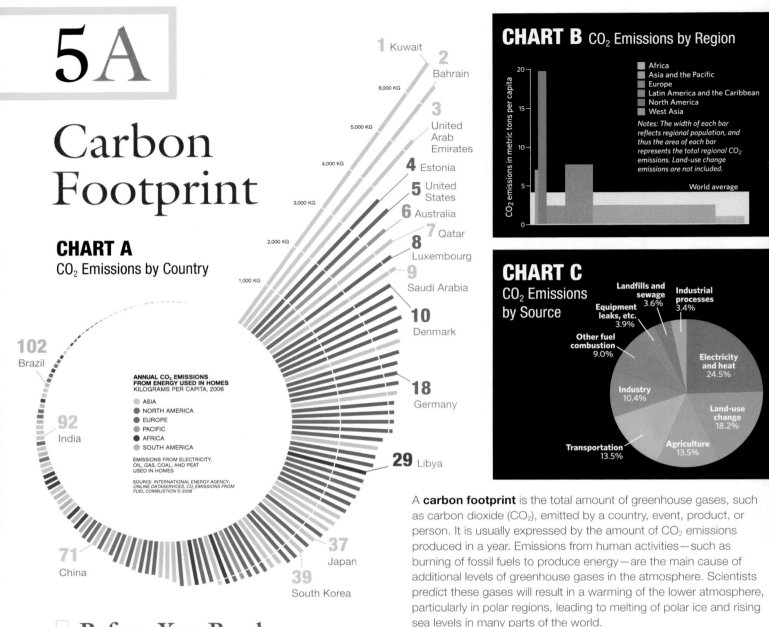

CHART A

CO₂ Emissions by Country

1 Kuwait
2 Bahrain
3 United Arab Emirates
4 Estonia
5 United States
6 Australia
7 Qatar
8 Luxembourg
9 Saudi Arabia
10 Denmark
18 Germany
29 Libya
37 Japan
39 South Korea

6,000 KG
5,000 KG
4,000 KG
3,000 KG
2,000 KG
1,000 KG

102 Brazil
92 India
71 China

ANNUAL CO₂ EMISSIONS FROM ENERGY USED IN HOMES
KILOGRAMS PER CAPITA, 2006

○ ASIA
● NORTH AMERICA
● EUROPE
○ PACIFIC
● AFRICA
○ SOUTH AMERICA

EMISSIONS FROM ELECTRICITY, OIL, GAS, COAL, AND PEAT USED IN HOMES

SOURCE: INTERNATIONAL ENERGY AGENCY, ONLINE DATASERVICES, CO₂ EMISSIONS FROM FUEL COMBUSTION © 2008

CHART B CO₂ Emissions by Region

■ Africa
■ Asia and the Pacific
■ Europe
■ Latin America and the Caribbean
■ North America
■ West Asia

CO₂ emissions in metric tons per capita

20
15
10
5
0

Notes: The width of each bar reflects regional population, and thus the area of each bar represents the total regional CO₂ emissions. Land-use change emissions are not included.

World average

CHART C

CO₂ Emissions by Source

Landfills and sewage 3.6%
Industrial processes 3.4%
Equipment leaks, etc. 3.9%
Other fuel combustion 9.0%
Electricity and heat 24.5%
Industry 10.4%
Land-use change 18.2%
Transportation 13.5%
Agriculture 13.5%

A **carbon footprint** is the total amount of greenhouse gases, such as carbon dioxide (CO₂), emitted by a country, event, product, or person. It is usually expressed by the amount of CO₂ emissions produced in a year. Emissions from human activities—such as burning of fossil fuels to produce energy—are the main cause of additional levels of greenhouse gases in the atmosphere. Scientists predict these gases will result in a warming of the lower atmosphere, particularly in polar regions, leading to melting of polar ice and rising sea levels in many parts of the world.

☐ Before You Read

A. Understanding Charts. Use the information above to decide if each statement is true (**T**) or false (**F**).

1. Brazilian households have relatively low levels of per capita (per person) CO₂ emissions.   T   F

2. The country with the world's highest per capita household CO₂ emissions is the United States.   T   F

3. Overall, per capita CO₂ emissions in Europe are below the world average.   T   F

4. The amount of CO₂ produced by the generation of electricity and heat is more than double the amount produced by industry.   T   F

B. Skim and Predict. Skim the passage on pages 81–83, looking especially at the title, section headings, captions, and the first sentence of each paragraph. Try to answer the questions below. Then read the passage to check your ideas.

What kind of experiment is the author participating in? What do you think he found out?

It Starts at Home

▲ Thermal imaging lets us see where energy is being wasted in a house in New Haven, Connecticut. Red and yellow patches indicate escaping heat, while windows which seal in heat appear cool blue.

1 With a little effort, and not much money, most of us could reduce our energy diets by 25 percent or more. So what's holding us back? Writer Peter Miller goes on a strict low-carbon diet to find out.

5 Not long ago, my wife and I tried a new diet—not to lose weight but to answer a question about climate change. Scientists have reported that the world is heating up even faster than they predicted just a few years ago. The consequences, they say,
10 could be severe if we don't keep reducing emissions of carbon dioxide and other greenhouse gases that are trapping heat in our atmosphere. But what can we do about it as individuals? And will our efforts really make any difference?

15 ## The Experiment

We decided to try an experiment. For one month we tracked our personal emissions of carbon dioxide (CO_2) as if we were counting calories. We wanted to see how much we could cut back.

20 The average U.S. household produces about 150 pounds (68 kg) of CO_2 a day by doing commonplace things like turning on air-conditioning or driving cars. That's more than twice the European average and almost five times
25 the global average. But how much should we try to reduce?

I checked with Tim Flannery, author of *The Weather Makers: How Man Is Changing the Climate and What It Means for Life on Earth*. In his
30 book, he challenged readers to make deep cuts in personal emissions to keep the world from reaching critical tipping points,[1] such as the melting of the ice sheets in Greenland or West Antarctica. "To stay below that threshold, we need to reduce CO_2
35 emissions by 80 percent," he said. "That sounds like a lot," my wife said. "Can we really do that?"

[1] A **tipping point** is a stage of a process when a significant change takes place, after which the process cannot be turned back.

◄ About 1,190 pounds of CO₂ is emitted by refrigerators alone in the U.S. every year. Scientists estimate that global CO_2 emissions have risen about 30 percent over the last decade, and show no signs of stopping.

It seemed unlikely to me too. Still, the point was to answer a simple question: How close could we come to a lifestyle the planet could handle? Finally we agreed to aim for 80 percent less than the U.S. average: a daily diet of only 30 pounds of CO_2.

Our first challenge was to find ways to convert our daily activities into pounds of CO_2. We wanted to track our progress as we went, to change our habits if necessary.

To get a rough idea of our current carbon footprint, I put numbers from recent utility bills into several calculators on websites. None was flattering.[2] The Environmental Protection Agency (EPA) website figured our annual CO_2 emissions at 54,273 pounds, 30 percent higher than the average American family with two people. The main culprit was the energy we were using to heat and cool our house. Clearly we had further to go than I thought.

The Diagnosis

We got some help in Week Two from a professional "house doctor," Ed Minch, of Energy Services Group in Wilmington, Delaware. We asked Minch to do an energy audit of our house. The first thing he did was walk around the outside of the house. Had the architect and builder created any opportunities for air to seep[3] in or out, such as overhanging floors? Next he went inside and used an infrared scanner to look at our interior walls. Finally his assistants set up a powerful fan in our front door to lower air pressure inside the house and force air through whatever leaks there might be in the shell of the house.

Our house, his instruments showed, was 50 percent leakier than it should be. Addressing this became a priority, as heating represents up to half of a house's energy costs, and cooling can account for a tenth. Minch also gave us tips about lighting and appliances. "A typical kitchen these days has ten 75-watt spots[4] on all day," he said. "That's a huge waste of money." Replacing them with compact fluorescents could save a homeowner $200 a year. Refrigerators, washing machines, dishwashers, and other appliances, in fact, may represent half of a household's electric bill.

Everywhere I looked I saw things sucking up energy. One night I sat up in bed and counted ten little lights in the darkness: cell phone charger, desktop calculator, laptop computer, printer, clock radio, cable TV box, camera battery recharger, carbon monoxide detector,

A study found that "vampire" power sucked up by electronics can add up to 8 percent of a house's electric bill.

cordless phone base, smoke detector. What were they all doing? A study by the Lawrence Berkeley National Laboratory found that "vampire" power sucked up by electronics in standby mode can add up to 8 percent of a house's electric bill. What else had I missed?

"You can go nuts[5] thinking about everything in your house that uses power," said Jennifer Thorne Amann, author of *Consumer Guide to Home Energy Savings.* "You have to use common sense and prioritize. Don't agonize[6] too much. Think about what you'll be able to sustain after the experiment is over. If you have trouble reaching your goal in one area, remember there's always something else you can do."

▲ The red glow of these adapter plugs show that while plugged in, they continue to use power even when the appliances themselves are turned off.

[2] Something that is **flattering** makes us look or seem better than we really are.
[3] If something **seeps** in or through, it leaks in or through slowly.
[4] The word "**spots**" is short for "spotlights," or strong, focused lights.
[5] If someone goes **nuts**, he or she is going crazy.
[6] When people **agonize** about something, they are very worried about it.

◀ Situated on a barge on the Hudson River in New York, this hydroponic farm saves energy by eliminating the need to transport produce from rural farms into the city.

The Results

By the last week in July, we were finally getting into the flow of the reduced carbon lifestyle. We walked to the neighborhood pool instead of driving, biked to the local farmers market on Saturday morning, and sat out on the deck until dark, chatting over the sound of the crickets. Whenever possible I worked from home, and when I commuted I took the bus and subway.

Our numbers were looking pretty good, in fact, when we crossed the finish line on August 1. Compared with the previous July, we cut electricity use by 70 percent, natural gas by 40 percent, and reduced our driving to half the national average. In terms of CO_2, we trimmed our emissions to an average of 70.5 pounds a day, which, though twice as much as we'd targeted as our goal, was still half the national average.

We can do more, of course. We can sign up with our utility company for power from regional wind farms. We can purchase locally grown foods instead of winter raspberries from Chile and bottled water from Fiji. We can join a carbon-reduction club, or set up one of our own.

The Future

Will it make any difference? That's what we really wanted to know. Our low carbon diet had shown us that, with little or no hardship and no major cash outlays,[7] we could cut day-to-day emissions of CO_2 in half—mainly by wasting less energy at home and on the highway. Similar efforts in office buildings, shopping malls, and factories throughout the nation, combined with incentives and efficiency standards, could halt further increases in U.S. emissions.

Yet efficiency, in the end, can only take us so far. To get the deeper reductions we need, as Tim Flannery advised, we must replace fossil fuels faster with renewable energy from wind farms, solar plants, geothermal facilities, and biofuels. We must slow deforestation, which is an additional source of greenhouse gases. And we must develop technologies to capture and bury carbon dioxide from existing power plants. Efficiency can buy us time—perhaps as much as two decades—to figure out how to remove carbon from the world's diet.

Not that there won't still be obstacles. Every sector of our economy faces challenges, says energy-efficiency guru Amory Lovins of the Rocky Mountain Institute. "But they all have huge potential. I don't know anyone who has failed to make money at energy efficiency. There's so much low-hanging fruit, it's falling off the trees and mushing up[8] around our ankles."

The rest of the world isn't waiting for the United States to show the way. Sweden has pioneered carbon-neutral houses, Germany affordable solar power, Japan fuel-efficient cars, the Netherlands prosperous cities filled with bicycles. Do Americans have the will to match such efforts?

Change starts at home with the replacement of a lightbulb, the opening of a window, a walk to the bus, or a bike ride to the post office. My wife and I did it for only a month, but I can see the low carbon diet becoming a habit. As my wife said, "What do we have to lose?"

[7] A **cash outlay** is the amount of money that has to be spent, often at the beginning of a project, for the project or business to get started.
[8] If a fruit is **mushing up**, it is becoming a soft pulpy mass, a process caused by rotting.

Reading Comprehension

A. **Multiple Choice.** Choose the best answer for each question.

Gist **1.** The best alternative title for this reading would be _____.
   a. One Family's Energy Diet
   b. How People Are Changing the Climate
   c. Replacing Fossil Fuels
   d. Our Current Carbon Footprint

Reference **2.** The word *it* in line 13 refers to _____.
   a. a new diet   b. an effort   c. climate change   d. the world

Detail **3.** About how much CO_2 does the average family in Europe produce a day?
   a. 30 pounds   b. 70 pounds   c. 150 pounds   d. 300 pounds

Inference **4.** The author is initially _____ reducing his family's CO_2 production by 80 percent.
   a. fairly agreeable to   c. not very interested in
   b. enthusiastic about   d. not confident about

Negative Detail **5.** Which of the following is NOT one of the steps Ed Minch took as part of his energy audit of the author's house?
   a. He used an infrared scanner to examine the interior walls of the house.
   b. He set up a powerful fan to detect leaks in the exterior of the house.
   c. He consulted with the architect and the builder to find ways to save energy.
   d. He gave the author hints about reducing the energy used by lights and appliances.

Detail **6.** What does the author say in paragraph 10 (from line 83) about the standby mode on electronic devices?
   a. Using it is an efficient way to save energy and money.
   b. It uses as much energy as leaving the device turned on.
   c. Using it can account for up to 8% of a household's electricity.
   d. It uses less energy than turning a device off and then on again.

Paraphrase **7.** Which of the following is closest in meaning to this sentence from lines 124–127:
   In terms of CO_2, we trimmed our emissions to an average of 70.5 pounds a day, which, though twice as much as we'd targeted as our goal, was still half the national average.
   a. The author and his family's goal was to reduce emissions to half the national average, but they were able to reduce emissions by twice that much.
   b. The author's family reduced their CO_2 output to 70.5 percent of the national average, but they still didn't reduce it as much as they had hoped.
   c. During the experiment, the author's family managed to reduce their CO_2 to half the national average, but this was only half their targeted cut.
   d. Although the author and his wife were not able to cut their CO_2 output to the level of the average U.S. family, they still met their goal.

Detail **8.** According to the information in paragraph 18 (from line 164), which of these countries are known for using "green" modes of transportation?
   a. The Netherlands and Sweden
   b. Germany and Japan
   c. Sweden and Germany
   d. Japan and the Netherlands

B. Matching. Write a letter (**A–J**) that corresponds to the main idea of each section of the article listed below. Then write the letter of a sentence that supports that idea. Two of the sentences contain incorrect information and are not needed.

A. According to the EPA website, the author's annual household CO_2 emissions totaled 54,273 pounds.

B. Increasing household energy efficiency is a first step, but other measures are needed to tackle global warming.

C. With some outside advice, the author learned his house was losing a lot of energy through heat leakage and household appliances.

D. The author's house did not leak energy as badly as he had originally thought.

E. Although there was more he could do, the author was pleased that he was able to significantly lower his carbon footprint.

F. To help reduce his carbon emissions, the author walked and cycled whenever possible.

G. The author decided to investigate his household carbon footprint and found it was surprisingly high.

H. The author learned that compact fluorescents can save house owners about $200 a year.

I. The author and his wife trimmed their annual emissions to 70% of the national average.

J. Countries such as Germany and Japan have developed some innovative ways to reduce carbon emissions.

Main idea of the article (thesis statement):
The author and his family performed an experiment to see if they could significantly reduce their carbon emissions.

Section 1: The Experiment
Main idea: _____ Supporting information: _____

Section 2: The Diagnosis
Main idea: _____ Supporting information: _____

Section 3: The Results
Main idea: _____ Supporting information: _____

Section 4: The Future
Main idea: _____ Supporting information: _____

C. Critical Thinking. Discuss these questions with a partner.

1. Is the author's attitude towards the experiment mainly positive or negative? How do you know?

2. What are some ways the author says individuals can cut carbon emissions? How about countries? Can you think of other ways in which we can cut emissions either as individuals or as societies?

3. Would you be willing to do a CO_2-cutting experiment similar to the author's? Why or why not? What do you think would be the most difficult challenges?

☐ Vocabulary Practice

A. Completion. Complete the information with the correct form of words from the box. Two words are extra.

audit	commute	emission	obstacle
commonplace	efficiency	mode	threshold

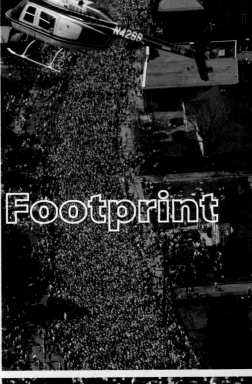

Managing a Marathon's Footprint

Marathon Monday is an official state holiday in Massachusetts, a day when citizens crowd the streets to watch some of world's top long-distance runners. Approximately 20,000 runners compete each year to win this famous race, or at the very least, to reach their personal **1.** _____ of endurance.

The 2009 race was the 113th marathon in Boston's history, and it was also the "greenest." For the first time, electric scooters followed the runners rather than motorcycles. A "green team" was employed to ensure that thousands of items discarded along the marathon route—including **2.** _____ items like plastic cups and bottles—found their way into recycling containers. It was the first step toward making the race more sustainable.

An energy **3.** _____ of the Boston Marathon, however, shows that it still has many **4.** _____ to overcome before it can claim to be a truly sustainable event. For example, only about two percent of the runners are from the surrounding area. So there is a considerable carbon footprint from airplane and car **5.** _____ as the runners travel long distances to get to the event.

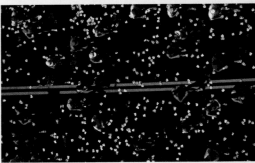

▲ Up to 20,000 people run the Boston Marathon every year, but they leave more than just their footprints. Each year, discarded drinking cups litter the Boston roads.

In recent years, other races in the U.S. have made efforts to improve their **6.** _____ in energy consumption. The Austin marathon uses solar power to run its stage, while Portland provides runners with medals made from recycled bicycle parts. The race to become the nation's greenest marathon has just begun.

B. Completion. Complete the sentences using the correct word from each pair.

1. Scientists warn we need to keep below the critical threshold / obstacle of polluting gases.

2. Turning on lights, driving cars, and using computers are all examples of compact / commonplace activities that consume energy.

3. Household modes / appliances are a major source of electricity consumption.

4. In the past, there have been many obstacles / audits to implementing solar and wind power projects.

5. Most threshold / compact cars use less gas and produce fewer emissions / appliances than larger, regular cars, so they are a more energy-efficient / -emission way to commute / audit to work.

Word Partnership

Use **obstacle** with: (n.) obstacle **course**, obstacle to **peace**; (v.) **be** an obstacle, **overcome** an obstacle, **hit** an obstacle; (adj.) **major** obstacle, **serious** obstacle.

5B Renewable Energy

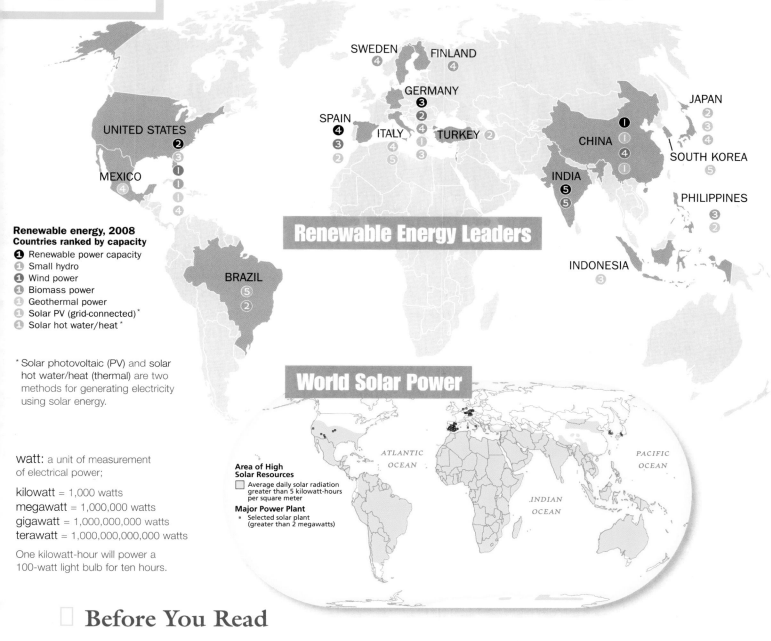

Renewable energy, 2008
Countries ranked by capacity
- ❶ Renewable power capacity
- ❶ Small hydro
- ❶ Wind power
- ❶ Biomass power
- ❶ Geothermal power
- ❶ Solar PV (grid-connected)*
- ❶ Solar hot water/heat*

*Solar photovoltaic (PV) and solar hot water/heat (thermal) are two methods for generating electricity using solar energy.

Renewable Energy Leaders

World Solar Power

Area of High Solar Resources
☐ Average daily solar radiation greater than 5 kilowatt-hours per square meter

Major Power Plant
▪ Selected solar plant (greater than 2 megawatts)

watt: a unit of measurement of electrical power;

kilowatt = 1,000 watts
megawatt = 1,000,000 watts
gigawatt = 1,000,000,000 watts
terawatt = 1,000,000,000,000 watts

One kilowatt-hour will power a 100-watt light bulb for ten hours.

☐ Before You Read

A. Understanding Maps. Look at the maps above and answer the questions.

1. Which countries are world leaders in renewable energy? Which has the highest capacity for solar PV energy? Which is top for solar thermal energy? Does any of the information surprise you?

2. Which parts of the world receive the greatest amount of solar radiation? Where are most of the largest solar power plants concentrated? Why do you think this is?

B. Scan. The article on pages 88–90 discusses solar power. Scan the article to find names of countries and places, and then answer these questions below:

1. Which countries does the article focus on? _____

2. What kinds of places in those countries does it mention? _____

Plugging into the Sun

Sunlight bathes us in far more energy than we could ever need— if we could just catch enough.

▲ At Nevada Solar One, rows of sun-catching mirror arrays stretch across the land. This one plant is estimated to produce about 134 million kilowatt hours of electricity per year.

1 EARLY ON A CLEAR November morning in the Mojave Desert, a full moon is sinking over the gigawatt[1] glare of Las Vegas. Nevada Solar One is sleeping. But the day's work is about to begin.

5 It is hard to imagine that a power plant could be so beautiful: 100 hectares of gently curved mirrors lined up like canals of light. Parked facing the ground overnight, they are starting to awaken— more than 182,000 of
10 them—and follow the sun.

"Looks like this will be a 700-degree day," says one of the operators in the control room.
15 His job is to monitor the rows of mirrors as they concentrate sunlight on long steel pipes filled with circulating oil, heating it as high as 750 degrees Fahrenheit (400°C). The heat produces steam, driving a turbine and dynamo, pushing as much as
20 64 megawatts onto the grid—enough to electrify 14,000 households, or a few Las Vegas casinos.

When Nevada Solar One came on line in 2007, it was the first large solar plant to be built in the United States in more than 17 years. During that
25 time, solar technology blossomed[2] elsewhere. The owner of Nevada Solar One is a Spanish company, Acciona; the mirrors were made in Germany.

Putting on hard hats and dark glasses, plant manager Robert Cable and I drive out to take a
30 closer look at the mirrors. Men with a water truck are hosing some down. "Any kind of dust affects them," Cable says. On a clear summer day with the sun directly overhead, Nevada Solar One can convert about 20 percent of the sun's rays into
35 electricity. Gas plants are more efficient, but this

> The total power needs of the humans on Earth is approximately 16 terawatts. The sunshine on the solid part of the Earth is 120,000 terawatts. From this perspective, energy from the sun is virtually unlimited.

fuel is free. And it doesn't emit planet-warming carbon dioxide.

"If we talk about geothermal or wind, all these other sources of renewable energy are limited
40 in their quantity," said Eicke Weber, director of the Fraunhofer Institute for Solar Energy Systems, in Freiburg, Germany. "The total power needs of the humans on Earth is approximately 16 terawatts," he said. (A terawatt is a trillion
45 (1,000,000,000,000) watts.) "In the year 2020 it is expected to grow to 20 terawatts. The sunshine on the solid part of the Earth is 120,000 terawatts. From this perspective, energy from the sun is virtually unlimited."

[1] One **gigawatt** is a billion (10⁹) watts.
[2] If something has **blossomed**, it has grown and developed well.

▲ In Albuquerque, New Mexico, mirror arrays concentrate light to make electricity.

Tapping the Sun

Solar energy may be unlimited, but its potential is barely tapped. "Right now solar is such a small fraction of U.S. electricity production that it's measured in tenths of a percent," said Robert Hawsey, an associate director of the National Renewable Energy Laboratory (NREL) in Golden, Colorado. "But that's expected to grow. Ten to 20 percent of the nation's peak electricity demand could be provided by solar energy by 2030."

Achieving that level will require government help. Nevada Solar One was built because the state had set a deadline requiring utilities to generate 20 percent of their power from renewable sources by 2015. During peak demand, the solar plant's electricity is almost as cheap as that of its gas-fired neighbor—but that's only because a 30 percent federal tax credit helped offset its construction costs.

The aim now is to bring down costs and reduce the need for subsidies and incentives. To achieve this, NREL's engineers are studying mirrors made from lightweight polymers instead of glass, and tubes that will absorb more sunlight and lose less heat. They're also working on solar power's biggest problem: how to store some of the heat produced during daylight hours for release later on.

Power plants such as Nevada Solar One use solar thermal energy (STE) technology, in other words collecting the sun's rays via mirrors to produce thermal energy (heat). Another method is to convert sunlight directly into electricity with photovoltaic (PV) panels made of semiconductors such as silicon. Back in the 1980s, an engineer named Roland Hulstrom calculated that if PV panels covered just three-tenths of a percent of the United States, they could electrify the entire country.

Twenty years later, PV panels still contribute only a tiny amount to the nation's electricity supply. But on rooftops in California, Nevada, and other states with good sunshine and tax incentives, they are increasingly common, almost as familiar as air conditioners. Though not yet as developed as solar thermal, they may have a brighter future. Two American companies, First Solar and Nanosolar, say they can now manufacture thin-film solar cells at a cost of around a dollar a watt—close to what's needed to compete with fossil fuels.

Germany's Solar Solution

On a cold December morning west of Frankfurt, Germany, fog hangs frozen in the trees, and clouds block the sun. In the town of Morbach, the blades of a 330-foot-high wind turbine appear and disappear in the gloom.[3] Down below, a field of photovoltaic panels struggle for light. Considering

▲ In Bavaria, Germany, solar photovoltaic panels appear on rooftops and farmhouses. Such facilities are not only eco-friendly, they often absorb more energy than is needed, earning a profit for the owners and residents.

[3] Something that is in the **gloom** is in partial or total darkness.

▲ Transmission towers like this one carry electricity across southern California, where, as in other sunny states, the business of solar energy is beginning to blossom.

its unpredictable weather, who would have thought that Germany would transform itself into the largest producer of photovoltaic power in the world?

A fraction of Germany's five gigawatt photovoltaic power comes from centralized plants like the one at Morbach. With land at a premium in Germany, solar panels can be found mounted on rooftops, farmhouses, even on soccer stadiums and along the autobahn.[4] The panels, dispersed across the German countryside, are all connected to the national grid.

The solar boom has completely transformed towns like "sunny Freiburg," as the tourist brochures call it, which sits at the edge of the Black Forest in the southern part of the country. Towering walls of photovoltaics greet visitors as they arrive at Freiburg's train station. Across the street from a school covered with photovoltaic panels is Solarsiedlung ("solar settlement"), one of the town's condominium complexes.[5]

"We are being paid for living in this house," said Wolfgang Schnürer, one of Solarsiedlung's residents. The day before, when snow covered the roof, Schnürer's system produced only 5.8 kilowatt-hours, not enough power for a German household. But on a sunny day in May it yielded more than seven times that much.

In Germany, regulations require utility companies to pay even the smallest PV producers a premium of about 50 euro cents a kilowatt-hour. In 2008,

Schnürer's personal power plant yielded over 6,000 kilowatt-hours, more than double what the family consumed. When they subtracted their usage from the amount they produced, the family found they were more than 2,500 euros (nearly $3,700) in profit.

Anybody who installs a PV system is guaranteed above-market rates for 20 years—the equivalent of an 8 percent annual return on the initial investment. "It is an ingenious mechanism," Eicke Weber said. "I always say the United States addresses the idealists, those who want to save the planet. In Germany the law addresses anyone who wants to get 8 percent return on his investment for 20 years."

In total, Germany now generates more than 2,000 gigawatt-hours of electricity annually from solar energy, whereas the U.S. generates less than half this amount. The largest photovoltaic installation in the United States—at Nellis Air Force Base just outside Las Vegas—is only about the 25th largest in the world. Nearly all the bigger ones are located in either Germany or Spain. But in the U.S., too, there is a gathering sense that the time for solar energy has arrived—if there is a commitment to jump-start[6] the technology. "Originally it seemed like a pie-in-the-sky idea," said Michelle Price, the energy manager at Nellis. "It didn't seem possible." Many things seem possible now.

[4] **Autobahn** is a word used to describe super highways in Austria, Germany, and Switzerland, on which vehicles travel very fast.
[5] **Condominium complexes** are apartment compounds, or living areas.
[6] To **jump-start** a process is to get it started very quickly.

Reading Comprehension

A. Multiple Choice. Choose the best answer for each question.

Inference
1. The author seems surprised by Nevada Solar One because it _____.
    a. is more attractive than a typical power plant
    b. can provide electricity for many households
    c. is more efficient than other solar power plants
    d. heats oil to very high temperatures

Detail
2. What is the job of the men with the water truck in paragraph 5 (from line 28)?
    a. to pump water that will then be heated
    b. to clean the surface of some of the mirrors
    c. to provide the workers with drinking water
    d. to cool the solar plant

Detail
3. By how much will the Earth's energy needs increase from the time the article was written to 2020?
    a. 4 terawatts   c. 20 terawatts
    b. 16 terawatts   d. 24 terawatts

Vocabulary/Inference
4. The phrase *barely tapped* (line 52) indicates that _____.
    a. the use of solar energy has been growing rapidly
    b. someday, much more solar energy can be utilized
    c. the supply of solar power will never meet the demand
    d. no one knows how much solar energy can be generated

Negative Detail
5. Which of these is NOT mentioned in paragraph 9 (from line 69) as a way to cut prices for solar energy production?
    a. making mirrors from different materials
    b. designing tubes that take in more sunlight and hold heat better
    c. obtaining more subsidies from the government
    d. finding a way to store heat for use at night

Inference
6. What does the author imply in paragraph 14 (from line 125) about the town of Freiburg, Germany?
    a. It was the first town with a large-scale solar plant.
    b. It does not really get that much sunshine.
    c. Its solar industry helps to attract tourists.
    d. It is sunny there throughout the year.

Paraphrase
7. What does Wolfgang Schnürer mean when he says, "We are being paid for living in this house" (line 134)?
    a. "The money we get for producing electricity is greater than our total living costs."
    b. "The government pays us a salary for maintaining a personal solar power plant."
    c. "The income from our personal power plant is greater than our energy costs."
    d. "We receive free housing in exchange for our work for the utility company."

Vocabulary
8. The phrase *pie-in-the-sky* in paragraph 18 (line 175) is closest in meaning to _____.
    a. unrealistic   c. believable
    b. brilliant   d. unwelcome

A major part of this article consists of a comparison between the solar power industry in the United States and in Germany. To understand a comparison between X and Y, you first need to identify which ideas and information relate to each category.

B. Classification. Write the letter of each sentence below in the correct place in the chart, depending on whether it refers to Germany, the United States, both, or neither.

A. Despite unpredictable weather, it has the world's largest PV solar industry.

B. The mirrors for Nevada Solar One were made here.

C. The government here has given incentives for the increased use of solar power.

D. Solar power produces less than one percent of the country's electricity production.

E. The company that owns Nevada Solar One is from this country.

F. According to one expert, the government policies here regarding solar energy appeal to people who want to make money on their investment.

G. Manufacturers here have recently developed very cheap, thin solar cells.

H. Even the smallest solar providers here are connected to the national electrical grid.

I. According to one expert, the government policies here regarding solar energy appeal to idealists.

J. It is the second largest producer of photovoltaic power.

K. It generates less than 1,000 gigawatt-hours of electricity every year from solar power.

L. There is optimism that solar electricity production here will be more significant in the future.

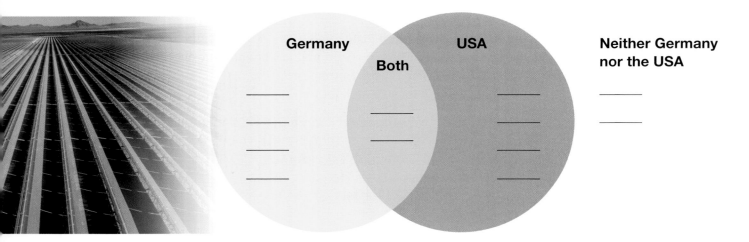

Germany   Both   USA   Neither Germany nor the USA

C. Critical Thinking. Discuss these questions with a partner.

1. Do you think the author of this article is generally optimistic or pessimistic about this topic? Find places in the article that support your opinion.

2. What do you think the author of the previous article, "It Starts at Home," would feel about the information in this article?

3. Is your country or region a good place for solar power production? Are there incentives for people to try solar power or other renewable sources of energy?

Vocabulary Practice

A. Completion. Complete the information with the correct form of words from the box. Three words are extra.

absorb	deadline	manufacture	premium
subtract	circulation	invest	panel
renewable	yield		

Fish + Wind = Energy Solution?

Germany needs a place to store its wind power. And in the small town of Cuxhaven on the windy North Sea coast, they think they've found an answer—in frozen fish.

▲ Globally, wind supplies less than one percent of electric power. But its share is growing, particularly in European countries such as Germany and (pictured) Denmark.

One of **1.** _____ energy's most problematic issues is the uncertainty of wind and solar power. Customers need a steady, predictable stream of electricity. But how do you produce a steady **2.** _____ of electricity from wind power, when winds are so unpredictable? This is particularly an issue in Germany, where seven percent of electricity is **3.** _____ from wind energy.

One possible solution is cold storage. When fish from the North Sea are stored in a warehouse, such as Erwin GOOSS warehouse in Cuxhaven, they need to be kept cold. Ordinarily, air **4.** _____ inside the warehouse is controlled so temperatures remain at about -20°C (-4°F). But during peak hours of wind production, the temperature can be pushed as low as -30°C (-22°F). The frozen fish **5.** _____ and "store" this extra energy. When winds die down, the cooling is switched off, but the warehouse remains cold enough for fish to stay frozen. This keeps cooling costs to a minimum, especially during the summer when electricity is at a **6.** _____.

"It's not that we're using less power, it's just that we're using it when it's cheaper," says Gunter Krins, technical director of Erwin GOOSS. By **7.** _____ in storage methods such as Cuxhaven's, it is hoped that wind power could become an efficient long-term solution to Germany's energy needs— no matter how hard the wind is blowing.

B. Definitions. Use the correct form of words in the box in **A** to complete the definitions.

1. move around easily _____

2. natural, can be used again _____

3. specific time for completion _____

4. take away, deduct _____

5. higher price, usually due to short supply _____

6. amount or quantity produced _____

7. take in, soak up _____

8. flat, rectangular piece of material _____

Word Link

The prefix **sub–** often has the meaning of *below*, e.g., **sub**tract, **sub**marine, **sub**merge, **sub**divide, **sub**conscious, **sub**head, **sub**ordinate.

Our Stormy Star

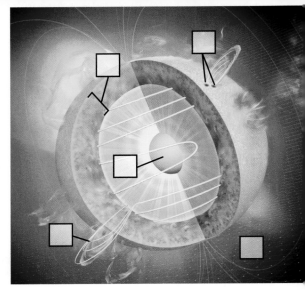

A. Preview. This unit's video is about our closest star—the sun. Read the sentences describing parts of the sun, and label the picture (**1–5**).

At the center of the sun is its **1** core, a thermonuclear reactor where hydrogen is converted to helium. These hot, electrified gases are in a state of matter called plasma.

It takes hundreds of thousands of years for light to travel out through the sun's dense interior to the **2** convection zone, the layer beneath the sun's surface.

The **3** corona is the sun's outer atmosphere. Here plasma particles flow nonstop into space as solar winds.

The sun's rotational movement stretches its magnetic field, sometimes causing **4** magnetic field lines to extend through the surface into the corona.

Intense magnetic activity creates areas of reduced surface temperature, known as **5** sun spots. These appear as dark areas which may be visible from Earth.

B. Summarize. Watch the video, *Our Stormy Star.* Then complete the summary below using the correct form of words in the box. One word is extra

circulation	manufacture	nevertheless	nuclear	panel	principal
proximity	renewable	release	so-called	virtually	volume

It might seem like a great ball of fire, but the sun is really a sphere of super-hot hydrogen and helium gas. Powerful **1.** _____ reactions inside the sun **2.** _____ huge amounts of energy in a process called fusion, providing the source for **3.** _____ all of the Earth's energy.

The sun's **4.** _____ is so great that it could contain more than one million Earths. Yet compared to some other stars in our galaxy, the sun is not particularly large. **5.** _____, in one respect, the sun is very special: it is the **6.** _____ energy provider for life on our planet. Its light powers the photosynthesis that plants need to grow; the plants, in turn, **7.** _____ the food and oxygen that animals need to eat and breathe.

The sun has other dramatic effects. Strong solar winds striking our magnetic field create amazing light shows in the polar skies—the **8.** _____ "Northern and Southern Lights," or auroras. The sun's **9.** _____ to the Earth also has a major effect on our planet: the slight tilting of the Earth's axis toward and away from the sun creates our seasons. And the sun's energy also powers the **10.** _____ of our air and sea currents.

The sun is expected to die out about five billion years from now. Until then it offers an almost limitless supply of **11.** _____ energy, which could potentially solve our planet's energy problems.

C. Think About It.

1. The sun's energy is virtually unlimited, but solar energy contributes just a small fraction of the global energy supply. Why do you think this is?

2. Of the energy solutions discussed in this unit, which have the best potential for solving our planet's energy problems?

To learn more about energy problems and solutions, visit elt. heinle.com/explorer

UNIT 6
Light

Light falls through a window frame in Agra, India, 1936.

95

6A From Light to Sight

Electromagnetic Spectrum

When light moves through space, it is best understood as a wave. **Shortwave energy (S)** has wavelengths below 400 nanometers (nm) and includes ultraviolet (UV) rays, X-rays, and gamma rays. **Visible wavelengths (V)** range from 400 to 750 nm and are sensed as a band of colors. We know these as the seven rainbow colors (from violet to deep red), although the human eye can actually detect up to ten million shades. Invisible **long-wave energy (L)** above 750 nm includes infrared, microwaves, and radio waves.

Seeing Color

When light waves encounter the eye, light acts as a particle of energy, or **photon**. Photons stimulate the **rods and cones** in our **retina** (at the back of our eye), allowing us to sense color. Each type of cone (blue, green, red) is sensitive to a specific range of wavelengths. For example, a sheet of green glass will absorb all visible wavelengths except those in the middle of the spectrum. These wavelengths will then stimulate mainly the green cones (**A**) and a person will "see" this color. Longer wavelengths will stimulate both red and green cones to make yellow (**B**). If all three are stimulated, the result is white (**C**). This information is sent to the person's brain via **nerve cells** in the eye.

1 **nanometer** (nm) = one billionth of a meter

☐ Before You Read

A. Quiz. Read the information above and circle **T** (true) or **F** (false) for each sentence. If a statement is wrong, change it to make it true.

1. Humans are unable to see wavelengths below 400 and above 750 nanometers. **T** **F**

2. Humans can only detect a limited number of color shades. **T** **F**

3. Light photons stimulate rods and cones in the eye, which enable us to see color. **T** **F**

4. When all three cones are stimulated, a person sees the color green. **T** **F**

B. Skim and Predict. The passage on pages 97–99 has four main sections. Skim and match each section with its topic. Then read the article to check your ideas. Underline key information to help you recall it later.

Section	What it's about
1. Seeing the World	_____ what light means to us today
2. Fire in the Eye	_____ recent theories about the nature of light
3. Light, Time, and Space	_____ what light is and how we're able to sense it
4. Pure But Not Simple	_____ how early thinkers explained light and vision

What Is Light?

▲ One of Sir Isaac Newton's original prisms breaks light into a spectrum of colors on a man's face.

1 THERE HAS BEEN LIGHT from the
beginning. There will be light, feebly,[1] at the end.
In all its forms—visible and invisible—it saturates
the universe. But light is more than a little bit
5 mysterious. No one is exactly sure how to describe
it. A wave? A particle? Yes, the scientists say. Both.

Seeing the World

What we call light is really the same thing—in a
different set of wavelengths—as the radiation that
10 we call radio waves or gamma rays or X-rays. But
in practice, scientists often use the term "light" to
mean the portion of the electromagnetic spectrum
that makes up visible light.

Visible light is unlike any other fundamental
15 element of the universe: It directly, regularly, and
dramatically interacts with our senses. Light offers
high-resolution information across great distances
(you can't hear or smell the moons of Jupiter or
the Crab Nebula). So much information is carried
20 by visible light that almost everything from a fly to
an octopus has a way to capture it—an eye, eyes, or
something similar.

Our eyes each have about 125 million rods and
cones—specialized cells so sensitive that some can
25 detect a mere handful of photons. "About one-fifth
of your brain does nothing but try to deal with
the visual world around you," says physicist Sidney
Perkowitz, author of *Empire of Light*.

It's worth noting that our eyes are designed
30 to detect the kind of light that is radiated in
abundance by the particular star—the sun—that
gives life to our planet. Visible light is powerful
stuff, moving at relatively short wavelengths, which
makes it biologically convenient. To see long,
35 stretched-out radio waves, we'd have to have huge
eyes, like satellite dishes. Nor would it make sense
for our eyes to detect light in the near infrared:
we'd be constantly distracted,[2] because any heat-
emitting object glows in those wavelengths.

40 "If we were seeing infrared," says physicist Charles
Townes, "all of this room would be glowing. The
eye itself is infrared—it's warm. We don't want to
detect all of that stuff."

---

[1] If something is moving or existing **feebly**, it is very weak.
[2] If someone is **distracted**, they are unable to concentrate because
they are thinking about or looking at other things.

▲ A Cuban tree frog displays a swallowed Christmas light.

Fire in the Eye

45 If it is hard for us to understand light, for the ancients it was much harder. Lacking scientific instruments, they could probe the nature of light only with their inventive minds. "Light is the activity of what is transparent,"[3] declared the Greek 50 philosopher Aristotle. This transparency was an essential property of various substances; when activated by sun or fire, it was said to produce light and color.

The fifth-century B.C. philosopher and poet 55 Empedocles had the brilliant idea that light is a substance emitted by the sun and that we are not conscious of its movement because it moves too fast. But he also subscribed to the notion of "fire within 60 the eye," comparing the eyes to lanterns. Many Greeks, including Plato and Euclid, shared this belief that the eyes produce a kind of visual ray. It explained the curious fact that sometimes we look in the direction of an object but fail to notice it 65 immediately. The ray, it was assumed, must strike the object directly before it can be seen. Aristotle was among those to point out that if this were true, we'd be able to see in the dark.

A thousand years ago, the Arab scientist Alhazen 70 advocated the idea that light enters the eye, citing as evidence the pain we feel when we look directly at the sun. Centuries later Leonardo da Vinci realized that the eye is akin to the camera 75 obscura, pioneered by Alhazen, in which light passes through a pinhole into a darkened room and casts an inverted[4] 80 image of the exterior world onto a wall.

In the early 17th century, French philosopher René Descartes did a rather 85 dramatic examination of the eyeball of an ox, scraping away the back of the eye and peering through it. He saw that 90 the eye captures an inverted, upside-down image of the world. Why doesn't the world look upside down? Because our minds correct the image. Sight has both a physical 95 and psychological element.

Light soon passed through the laboratory of Isaac Newton and never looked the same again. In the 1660s, Newton demonstrated that white light is composed of all the colors of the spectrum. Using a 100 prism,[5] he broke sunlight into a rainbow, then later used a second prism to cohere the colors back into white light.

> Light passed through the laboratory of Isaac Newton and never looked the same again.

Newton believed that light was made of "unimaginable small and swift" particles. Newton's 105 views were so respected that the wave theory only resurfaced in the 1860s, when James Clerk Maxwell made an essential breakthrough. Maxwell had been studying electricity and magnetism, and realized that they propagated[6] through space 110 at—coincidence?—the speed of light. Light, he concluded, is an "electromagnetic" wave.

---

[3] Something that is **transparent** is clear, colorless, and can be looked through, for example, clear glass.

[4] Something that is **inverted** is turned upside down or inside out from the way it usually is seen.

[5] A **prism** is a transparent block, often with triangular ends and rectangular sides, used to manipulate light.

[6] Something that is **propagated** is spread and transmitted to a wide area.

Light, Time, and Space

115 The particle versus wave debate eventually developed a kind of truce, governed by quantum

120 mechanics:[7] light is produced by changes in the energy level of electrons. Light moves through

125 space as a wave, but when it encounters matter it behaves like a particle. It simply doesn't fit into

130 one of our neat little categories. "Light, indeed, is different from anything else we know," writes Sidney Perkowitz.

The era of permanent uncertainty began in 1900, when Max Planck's experiments with heat radiation

135 implied that light strikes against matter in discrete chunks—quanta, he called them—like bullets from a machine gun. This seemed contrary to Maxwell's equations, and Planck was reluctant to believe it.

Enter Albert Einstein, whose special theory of

140 relativity rejected the rigid, mechanical Newtonian universe. He achieved this theoretical breakthrough by thinking about light. Einstein did "thought experiments," and in one he asked what would happen if you could ride a beam of light and look

145 at an adjacent beam. Wouldn't the adjacent beam of light appear motionless? Maxwell's equations didn't seem to allow light to slow down or stop when moving through space. Einstein's answer— that light's speed is constant for all observers

150 regardless of their own speed—destroyed the classical concepts of space and time.

Einstein's relativity presents all manner of head-scratching[8] implications. It reveals that as objects approach the speed of light, time slows down. At

155 the speed of light itself, time stops. This fact can help us understand the journeys made by starlight and galaxylight and quasarlight across cosmic

▲ Candles and lamps are lit during the celebration of Diwali, the Festival of Lights. Diwali is one among many festival and cultural events around the globe in which light plays an essential part.

distances. We use the term light-year to express a unit of distance (about ten trillion kilometers,

160 or six trillion miles). But if you were the light itself—if you could be a traveling photon—you'd experience no time. That long journey would be instantaneous.

Pure But Not Simple

165 We have come a way in our understanding of light. Yet it is perhaps a measure of light's importance in our daily lives that most of us hardly pay any attention to it. Light is almost like air. It's a given. We would no more linger over[9] the concept of

170 light than a fish would consider the notion of water.

Perhaps it is just as well. For those who have attempted to study and capture it, from Aristotle to Alhazen to Einstein, light has proven an extremely

175 difficult quantity to explain. While physicists have been able to slice most of nature into ever smaller constituents, they have found that light won't reduce. In the end, it seems that light is light— pure, but definitely not simple.

[7] **Quantum mechanics** is a branch of mathematical physics that deals with the structure, nature, and behavior of molecules, atoms, and subatomic particles.

[8] If an idea is described as **head-scratching**, it is confusing or hard to understand.

[9] If you **linger over** an idea or task, you spend a lot time patiently thinking about it or doing it.

Reading Comprehension

A. Multiple Choice. Choose the best answer for each question.

Purpose **1.** What is the main purpose of this article?
  a. to trace the history of humankind's study of light
  b. to explain how the human eye interacts with light
  c. to discuss how ancient people investigated light
  d. to show how Einstein changed our understanding of light

Detail **2.** What does the author say about rods and cones in paragraph 4 (from line 23)?
  a. Only about one-fifth of them can actually detect light.
  b. Every human eye has about 125 million of them.
  c. None of them can detect more than a few photons.
  d. Their existence was discovered by Sidney Perkowitz.

Reference **3.** What does *that stuff* refer to in line 43?
  a. things emitting infrared
  b. parts of the human eye
  c. electrical lights in a room
  d. objects emitting radio waves

Detail **4.** According to the author, if humans were able to detect radio waves, _____.
  a. they would no longer be able to detect visible light
  b. their eyes would probably be shaped like giant disks
  c. everything that they saw would seem to be glowing
  d. their eyes would probably be long and narrow

Detail **5.** Who developed the camera obscura?
  a. Alhazen   c. da Vinci
  b. Aristotle   d. Descartes

Main Idea **6.** The main idea of paragraph 13 (from line 114) is that _____.
  a. the particle theory was eventually replaced by the wave theory
  b. scientists realized that neither the wave nor the particle theory was correct
  c. quantum physics provided a way to combine the wave and particle theories
  d. quantum theory provided a simple way to categorize the behavior of light

Inference **7.** The information in paragraph 16 (from line 152) suggests that astronauts traveling at the speed of light for 10 years would _____.
  a. return to the place from which they departed
  b. travel backwards in time to ten years in the past
  c. be no older when they arrived than when they had left
  d. travel about 10 trillion kilometers across space

Detail **8.** In the final paragraph, the author suggest that light is different from other natural phenomena because scientists _____.
  a. are not able to divide light into its components
  b. have been studying it for a much longer time
  c. understand it but can't explain it well to non-scientists
  d. have not been able to design many instruments to study it

Much of this article focuses on the contributions of various scientists and thinkers to the study of light, from ancient times until recent times. To identify connections between individuals and their accomplishments, scan for instances of the person's name and then read the surrounding sentences.

B. Matching. Match each name (**1–10**) with the idea or the accomplishment described in the article (**a–j**).

1. _____ Albert Einstein
2. _____ Alhazen
3. _____ Aristotle
4. _____ Empedocles
5. _____ Isaac Newton
6. _____ James Clerk Maxwell
7. _____ Leonardo da Vinci
8. _____ Max Planck
9. _____ Plato and Euclid
10. _____ René Descartes

a. said that light must actually enter the eye because looking at the sun was painful

b. believed light was a substance released by the sun, but it moved too rapidly to be visible

c. proposed that light interacted with matter in packages called quanta

d. proved that white light was made up of a rainbow of colored light

e. gave one reason why the "fire in the eye" theory could not be correct

f. realized that our eyes were similar to a camera obscura

g. theorized that time stops for something travelling at the speed of light

h. by looking through the eye of an animal, learned that the eye sees images upside down

i. discovered that light is part of the electromagnetic spectrum

j. believed that the eye itself produced a visual ray

C. Critical Thinking. Discuss these questions with a partner.

1. The author uses various verbs to describe individuals' opinions and discoveries, e.g., *declared* (line 49) and *realized that* (line 109). What other similar verbs can you find? Which ones relate to an individual's opinion and which relate to the discovery of a fact?

2. In paragraph 10 (lines 94–95), the author says that "Sight has both a physical and psychological element." What do you think he means? Explain in your own words.

3. In paragraph 17, the author says, " . . . most of us hardly pay any attention to it. Light is almost like air." What does he mean by this? How is light similar to air? Do you agree with him? Can you think of other things in life that are like light and air in this respect?

Vocabulary Practice

A. Completion. Complete the information using the correct form of the words in the box.

conscious	concept	discrete	element
encounter	equation	implication	reluctant
saturate	subscribe		

Just about anywhere astronomers' observations take them—from the largest stars to the tiniest **1.** _____ of our galaxy—they **2.** _____ Einstein's world, a place where time is relative, mass and energy are interchangeable, and space can stretch and bend.

At the turn of the 20th century, physics was in a state of uncertainty. Most physicists at that time still **3.** _____ to the laws of the physical world first proposed by Isaac Newton more than 200 years previously. But physicists were becoming increasingly **4.** _____ of the fact that their current theories were insufficient. For one thing, they could not fully explain the behavior of the various **5.** _____ particles that were being discovered at the subatomic level. One scientist who was **6.** _____ to accept the Newtonian view of the universe was Albert Einstein.

▲ An artist's view of how the universe might end, 20 billion years from now. According to Einstein's theories, space-time is curved by gravity. However, a mysterious force known as dark energy appears to be counteracting gravity's pull, causing the universe to expand at an increasing rate. Ultimately, all matter could be torn apart.

Einstein realized that space and time are "relative," flowing differently for each of us depending on our motion. His special theory of relativity, published a hundred years ago, revealed that energy and mass are two sides of the same coin, forever linked in his famous **7.** _____, $E = mc^2$. (E stands for energy, m for mass, and c for the speed of light.) The radical **8.** _____ of Einstein's general relativity later led to the **9.** _____ of dark energy and dark matter, mysterious and invisible substances that **10.** _____ our universe.

B. Definitions. Use the correct form of the words in the box in **A** to complete the definitions.

1. (to) fill completely _____

2. something likely to happen as a result _____

3. unwilling, unenthusiastic _____

4. separate and distinct from each other _____

5. substance consisting of one type of atom _____

6. aware (of something) _____

7. (to) believe in an opinion or idea _____

8. (to) come across, meet unexpectedly _____

9. mathematical statement of equality _____

10. idea, abstract principle _____

Usage

If you are **conscious** of something, you notice or realize that it is happening. A **conscious** decision or action is made or done deliberately and intentionally. Someone who is **conscious** is awake rather than asleep or unconscious.

6B | Laser Technology

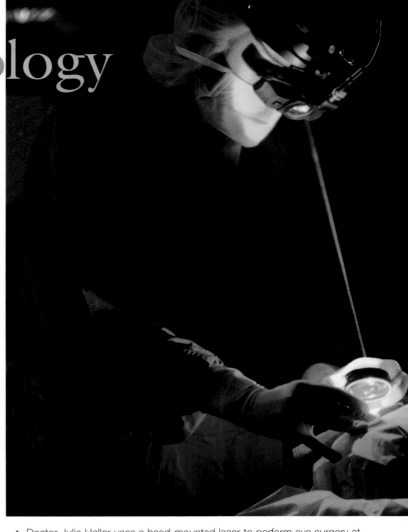

A **laser** achieves its power by emitting, or sending out, specific wavelengths of light. These wavelengths are highly concentrated, producing a beam like the one seen in the photo on the right.

Some lasers are extremely powerful and can be used to cut or repair things. Other lasers (like those used at the nightclub shown below) emit beams that are much less intense and therefore less dangerous.

☐ Before You Read

A. Completion. Read the information above and complete the first column of the chart with your ideas.

	What I already know	What I learned from the passage
What is a laser?		
How does a laser work?		
What are some common uses of lasers today?		
What are some possible uses of lasers in the future?		

▲ Doctor Julia Haller uses a head-mounted laser to perform eye surgery at Johns Hopkins University. Using the intense beam of light, Haller is able to destroy tumors (abnormal tissue growth) and repair eye damage.

B. Skim and Predict. Skim the passage on pages 104–106 to see if any questions in **A** are discussed. Then read the article and add information you learn to the second column of the chart.

Light
Engineering

▲ Fiber-optic strands from Lucent Technologies, when pulsed with infrared light, can each transmit ten million phone conversations at once.

1 We use light today for everything from laser eye surgery to telephone technology. In fact, the more you look at the topic, the more you realize that our lives are built around light, that our daily existence
5 is continuously shaped—and made vivid—by that ambiguous stuff that dates from the beginning of time.

"THIS IS A VERY PURE, STRAIGHT BEAM." Charles Townes was showing me a helium-neon laser in
10 his laboratory at the University of California at Berkeley. He has hundreds of lasers, including some that arrive in the mail as gifts, lasers smaller than matchboxes, green lasers soothing to the eye—all the various descendants of technology that
15 Townes, together with his brother-in-law Arthur Schawlow, invented in the 1950s.

Light normally spreads out rapidly in all directions; a laser coheres and amplifies the light in a narrow beam. The key to producing this beam is the basic
20 atomic principle that says that photons—light as particles—can be captured or emitted by atoms. When an electron changes from a high-energy, or excited, state to a low-energy state, its atom will emit a photon. A laser exploits this process.

25 A laser starts with a crystal or other medium whose atoms are prone to[1] excitement. These atoms are hit with light, causing their electrons to do a little dance. When they calm down, they release excess energy as photons. Those photons, in turn,
30 induce more electron dancing, which creates more photons—a chain reaction. It is physics, not magic, that causes more light to come out than went in.

The arrival of the laser was greeted by some parts of the media as the start of a new era of military
35 death rays, similar to the Martian Heat-Ray in H.G. Wells' *The War of the Worlds.* But a half century ago, Townes and Schawlow weren't actually sure what could be done with their invention. They just knew they'd figured out[2] a way to make light shine
40 strong and straight.

It's hard to overstate the usefulness of a tool that makes light shine straight. "People used to kid me, 'Lasers are a solution looking for a problem,'" Townes says. He thinks about that every time he
45 goes to the checkout line at the grocery store, where light is used to scan the price of every product. When you make a long-distance phone call, your words are transmitted by laser light along a fiber-optic cable. A laser reads the CD in a CD
50 player. "When a friend comes to me and says laser surgery saved his eyesight, that's a very emotional thing," Townes says.

[1] Someone or something that is **prone to** do something is more likely to do it.
[2] If you have **figured out** a concept, you have thought hard about it and now understand it.

▲ The theoretic foundations for LASER, or Light Amplification by Stimulated Emission of Radiation, were established in 1917 by Albert Einstein. In 1957, Townes and Schawlow began the first serious study of lasers using visible light.

THE WORLD'S LARGEST LASER is about an hour east of San Francisco, in the National Ignition Facility
55 (NIF) at the Lawrence Livermore National Laboratory. The laser is actually 192 individual beams of light, grouped in bundles of four, which travel the length of a building 213 meters (700 feet) long and 122 meters (400
60 feet) wide. Each laser bounces off a mirror into a target chamber—a 9-meter diameter sphere that looks somewhat like an enormous golf ball from outer space.

65 Inside the chamber the laser beams crash into a gold-plated cylinder containing a gas-filled pellet. The gases in the pellet, under the pressure of all this light, compress to the point where they induce nuclear fusion. "The goal is to create a miniature
70 star in the laboratory," says Ed Moses, the NIF project manager. In the long term, the scientists at NIF hope to clear a path toward a source of cheap, endless, pollution-free electricity.

According to physicist Vaughn Draggoo,
75 "NIF will produce more power in a one-nanosecond[3] laser pulse than all the power generated in the rest of the world at that moment." How is it that light is such a useful source of energy? "Because you can
80 compress a lot of light's energy in a very small point," says Moses. Children, he notes, discover this when they play with a magnifying glass on a sunny summer day. Here we come to one facet of the
85 miracle of light. It has no volume. And photons have no charge, so when they are concentrated into a very small space,

they don't repulse each other as negatively charged electrons do. "They don't bother one another" is
90 the way Moses puts it.

THE TELECOMMUNICATIONS INDUSTRY loves light. When you visit Lucent Technologies Bell Labs in Holmdel, New Jersey, you're greeted with a sign saying, "Welcome to Photon Valley."

95 Kathy Szelag, a vice president with Lucent's Optical Networking Group, told me, "People like my parents think we're in the *Star Wars* part of optical networking. We're really in the crude oil part of optical networking. We're just at the
100 beginning." Her colleague Bob Windeler, an optical-fiber researcher, added, "The amount of information you can put on a fiber more than doubles every year." In theory a single fiber could someday transmit every phone call on Earth
105 simultaneously.

Lasers are used to beam different wavelengths of infrared light down a single fiber. Each wavelength

"NIF will produce more power in a one-nanosecond laser pulse than all the power generated in the rest of the world at that moment."

is its own data channel—its own pipe. Right now, a fiber can carry dozens of these channels, but that
110 could become thousands or even millions. "It's as close to a miracle as there is," says Dave Bishop, Lucent's vice president of optical research.

³ A **nano-second** is one billionth of a second.

▼ In this 1950 photo, a tiny model farm is used for lightning research and to conduct power line tests.

▲ In Lovozero, Russia, where the sun does not shine at all during the winter months, children are exposed to ultraviolet light. The light makes the body produce vitamin D, which is necessary to a healthy human body meant to live in the presence of sunlight.

George Gilder, an influential technology guru, has declared that light will be the medium of a
115 communications revolution. "You can envision⁴ a point where everyone in the world could have his own wavelength," says Gilder. "You'd have one wavelength that connected you to the person you wanted to address in Vienna or Tokyo or
120 Tierra del Fuego, and this wavelength could easily accommodate three dimensional images. You could have conversations in which you forget within literally seconds that the person is not present. You see a face, the image saturates your own
125 optical capabilities."

MODERN PHYSICS EMERGED from the study of matter and light. Modern cosmology, including the revelation that the universe is expanding, came from the detection of faint galactic light. So,
130 what's next for light?

Some scientists predict that computing will eventually be based on light. Computer engineers could create devices that, instead of silicon chips, have light beams at their core. Light could even
135 become the main power source for long-distance space travel. The spaceship would have an ultra thin sail to catch the "wind" of light beamed from an Earth-based laser. In theory, such a craft could accelerate to a sizable fraction of the speed of
140 light—without carrying fuel.

What's certain is that light is going to remain extremely useful—for industry, science, art, and our daily comings and goings. It's an amazing tool, a carrier of beauty, a giver of life. It surely has a very
145 bright future.

▲ The applications of light are seemingly unlimited. These men are undergoing treatments against infection using ultraviolet light.

⁴ When you **envision** something, you imagine it, and picture it in your mind.

Reading Comprehension

A. Multiple Choice. Choose the best answer for each question.

Detail   **1.** What do all the "hundreds of lasers" mentioned in paragraph 2 have in common?
a. They are all much smaller than standard lasers.
b. All are based on an invention of Townes and Schawlow.
c. Every one of them was developed back in the 1950s.
d. Each of them was sent to Charles Townes as a gift.

Vocabulary   **2.** The word *soothing* in line 13 is closest in meaning to _____.
a. comforting   c. damaging
b. helpful   d. invisible

Detail   **3.** According to the information in paragraphs 3 and 4 (from line 17), an atom emits a photon when its electrons _____.
a. are in a high-energy, or excited state
b. have just begun to "dance"
c. change from high- to low-energy state
d. are first struck by a beam of light

Cohesion   **4.** Where would be the best place to insert this sentence in paragraph 6 (from line 41)?
Laser surgery corrects faulty vision in an increasingly routine procedure.
a. after the second sentence (". . . *says*.")
b. after the third sentence (". . . *product*.")
c. after the fourth sentence (". . . *cable*.")
d. after the fifth sentence (". . . *player*.")

Detail   **5.** In the laser at the National Ignition Facility, how many beams of light are contained in each bundle?
a. 4   c. 192
b. 48   d. 700

Detail   **6.** What is the goal of the scientists working on the world's largest laser?
a. to help design a new military weapon
b. to test the strength of various materials
c. to develop a new means of space travel
d. to produce a new source of energy

Rhetorical Purpose   **7.** The author quotes Kathy Szelag in paragraph 11 in order to _____.
a. explain a number of exciting new developments in the field of optical networking
b. show how optical fibers have become more advanced than people expected
c. challenge the idea that someday one fiber can transmit all the phone calls on Earth
d. point out there are many advances that can still be made in optical engineering

Rhetorical Purpose   **8.** In line 137, why does the author place quotations marks around the word *wind*?
a. to indicate that the word *wind* is directly quoted from another magazine
b. to emphasize that the wind in the article is actually light, not moving air
c. to show that the author is not sure if this method of propulsion will work
d. to express the author's surprise that wind could be useful for space travel

B. Matching. Find the four most appropriate section titles from the list (**A–H**) and put them in the correct order below.

A. From Martian Heat Rays to Today's Weapon Systems
B. Light's Impact, Past and Future
C. Laser Surgery: Hope for the Blind?
D. Telecommunications at the Speed of Light
E. Computers That Run on Light
F. Cheap Green Energy from a Mini-Star
G. Long Distance Chats with 3-D Friends
H. An Invention That Changed the World

Light Engineering

Section 1 (from line 8): _____

Section 2 (from line 53): _____

Section 3 (from line 91): _____

Section 4 (from line 126): _____

C. Critical Thinking. Discuss these questions with a partner.

1. Do you think the author is generally optimistic or pessimistic about the future of light technology? Find lines from the article that support your opinion.

2. Why does George Gilder think lasers will create a "communications revolution" (line 115)?

3. How has the way people communicate changed in recent years? Have the changes generally been positive or negative? How do you think it will change in the future?

Vocabulary Practice

▲ Physicists such as Lene Hau (above) continue to push the limits of laser technology. In a series of experiments, Hau used super-cooled gases to slow the speed of light to zero.

A. Completion. Complete the information by circling the most appropriate word in each pair.

Laser "light bullets" that can curve through the air might someday help scientists monitor air pollution, a new study reports.

The bullets are created by extremely rapid, high-intensity laser pulses, in which the brightest part of the beam bends as the light speeds away. The intensity of the laser can cause it to change shape as it moves: at times, it can look like a short needle, or it can **1.** compress / repulse so that it **2.** somewhat / ambiguously resembles a flattened pancake. Within the laser, the light intensity is **3.** amplified / communicated to such a high degree that the air around it becomes electrically charged, briefly creating a curving plasma trail that emits its own light.

Previous research suggested that light bullets might be used to create a certain type of **4.** human-induced / -communicated lightning. This has implications for the testing of lightning control around tall buildings and airplanes. These new plasma-producing "needle" bullets might have other uses too, such as providing a way to monitor air pollution without the need for airplanes or weather balloons.

This new **5.** facet / sphere of the laser—curved light pulses—is an important development in emerging laser technologies, says Jerome Kasparian, a physicist at the University of Geneva. "Up to now, it has only been possible to bend a beam through the interaction with a **6.** medium / facet," such as a lens, he says. "This is the first time you can have [a] laser [with its own] curving capability."

B. Words in Context. Complete each sentence with the best answer.

1. If something is ambiguous, it is _____.
   a. confusing or unclear   b. easily understood   c. narrow or limited

2. If you compress something, or it compresses, it becomes _____.
   a. faster or more active   b. lighter or less dense   c. smaller or shorter

3. If an army or other group repulses another group, they _____.
   a. destroy it completely   b. force it to go back   c. negotiate with it

4. A globe is an example of a _____.
   a. facet   b. medium   c. sphere

5. Fiber optic technologies are likely to transform _____ in the near future.
   a. amplifications   b. communications   c. facets

> **Usage** A **medium** (*n. sing.*) is a way or means of expressing ideas or communicating with people. The **media** (*n. plur.*) commonly refers to TV, radio, newspapers, and magazines: **mass media**, **multimedia**. A **medium** is also a substance or material used for a particular effect. As an adjective, **medium** is used to describe something that is average or halfway.

Lighting the Dark

A. Preview. You will hear these words in the video. Match each word with its definition.

1. lantern _____
2. abyss _____
3. glimpse _____
4. descend _____
5. drowning _____

a. a brief or incomplete view; a vague indication
b. death caused by suffocating in water or another liquid
c. to move from a higher to a lower place
d. a light with a transparent or translucent protective case
e. an immeasurably deep and dark chasm, depth, or void

▲ A spotlight from a remotely operated submarine reveals a giant female spider crab.

Surugu Bay

B. Summarize. Watch the video, *Lighting the Dark*. Then complete the summary below using the correct form of words in the box. Two words are extra.

ambiguous	chart	discrete	encounter	facet
impose	release	repulsive	saturate	somewhat

Deep beneath the surface of Japan's Surugu Bay, marine scientists are starting to **1.** _____ mysterious creatures that live **2.** _____ in the depths, hidden in the darkness close to the ocean floor.

It is only through today's technological advances that these scientists are able to **3.** _____ the seafloor. At such depths, there are too many difficulties **4.** _____ on human divers for exploration by scuba diving to be possible. Hence, scientists use an ROV—a remotely-operated vehicle— to take pictures of the secretive—and **5.** _____ unusual—creatures that live down here. Such remotely operated submarines enable the scientists to explore the sea floor and reveal to us these mysterious **6.** _____ of marine life for the first time.

One dweller of the dark is the deep-sea anglerfish; some of these possess fins that appear to have elbows. Another creature hiding in the darkness is the giant spider crab—the largest crab in the world. They can grow up to three meters across, and are known as the "Dead Man's Crab" for reasons that some may find **7.** _____ (they have been found feeding on drowning victims).

The ROV also manages to catch the first moving images of the Abyssal Cusk eel, a species of fish that can live deeper in the sea than any other known fish. And finally, in a rarely-seen occurrence, a female Chimera is seen in the process of **8.** _____ her eggs.

C. Think About It.

1. What kind of challenges do you think marine scientists face when exploring the ocean floor? How do you think these compare with the challenges faced by astronauts?
2. Is light always useful? Are there harmful kinds of light?

To learn more about light, visit elt.heinle. com/explorer

A. World Heritage Spotlight. Read the information about Waterton-Glacier International Peace Park on pages 112–113 and answer the questions (**1–3**).

1. Sequencing. Number the events in the order they occurred (**1–8**).

_____ Glacier Park is named a U.S. National Park.
_____ Thick glaciers move over much of northwestern America.
_____ High mountain ranges emerge as glaciers retreat.
_____ Sea bed is pushed eastward over land now covered by the park.
_____ Tiny marine creatures are deposited on an ancient sea bed.
_____ Total number of glaciers in Glacier Park drops below 30.
_____ Waterton-Glacier Park becomes the first international peace park.
_____ Waterton-Glacier Park is made a World Heritage Site.

2. Vocabulary from Context. Find words or phrases on page 112 that are closest in meaning to the following (**a–f**).

a. at the most, or at the latest _____
b. at the same time _____
c. formally awarded the title of _____
d. sufficient means to stop (something) _____
e. includes; covers the whole of _____
f. eventually moved back; retreated _____

3. Discussion. Should the responsibility for protecting threatened environments like Glacier Park be largely regional, national, or international? What criteria do you think should determine who is responsible?

B. A Global View. Read the information on pages 114–115 and discuss the following questions with a partner.

1. What reasons are given for the loss of biodiversity? Can you think of other possible causes that are not mentioned?

2. Why are Laos and Brazil mentioned in connection with access to safe drinking water?

3. What does the chart "Assessing Water Use" show? How does it relate to environmental sustainability?

4. Where are the world's "biodiversity hotspots" located? Do their locations share similar characteristics?

5. Have there been any oil spills or other environmental disasters in or near your region? What caused them, and what do you think could be done to prevent them?

6. Do you think people in your country generally have an environmentally sustainable lifestyle? In what ways could they be more environmentally sustainable?

Glacier Park

Site: **Waterton-Glacier International Peace Park**

Location: **Alberta, Canada; Montana, USA**

Category: **Natural**

Status: **World Heritage Site since 1995**

Waterton-Glacier International Peace Park

In northwestern America, a stretch of the Rocky Mountains runs virtually unbroken for 400 kilometers (250 miles) from central Montana into southern Canada. The centerpiece, Glacier National Park, embraces more than 400,000 hectares (over a million acres). Its elevated peaks reach three kilometers into the sky. Below them are over 700 lakes, ranging in appearance from milky turquoise to so diamond clear you can see stones 15 meters (50 feet) deep.

One of the largest lakes has its head in Glacier Park and its body in a 50,000 hectare sister reserve, Waterton Lakes National Park, just across the border in Alberta, Canada. The adjoining protected areas were officially proclaimed the world's first international peace park in 1932. Both were named international biosphere reserves during the 1970s, and in 1995, Waterton–Glacier International Peace Park was made a World Heritage site.

Over the past two million years, glaciers more than a kilometer thick flowed over all but the highest points of the region. The Rockies, meanwhile, kept rising. When the tide of ice finally withdrew, the so-called Crown of the Continent emerged spectacularly cut and polished, its peaks taller than ever and their sides far steeper, soaring above serene valleys carved into broad U shapes. Small alpine glaciers persisted on the highest summits, or beneath walls too high and steep for the sun to reach into even in midsummer. About 150 glaciers existed when the park was established in 1910. Today, with increased carbon dioxide and other greenhouse emissions, a warming climate has reduced the number of moving glaciers to fewer than 30. Dan Fagre, a U.S. Geological Survey ecologist working in the reserve, says, "The last one will probably disappear by the year 2030, tops." Without adequate preventative measures, the park will soon have to be renamed Glacierless National Park.

▲ Mountain goats in Montana's Glacier National Park may travel hundreds of meters a day—vertically. This one negotiated a sheer rock wall to lick salt and other exposed minerals. The nutritious plant life on the mountain sides also draws bighorn sheep, and the occasional grizzly bear.

Framed against a winter sunrise, Vulture Peak shines as one of Glacier Park's most spectacular natural treasures.

The Origins of Life

Around 75 million years ago, tectonic forces acting on the Earth's crust sent a slab of rock kilometers thick sliding eastward across what is now Waterton-Glacier Park. This rock, formed between 1.5 billion and 800 million years ago in a shallow inland sea, still preserves fossilized traces of an ancient lifeform called cyanobacteria. These microbe colonies, termed stromatolites, may not seem very striking; nevertheless they represent some of the oldest organisms on Earth. More important, they may have been the first to practice photosynthesis, manufacturing sugar for food with the help of energy captured from the sun. The process yielded oxygen, which changed the atmosphere and transformed the course of life. Ultimately, the humble cyanobacteria and their successors made breathing air possible, and led to the emergence of all life forms we see today.

When naturalist George Bird Grinnell began campaigning for the creation of a national park here over a century ago, his namesake glacier covered more than 200 hectares. Today Grinnell Glacier's remnants are just over a third that size. All of Glacier Park's glaciers are expected to vanish within decades.

Environmental Sustainability

A Global View

Goal 7 of the UN MDGs is to achieve global environmental stability. This includes protecting environmental resources, reducing the loss of biodiversity, and reducing the proportion of people without sustainable access to safe drinking water and sanitation.

Despite increased investment in conservation, the main causes of biodiversity loss—high rates of consumption, habitat loss, invasive species, pollution, and climate change—are not being adequately addressed in order to meet the goal of reducing biodiversity loss. Nearly 17,000 species of plants and animals are currently at risk of extinction, and the number of threatened species continues to grow. On the plus side, overall deforestation rates have slowed, but they remain highest in some of the world's most biologically diverse regions, including many parts of South America and Africa.

Many examples of sustainable progress have been achieved on a local scale. In 2007, a million hectares of conservation land were established in Madagascar to protect the island's unique species. There has also been progress in providing access to safe drinking water and sanitation. Laos, for instance, has seen a rapid increase in access to improved sanitation in rural areas, from an estimated 10 percent in 1995 to 38 percent in 2008. Brazil has been implementing a program since 2002 to bring clean water to about 36 million people in the semi-arid northeastern part of the country. Globally, some 1.7 billion people have gained access to safe drinking water since 1990. Nevertheless, more than 880 million people worldwide still do not have access to drinkable water, and 2.6 billion lack toilets and other basic sanitation services.

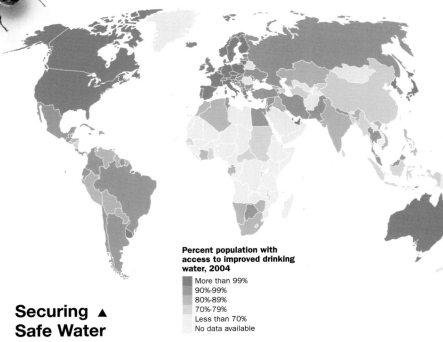

Percent population with access to improved drinking water, 2004
- More than 99%
- 90%-99%
- 80%-89%
- 70%-79%
- Less than 70%
- No data available

Securing ▲ Safe Water

More than one in eight people in the world lack access to clean drinking water, particularly in the developing world. As a result, many people die because of waterborne diseases—an estimated 1.8 million in 2006. Boiling water can make water safe for drinking, but the necessary fuel is often in short supply and used for cooking or heating instead.

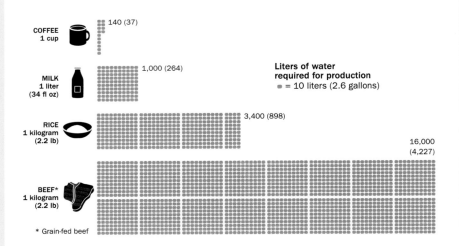

COFFEE 1 cup — 140 (37)

MILK 1 liter (34 fl oz) — 1,000 (264)

RICE 1 kilogram (2.2 lb) — 3,400 (898)

BEEF* 1 kilogram (2.2 lb) — 16,000 (4,227)

* Grain-fed beef

Liters of water required for production
● = 10 liters (2.6 gallons)

Assessing Water Use ▲

Many agricultural products require thousands of liters of water in their production. Beef is one of the most water-intensive products, due to irrigation of animal feed, watering of the livestock, and meat processing. The planet's rice fields require 1.4 trillion (1,400,000,000,000) cubic meters (49 trillion cubic feet) of water annually, which accounts for more than 20 percent of global water use for crop production.

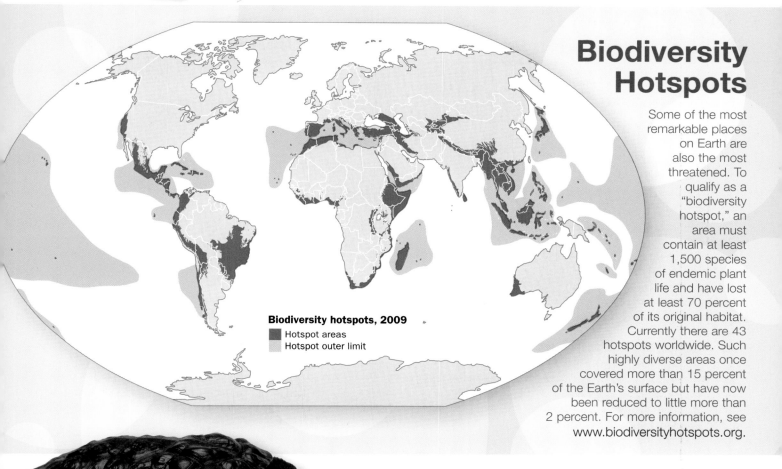

Biodiversity Hotspots

Some of the most remarkable places on Earth are also the most threatened. To qualify as a "biodiversity hotspot," an area must contain at least 1,500 species of endemic plant life and have lost at least 70 percent of its original habitat. Currently there are 43 hotspots worldwide. Such highly diverse areas once covered more than 15 percent of the Earth's surface but have now been reduced to little more than 2 percent. For more information, see www.biodiversityhotspots.org.

Biodiversity hotspots, 2009
- Hotspot areas
- Hotspot outer limit

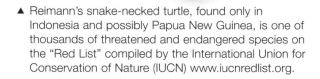

▲ Reimann's snake-necked turtle, found only in Indonesia and possibly Papua New Guinea, is one of thousands of threatened and endangered species on the "Red List" compiled by the International Union for Conservation of Nature (IUCN) www.iucnredlist.org.

The Deepwater Horizon spill of April 2010 ► devastated fisheries, local communities, and wildlife populations along more than a thousand kilometers of U.S. coastline. One of the many victims was this severely oiled brown pelican rescued off Queen Bess Island. "You could see the life draining out of it," says local official P.J. Hahn, who rescued the bird from the polluted waters.

A. Word Link. Each of the words in the box contains **circ/circum**, meaning *around*. Match each word with its definition. One word is extra. Use your dictionary to help you.

circuit	circuitous	circular	circulate
circulation	circumference	circumnavigate	circumstance

1. _____ the distance around the edge of a round object

2. _____ a condition which affects a situation

3. _____ complete route which an electrical current or path follows

4. _____ long and complicated rather than simple and direct

5. _____ movement of blood through the body

6. _____ (to) move around freely within a system

7. _____ (to) travel around (e.g. the globe), either by plane or ship

B. Word Forms. Complete the chart with the missing verb or noun form. Then use the correct forms of the words in the chart to complete the sentences below.

Noun	Verb
	absorb
concept	
	implicate
investment	
	impose
negotiation	
	renew
subscription	

1. Some people do not _____ to the theory of global warming.

2. Solar equipment _____ heat from the sun to produce energy.

3. Public protests sometimes follow the _____ of new taxes.

4. Einstein's _____ of relativity changed the field of physics.

5. The 2009 Copenhagen Summit was an attempt to _____ an international agreement on climate

6. The global climate change talks were _____ the following year in Cancun, Mexico.

7. Countries that _____ in new sources of energy can reduce harmful emissions.

8. Governments need to consider the long-term _____ of tourism on the environment.

C. Word Partnership. In each space below, write the word from the box that can precede all three words to form common word partnerships.

define	exert	induce	inflict	implement	repulse

1. _____ punishment, damage, losses

2. _____ armies, attacks, electricity

3. _____ influence, pressure, authority

4. _____ words, behavior, boundaries

5. _____ policies, plans, rules

6. _____ responses, changes, stress

D. Choosing the Right Definition. Study the numbered definitions for *conscious*. Then write the number of the definition (**1–6**) that relates to each sentence below. One definition is extra.

conscious /kɒnʃəs/ **1** ADJ If you are **conscious of** something, you notice it or realize that it is happening. **2** ADJ If you are **conscious of** something, you think about it a lot, especially because you have some negative feelings about it. **3** ADJ A **conscious** decision or action is made or done deliberately after a good deal of thought. ADV **consciously**. **4** ADJ Someone who is **conscious** is awake rather than asleep or unconscious. **5** ADJ **Conscious** memories or thoughts are ones that you are aware of. ADV **consciously**. **6** COMB in ADJ **-conscious** combines with other words to form adjectives which describe someone who believes that the aspect of life indicated is very important.

a. _____ Each year, thousands of students make a **conscious** choice about the university they wish to attend.

b. _____ People who are environmentally-**conscious** try to inflict as little damage as possible on the environment.

c. _____ People who are abnormally tall are often **conscious** of their height.

d. _____ It may take several hours or days for a person to regain **consciousness** following a serious accident.

e. _____ Although they cannot see, blind people are still **conscious** of events occurring around them.

E. Crossword. Use the definitions below to complete the missing words.

Across

1. If something is at a(n) _____, it is wanted or needed, but difficult to get.

4. A(n) _____ of something is a single side or aspect of something

7. to put money, energy, or time into something, because you think it will be successful

9. _____ is used to indicate that something is generally referred to by a particular name.

10. to surround an object or scene in a way that makes it more attractive

13. to meet someone or experience something; to come into contact with

14. enough; sufficient

16. happens often, or is often found, and therefore is not surprising

18. a way or means of communication

19. When an object or person is moved to a higher position, it is _____.

20. If something is a(n) _____ to another thing, they go well together

21. to forcefully drive (something) back

Down

1. a rectangular piece of material that forms part of a larger structure

2. A(n) _____ of something is a part or component of it.

3. to make something in a factory, usually in large quantities

5. an idea or abstract principle

6. If things _____ to happen, they often or usually happen.

8. to complete a course of studies successfully

9. take away; minus

11. Something is _____ if it can be replaced and is thus always available.

12. to make something as great in amount or importance as you can

14. a machine in your home that you use to do a job, like cleaning

15. to pass around something; to move freely and easily within a closed space or system

17. to cause something to happen, or someone to do something

18. a particular way of living or behaving

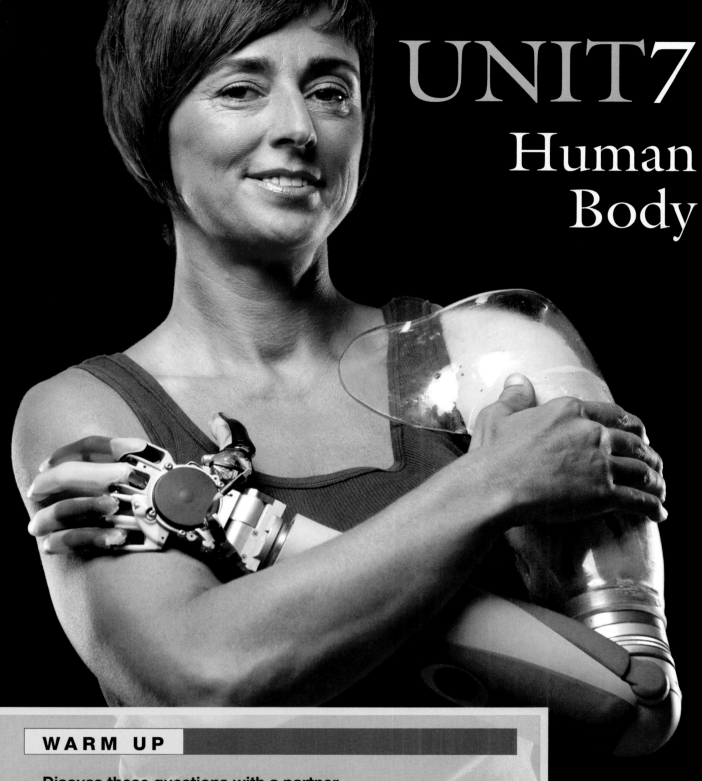

Human
Body

WARM UP

Discuss these questions with a partner.

1. What advantages does the human body have over other animals? What things are we not able to do?

2. In what ways do people today use technology to alter or improve their body?

3. What do you think the human body will be like 50 years from now? How about 100 years?

▲ A new generation of bionic technology provides hope to people with damaged body parts, including amputee Amanda Kitts.

119

7A How We Walk

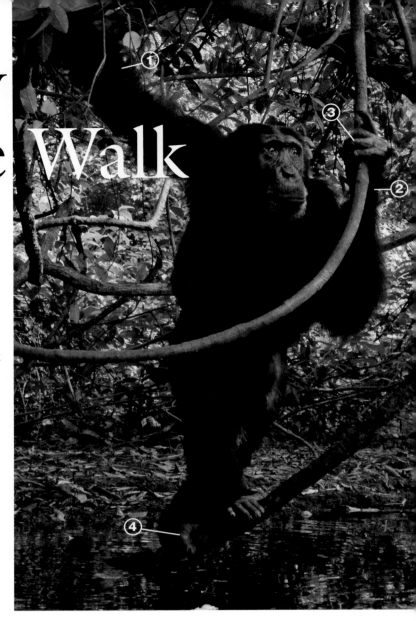

Chimpanzees are our closest living relatives, sharing approximately 96 percent of our DNA. Nevertheless, it's not hard to see the differences that 4 percent of DNA and millions of years of evolution have made. Some distinguishing features include:

Chimps

Long arms (**1**) and hands make climbing and hanging from trees possible. Specialized wrist (**2**) bones and extra flesh on the back of the hand allow chimps to walk on their knuckles (**3**)—their main method of locomotion (movement) on the ground. This is effective for short bursts of speed but is inefficient over long distances. Flat feet and an opposable toe (**4**) make it possible for chimps to use their feet not only for running, walking, and climbing, but also for grasping and holding things.

Humans

Smaller, highly specialized hands make it uniquely possible for humans to grasp and use objects (e.g., tools) with great precision. A wide, flat pelvis and hips, a curved lower spine, and the ability to fully extend our knees into a straight line make it possible to walk regularly on two legs. Over the same distance, humans use less energy walking upright than chimps walking on all fours. Two arched (curved) feet support the body's weight when a person stands, walks, or runs.

Before You Read

A. Discussion. Look at the photo and read the information above. Then answer the questions.

1. What are some of the differences between how chimps and humans move?
2. What are the advantages and disadvantages of walking on all fours, like chimps normally do? How about walking upright, the way humans do?

B. Skim and Predict. The passage on pages 121–124 is about bipedalism (walking on two legs). Read the title, subtitle, and first paragraph, and skim each of the five sections. In your own words, list what you think each section is going to be mainly about. Then read the article to check your ideas.

1. Yesterday's model _____
2. Upright citizens _____
3. Aching back _____
4. Unlikely feat _____
5. What do we stand for? _____

Bipedal Body

Our aching backs may be trying to tell us something:
It's part of the price we pay for walking on two legs.

◀ A chimpanzee can grasp and hold
objects in its hand-like feet, using
opposable toes that human beings lack.

1   WE HUMANS ARE ODD creatures: tailless bipeds with
curved spines, long limbs, arched feet, agile hands,
and enormous brains. Our bodies are a mosaic[1]
of features shaped by natural selection over vast
5   periods of time—exquisitely capable yet deeply
flawed. We can stand, walk, and run with grace
and endurance, but we suffer aching feet and knee
injuries; we can twist and torque our spines, and
yet most of us are plagued by back trouble at some
10 point in our lives. Scientists have long pondered
how our bodies came to be the way they are. Now,
using new methods from a variety of disciplines,
they are discovering that many of the flaws in
our "design" have a common theme: They arise
15 primarily from evolutionary compromises that
occurred when our ancestors stood upright—the
first step in the long path to becoming human.

Yesterday's model

Humans come from a long line of ancestors, reptile
20 to mammal to ape, whose skeletons were built to
carry their weight on all fours. Our ape ancestors
probably evolved around 20 million years ago from
small primates that carried themselves horizontally.
Over the next several million years, some apes grew
25 larger and began to use their arms to hold overhead
branches. Then, six or seven million years ago, our
ancestors stood up and began to move about on
their hind[2] legs.

It was a radical shift. "Bipedalism is a unique and
30 bizarre form of locomotion," says Craig Stanford,
an anthropologist at the University of Southern
California. "Of more than 250 species of primates,
only one goes around on two legs." Stanford and
many other scientists consider bipedalism the key
35 defining feature of being human.

Evolutionary biologists agree that shifts in behavior
often drive changes in anatomy. Standing upright
launched a series of anatomical alterations. The
method of upright walking is so different from
40 walking on all fours that bones from the neck down
had to change. To support the body's weight and
absorb the forces of upright locomotion, joints in
limbs and the spine enlarged, and the foot evolved
an arch. The pelvis evolved from the ape's long,
45 thin paddle into a wide, flat saddle shape, which
thrust the weight of the trunk down through the
legs and allowed for the attachment of
large muscles.

[1] A **mosaic** is a design made up of small pieces of different colors.
[2] **Hind** legs are back legs.

◄ Designed to walk on all fours, a chimp's two-legged walking is transitory and uses more energy than a human's bipedal strides.

Upright citizens

50 At his laboratory in the anthropology department at Harvard University, Dan Lieberman uses biomechanical studies to see how we use our body parts in various aspects of movement. These experiments on walking and running illuminate just

55 how astonishing a feat of balance, coordination, and efficiency is upright locomotion. The legs on a walking human body act not unlike inverted pendulums.[3] Using a stiff leg as a point of support, the body swings up and over it in an arc, so that

60 the potential energy gained in the rise roughly equals the kinetic energy generated in the descent. By this trick the body stores and recovers so much of the energy used with each stride that it reduces its own workload by as much as 65 percent.

65 "Compare this with the chimp," Lieberman says. "Chimps pay a hefty price in energy for being built the way they are. They can't extend their knees and lock their legs straight, as humans can. Instead, they have to use muscle power to support their

70 body weight when they're walking upright, and they waste energy rocking back and forth."

Chimps are our closest living evolutionary relatives and, as such, are well suited to teach us about ourselves. Almost every bone in a chimp's body

75 correlates with a bone in a human body. Whatever skeletal distinctions exist are primarily related to the human pattern of walking upright.

Two-legged walking in a chimp is an occasional, transitory behavior. In humans, it is a way of life,

80 one that carries with it several benefits, including freed hands. But upright posture and locomotion come with a number of uniquely human maladies.[4]

Aching back

Back pain is one of the most common health

85 complaints. That most of us will experience back pain at some point in our lives raises the question of the spine's design.

"The problem is that the vertebral column was originally designed to act as an arch," explains

90 Carol Ward, an anthropologist and anatomist at the University of Missouri in Columbia. "When we became upright, it had to function as a weight-bearing column." To support our head and balance our weight directly over our hip joints and lower

95 limbs, the spine evolved a series of S curves—a deep forward curve, or lordosis, in the lower back, and a backward curve, or kyphosis, in the upper back.

"This system of S curves is energetically efficient

100 and effective for maintaining our balance and for bipedal locomotion," Ward says. "But the lower region of the column suffers from the excessive pressure and oblique[5] force exerted on its curved structure by our upright posture."

105 Lean back, arching your spine. You're the only mammal in the world capable of this sort of backbend. Feel a cringing tightness in your lower back? That's the vertical joints between your vertebrae pressing against one another as their

110 compressive load increases. The curvature in your lower spine requires that its building blocks take the shape of a wedge, with the thick part in the front and the thin part in the back.

[3] A **pendulum** is a weight hung from a single point that is allowed to swing freely under the influence of gravity.
[4] **Maladies** are illnesses or diseases.
[5] Something that is **oblique** has a slanting or sloping direction.

But in the lower back region, where the load is
heaviest and the wedging most dramatic, strains
such as heavy lifting or hyperextension can cause
your lowest vertebrae to slip or squish together.
When the vertebrae are pressured in this way, the
disks between them may herniate, or bulge out,
impinging on spinal nerves and causing pain. Or
the pressure may pinch the delicate structures at
the back of the vertebrae, causing a fracture
called spondylolysis.

Considering the pressures of natural selection,
why are such seriously debilitating diseases still
prevalent? Latimer believes the answer lies in
the importance of lordosis for upright walking:
"Selection for bipedality must have been so
strong in our early ancestors that a permanent
lordosis developed despite the risk it carries for
spondylolysis and other back disorders."

Unlikely feat

And where does the buck finally stop?[6] What finally
bears the full weight of our upright body? Two
ridiculously tiny platforms.

"The human foot has rightfully been called the
most characteristic peculiarity in the human body,"
says Will Harcourt-Smith, a paleontologist at the
American Museum of Natural History. "For one
thing, it has no thumblike opposable toe. We're
the only primate to give up the foot as a
grasping organ."

This was a huge sacrifice. The chimp's foot is a
brilliantly useful and versatile feature, essential
to tree climbing and capable of as much motion
and manipulation as its hand. The human foot
is designed to do just two things, propel the
body forward and absorb the shock of doing so.
Bipedality may have freed the hands, but it also
yoked the feet.

Harcourt-Smith studies foot bones of early
humans with the new technique of geometric
morphometrics—measuring objects in three
dimensions. In all the fossil feet Harcourt-Smith
studies, some type of basic human pattern is clearly
present: a big toe aligned with the long axis of the
foot, or a well-developed longitudinal arch, or in
some cases a humanlike ankle joint—all ingenious
adaptations but fraught[7] with potential problems.

▲ The first stone tools appeared 2.6 million years ago. From that
time, the ancestors of modern humans were able to exploit their
bipedalism and their tool-making skills to become successful
scavengers on the African plains.

"Because the foot is so specialized in its design,"
Harcourt-Smith says, "it has a very narrow window
for working correctly." In people with a reduced
arch, fatigue fractures often develop. In those with
a pronounced arch, the ligaments[8] that support
the arch sometimes become inflamed. When the
carrying angle of the leg forces the big toe out of
alignment, bunions may form—more of a problem
for women than men because of their wider hips.

[6] The phrase "**where the buck stops**" refers to a point at which someone
takes responsibility for something, rather than passing it on.

[7] If something is **fraught** with difficulties, it involves many difficulties.

[8] A **ligament** is a band of tough tissue that connects bones and cartilage
within the body.

▲ Despite its quirks, the human leg is a key to humanity's unique place in the world.

What do we stand for?

170 We humans gave up stability and speed. We gave up the foot as a grasping tool. We gained spongy bones and fragile joints and vulnerable spines. Given the trade-offs—the aches and pains and severe drawbacks associated with bipedalism—why
175 get upright in the first place?

Theories about why we got upright have run the gamut[9] from freeing the arms of our ancestors to carry babies and food to reaching hitherto[10] inaccessible fruits. "But," says Mike Sockol of the
180 University of California, Davis, "one factor had to play a part in every scenario: the amount of energy required to move from point to point. If you can save energy while gathering your food supply, that energy can go into growth and reproduction."

185 Studies suggest that at the time our ancestors first stood upright, perhaps six to eight million years ago, their food supplies were becoming more widely dispersed. "If our ape ancestors had to roam[11] farther to find adequate food, and doing
190 so on two legs saved energy, then those individuals who moved across the ground more economically gained an advantage."

Scientists are the first to admit that much work needs to be done before we fully understand the
195 origins of bipedalism. But whatever drove human ancestors to get upright in the first place, the habit stuck. They eventually evolved the ability to walk and run long distances. They created and manipulated a diverse array of tools. These were
200 essential steps in evolving a big brain and a human intelligence, one that could make poetry and music and mathematics, develop sophisticated technology, and consider the roots of its own quirky[12] and imperfect upright being.

[9] A **gamut** is a range or scale of something.
[10] **Hitherto** is another way of saying "until this time."
[11] To **roam** is to walk about with no fixed purpose or direction.
[12] If something is **quirky**, it has strange or unusual characteristics.

Reading Comprehension

A. Multiple Choice. Choose the best answer for each question.

Main Idea **1.** What is the main idea of this article?
   a. Scientists have recently discovered many flaws in our bodies' "design."
   b. Walking on all fours gives chimps many advantages over humans.
   c. Standing upright has both advantages and disadvantages for humans.
   d. The change to an upright posture led to major changes in human behavior.

Vocabulary **2.** The word *pondered* in line 10 is closest in meaning to _____.
   a. wondered   c. confirmed
   b. decided   d. argued

Inference **3.** In paragraph 3 (from line 29), the author implies that _____.
   a. all but one type of primate usually walk on four legs
   b. Stanford's theories about bipedalism are unique
   c. there are more types of primates than was once thought
   d. besides humans, only one type of primate is bipedal

Application **4.** The author states in lines 36–37 that "shifts in behavior often drive changes in anatomy." Which of the following is an example of this principle?
   a. Bees have learned that flowers of a certain color are richer in pollen and visit those flowers first.
   b. When penguins could no longer fly and began to swim, their wings became like the flippers of sea mammals.
   c. Dolphins have found that working together to herd fish into shallow water allows them all to catch more fish.
   d. Horses have legs that are good for running, but can't be used to scratch their backs.

Negative Detail **5.** Which of the following is NOT one of the changes that took place in human ancestors when they began walking on two feet?
   a. Their pelvises grew wider and flatter.
   b. Their arms became shorter and their legs longer.
   c. Their feet developed an arch.
   d. The joints of their limbs and spine grew larger.

Detail **6.** What does the author say about chimps in paragraph 8 (from line 78)?
   a. It's unusual to see them walk on four legs.
   b. Walking upright can cause them pain.
   c. They walk upright when they need to use their hands.
   d. They don't generally walk on two feet.

Detail **7.** According to the article, most back problems occur because of _____.
   a. the inability of humans to fully arch their spine
   b. weaknesses in the design of the upper spine
   c. the pressure placed on the lower curve of the spine
   d. slippage of the top vertebrae in the spinal column

Reference **8.** The phrase *doing so* in lines 189–190 refers to _____.
   a. saving energy by moving less   c. consuming more food
   b. moving on four legs   d. traveling a greater distance

Many words in English, called homonyms, have more than one meaning. By using context, you can generally determine the correct definition of the word. Sometimes one definition is a literal meaning and the other a figurative one. (See Unit 4A for more information about literal and figurative meanings of words.)

B. Definitions. Find these words in the article. Then decide which definition is correct according to how the word is used in the article.

1. common (line 14)
   a. (*adj.*) ordinary; happening often
   b. (*adj.*) shared; having the same qualities

2. step (line 17)
   a. (*n.*) the act of putting one foot in front of the other when walking
   b. (*n.*) one stage in a process

3. branches (line 26)
   a. (*pl. n.*) parts of something, such as a business or family
   b. (*pl. n.*) the parts of a tree that grow from the trunk

4. roughly (line 60)
   a. (*adv.*) not gently; forcefully
   b. (*adv.*) approximately; more or less

5. limbs (line 95)
   a. (*adj.*) arms or legs
   b. (*adj.*) parts of a tree; branches

6. lean (line 105)
   a. (*adj.*) thin; slender
   b. (*v.*) to bend the body

7. pressure (line 121)
   a. (*n.*) a condition that cause changes in the outcome of a situation
   b. (*n.*) a physical force

8. pressures (line 124)
   a. (*n.*) conditions that cause changes in the outcome of a situation
   b. (*n.*) physical forces

9. bears (line 134)
   a. (*pl. n.*) large animals that sometimes stand on two legs
   b. (*v.*) holds; supports

10. shock (line 148)
   a. (*n.*) an upsetting, unpleasant surprise
   b. (*n.*) a sudden impact; a blow

11. window (line 161)
   a. (*n.*) an opening in a wall to let in air or light or both
   b. (*n.*) a favorable time or condition

12. pronounced (line 164)
   a. (*past participle*) spoken in a specific way
   b. (*n.*) clearly indicated

C. Critical Thinking. Discuss these questions with a partner.

1. In your own words, explain how changing from a creature that walked on four legs to two legs affected humans.

2. Imagine that humans never began to walk on two legs. In what ways would life today be different?

3. In what other ways is the human body "imperfect"? How do you think the human body might evolve in the future?

Vocabulary Practice

A. Completion. Complete the information by circling the most appropriate word in each pair.

▲ A model of a human female pelvic skeleton, though which a baby's head can be passed to simulate the birth process.

Our emergence into this world—via the birth canal—is far from a smooth ride. The human baby is a **1.** delicate / manipulated thing, yet it has to pass through many obstacles and must be **2.** aligned / correlated just right for it to emerge safely. In many cases, a baby's broad shoulders and large skull become stuck in the passage. Once it gets past these obstacles, the **3.** fragile / versatile head emerges into the world backwards, facing in the opposite direction from the mother. It is no wonder that it often takes many hours and a doctor's intervention to **4.** compromise / manipulate the baby's safe passage. For this reason, there is a strong **5.** coordination / correlation between the availability of adequate medical care for women in childbirth and the survival of both mother and child.

Why do women possess a birth canal of such **6.** discipline / peculiarity? According to anthropologists, the human female pelvis is a classic example of evolutionary **7.** compromise / coordination. Its design reflects a trade-off between the demand for a skeletal structure that allows for walking on two feet and one that permits the passage of a baby with a big brain and wide shoulders. It is not, apparently, an ideal design.

B. Definitions. Match words in red from **A** with the correct definition.

1. adaptable, flexible _____

2. a field of study in a university _____

3. strange or unusual characteristic _____

4. connection, link between things _____

5. organization of activities to work together efficiently _____

6. (to) skillfully move and press (something) into a position _____

7. (to) reach an agreement, usually halfway between opposing sides _____

8. placed in a position relative to something else, usually parallel _____

9. easily damaged or injured (two words) _____   _____

Word Partnership

Use *correlation* with:
(*v.*) **find a** correlation; (*adj.*) **direct** correlation; **negative** correlation; **significant** correlation; **strong** correlation; **weak** correlation

7B Human Bionics

Bionics: from *bi* ("life") + *onics* ("electronics")

As scientists work to link machine and mind, artificial bones, organs, joints, and limbs (parts shaded orange and blue) are gaining many of the capabilities of human ones:

a. Signals are transmitted from the brain to the bionic arm via **electrodes** attached to remaining nerves in the injured arm. The result: a person is able to grasp and manipulate objects.

b. A bionic ankle copies the action of a real one by propelling (pushing) the wearer forward, making it possible for the person to walk again.

c. **Implants** stimulate nerves inside the ear, allowing people who are partially or completely deaf to hear.

d. Images captured by a video camera in the glasses are converted to signals and sent wirelessly to an implant in the eye. Electrodes in the eye send the visual signals to the optic nerve which sends them to the brain, and a person is able to "see" the images.

electrode a piece of metal or other substance that takes an electric current to or from a power source
implant a small device put inside the body

Before You Read

A. Labeling. Match parts of the bionic body (**1–4**) with the labels (**a–d**). Then choose two of the bionic parts and explain in your own words to a partner how they work.

B. Skim and Predict. You are going to read an article about a woman with a bionic body part. Skim the passage on pages 129–132 for two minutes to note some information about her. Then read the passage to check your ideas.

Name	Amanda Kitts
Bionic body part	
Why she needs it	
Things she can now do	
Things she can't do yet	

TOMORROW'S PEOPLE

◄ It takes 20 motors to animate this cutting-edge bionic arm, one of the latest designs that is revolutionizing the field of prosthetics.

1   AMANDA KITTS IS MOBBED by four- and five-year-olds as she enters the classroom. "Hey kids, how're my babies today?" she says, patting shoulders and ruffling[1] hair. Slender and energetic, she has
5   operated this Knoxville, Tennessee, daycare center and two others for almost 20 years. She crouches down to talk to a small girl, putting her hands on her knees.

"The robot arm!" several kids cry.

10   "You remember this, huh?" says Kitts, holding out her left arm. She turns her hand palm up. There is a soft whirring sound. If you weren't paying close attention, you'd miss it. She bends her elbow, accompanied by more whirring.

15   "Make it do something silly!" one girl says.

"Silly? Remember how I can shake your hand?" Kitts says, extending her arm and rotating her wrist. A boy reaches out, hesitantly, to touch her fingers. What he brushes against is flesh-colored
20   plastic, fingers curved slightly inward. Underneath are three motors, a metal framework, and a network of sophisticated electronics. The assembly is topped by a white plastic cup midway up Kitts's biceps, encircling a stump that is almost all that
25   remains from the arm she lost in a car accident in 2006.

Almost all, but not quite. Within her brain, below the level of consciousness, lives an intact image of that arm, a phantom. When Kitts thinks about
30   flexing[2] her elbow, the phantom moves. Impulses racing down from her brain are picked up by electrode sensors in the white cup and converted into signals that turn motors, and the artificial elbow bends.

35   "I don't really think about it. I just move it," says the 40-year-old, who uses both this standard model and a more experimental arm with even more control. "After my accident I felt lost. These days I'm just excited all the time, because they keep on
40   improving the arm. One day I'll be able to feel things with it and clap my hands together in time to the songs my kids are singing."

[1] If you **ruffle** someone's hair, you lightly rub it.
[2] When you **flex** something, usually a muscle, you bend and stretch it.

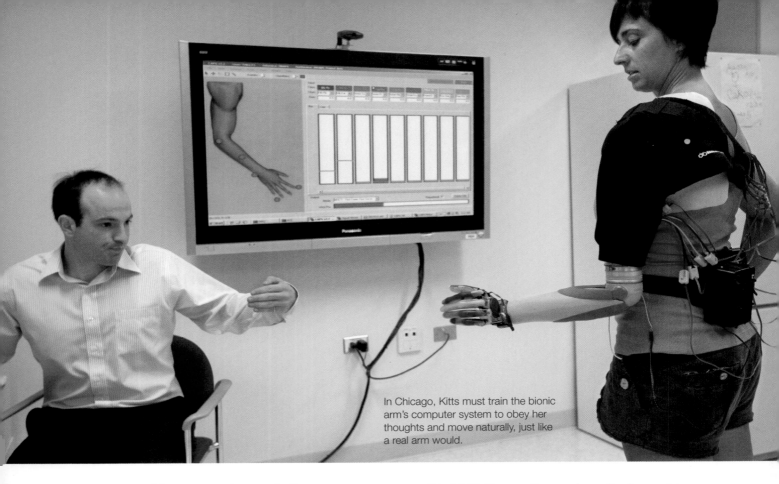

In Chicago, Kitts must train the bionic arm's computer system to obey her thoughts and move naturally, just like a real arm would.

Kitts is one of "tomorrow's people," a group whose missing or ruined body parts are being replaced by devices embedded in their nervous systems that respond to commands from their brains. The machines they use are called neural prostheses or—using a term made popular by science fiction writers—bionics.

THE KIND OF PROSTHESIS that Amanda Kitts uses is controlled by her brain. A technique called targeted muscle reinnervation uses nerves remaining after an amputation[3] to control an artificial limb. It was first tried in a patient in 2002. Four years later, Tommy Kitts, Amanda's husband, read about the research, which took place at the Rehabilitation Institute of Chicago (RIC). His wife lay in hospital at the time; the truck that had crushed her car had also crushed her arm, from just above the elbow down.

"I was angry, sad, depressed. I just couldn't accept it," she says. But the news Tommy brought her about the Chicago arm gave her some reassurance, and some hope. "It seemed like the best option out there, a lot better than motors and switches," Tommy says. "Amanda actually got excited about it." Soon they were on a plane to Illinois.

Todd Kuiken, a licensed medical practitioner and biomedical engineer at RIC, was the person responsible for what the institute had begun calling the "bionic arm." He knew that nerves in an amputee's stump could still carry signals from the brain. And he knew that a computer in a prosthesis could direct electric motors to move the limb. However, making the connection was far from straightforward. Nerves conduct electricity, but they can't be spliced together with a computer cable. (Nerve fibers and metal wires are not mutually compatible, and an open wound where a wire enters the body would be a dangerous avenue for infections.)

Kuiken needed an amplifier to boost the signals from the nerves, avoiding the need for a direct contact between nerve and wire. He found one in muscles. When muscles tense, they give off an electrical burst strong enough to be detected by an electrode placed on the skin. He developed a technique to reroute severed nerves from their old, damaged spots to other muscles that could give their signals the proper boost.

[3] An **amputation** occurs when a body part is cut off, usually for medical reasons.

In October 2006, Kitts
consented to have
Kuiken try out his new
technique on her. The
first step was to salvage
major nerves that once
went all the way down
her arm. "These are
the same nerves that
work the arm and hand,
but we had to create
four different muscle
areas to lead them to,"
Kuiken says. The nerves
started in Kitts's brain,
in the motor cortex,
which holds a rough
map of the body, but
they terminated at the
end of her stump. In
an intricate operation,
a surgeon rerouted
those nerves to different
regions of Kitts's
upper-arm muscles. For months the nerves grew,
millimeter by millimeter, moving deeper into their
newly assigned homes.

"At three months I started feeling little tingles
and twitches," says Kitts. "By four months I could
actually feel different parts of my hand when I
touched my upper arm. I could touch it in different
places and feel different fingers." What she was
feeling were parts of the phantom arm that were
mapped into her brain, now reconnected to flesh.
When Kitts thought about moving those phantom
fingers, her real upper-arm muscles contracted.

A month later she was fitted with her first bionic
arm, which had electrodes in the cup around the
stump to pick up the signals from the muscles.
Now the challenge was to convert those signals
into commands to adjust the elbow and hand. A
storm of electrical noise was coming from the small
region on Kitts's arm. Somewhere in there was
the signal that meant "straighten the elbow" or
"turn the wrist." A microprocessor inserted in the
prosthesis had to be programmed to differentiate
the right signal and send it to the right motor.

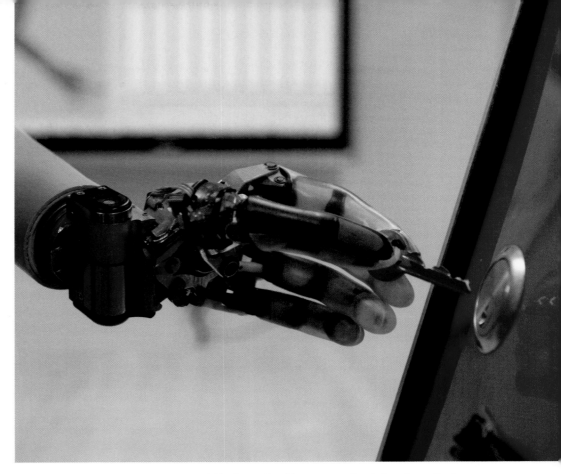

▲ A bionic arm like this one uses signals from the patient's nervous system to move, enabling the prosthesis to carry out daily tasks, like locking and unlocking doors.

Kitts practiced using her arm one floor below
Kuiken's office in an apartment set up by
occupational therapists. The apartment had a
kitchen with a stove, silverware in a drawer, a bed,
a closet with hangers, a bathroom, stairs—things
people use every day without a second thought
but that pose huge obstacles to someone missing
a limb. Watching Kitts make a peanut butter
sandwich in the kitchen is a startling experience.
With her sleeve rolled back to reveal the plastic
cup, her motion is fluid. Her live arm holds a slice
of bread, her artificial fingers close on a knife, the
elbow flexes, and she swipes peanut butter back
and forth.

"It wasn't easy at first," she says. "I would try
to move it, and it wouldn't always go where I
wanted." But she worked at it, and the more she
used the arm, the more lifelike the motions felt.
What Kitts would really like now is sensation. That
would be a big help in many actions, including one
of her favorites—gulping coffee.

"The problem with a paper coffee cup is that my hand will close until it gets a solid grip. But with a paper cup you never get a solid grip," she says. "That happened at Starbucks once. It kept squeezing until the cup went 'pop.'"

There are valid reasons for supposing that one day she'll get that sensation, says Kuiken. In partnership with bioengineers at the Johns Hopkins University Applied Physics Laboratory, RIC has been developing a new prototype[4] for Kitts and other patients that not only has more flexibility—more motors and joints—but also has pressure-sensing pads on the fingertips. The pads are connected to small rods that poke into Kitts's stump. The harder the pressure, the stronger the sensation in her phantom fingers.

"I can feel how hard I'm grabbing," she says. She can also differentiate between rubbing something rough, like sandpaper, and smooth, like glass, by how fast the rods vibrate. "I go up to Chicago to experiment with it, and I love it," she says. "I want them to give it to me already so I can take it home. But it's a lot more complicated than my take-home arm, so they don't have it completely reliable yet."

Today, Kitts has a new, more elastic cup atop her arm that better aligns electrodes with nerves that control the arm. "It means I can do a lot more with the arm," she says. "A new one up in Chicago lets me do lots of different hand grasps. I want that. I want to pick up pennies and hammers and toys with my kids." These are reasonable hopes for a substitute body part, Kuiken says. "We are giving people tools. They are better than what previously existed.

▲ Motorized springs in this bionic ankle push off like a real leg.

"The problem with a paper coffee cup is that my hand will close until it gets a solid grip. That happened at Starbucks once. It kept squeezing until the cup went 'pop.'"

But they are still crude, like a hammer, compared with the complexity of the human body."

The work of neural prostheses is extremely delicate, a series of trials filled with many errors. As scientists have learned that it's possible to link machine and mind, they have also learned how difficult it is to maintain that bond. Still, bionics represents a major leap forward, enabling researchers to give people back much more of what they've lost than was ever possible before.

"That's really what this work is about: restoration," says Joseph Pancrazio, program director for neural engineering at the National Institute of Neurological Disorders and Stroke. "When a person with a spinal-cord injury can be in a restaurant, feeding himself, and no one else notices, that is my definition of success."

[4] A **prototype** is an early model of a product that is tested so that the design can be changed if necessary.

Reading Comprehension

A. Multiple Choice. Choose the best answer for each question.

Gist **1.** The best alternative title for this reading would be _____.
- a. Bionics, the Next Generation of Prosthetics
- b. The Latest Varieties of Robots
- c. Amanda Kitts: A Brief Biography
- d. A Short History of Prosthetic Limbs

Vocabulary **2.** The phrase *brushes against* in line 19 is closest in meaning to _____.
- a. looks at carefully
- c. grasps tightly
- b. touches briefly
- d. pushes away quickly

Detail **3.** Who are "tomorrow's people"?
- a. Doctors who treat people who have lost limbs.
- b. All people who have a missing or damaged body part.
- c. Scientists who are developing advanced bionic limbs.
- d. People who have prosthetics controlled by their brains.

Detail **4.** According to the author, the term "bionics" _____.
- a. is older than the term "neural prosthesis"
- b. was popularized by science fiction authors
- c. is no longer in regular use today
- d. refers to the people who wear prostheses

Detail **5.** The "amplifier" (line 81) proposed by Kuiken _____.
- a. is an electric motor that is placed directly on the skin
- b. sends signals from damaged nerves to the brain
- c. is a muscle that helps to link nerve signals to electrodes
- d. receives a signal directly from a computer cable

Reference **6.** The word *It* in line 151 refers to _____.
- a. using her prosthetic arm
- b. experiencing sensation in her arm
- c. watching a startling experience
- d. holding a slice of bread

Inference **7.** The author implies that the paper coffee cup "went pop" (line 162) because Kitts _____.
- a. did not know how hard she was squeezing the cup
- b. could not feel how hot the coffee was
- c. did not realize how full the cup was
- d. could not tell that the cup was already empty

Detail **8.** According to information in lines 163–181, what is the main difference between Amanda Kitts' "prototype arm" and her "take-home arm"?
- a. She uses one at work and one when she is at home.
- b. One is more useful but is a lot more expensive.
- c. She uses one when she is awake, the other when she is asleep.
- d. One provides more control and sensation but is less reliable.

B. Classification. The following sentences are based on information from the article. Decide if this information is a fact (**F**) or an opinion (**O**).

1. _____ Signals run from Amanda Kitts' brain to electrode sensors in the white cup, where they are transmitted into signals that power motors, and she can then bend her elbow. (para starting line 27)

2. _____ The bionic arm seems like the best option, much better than the older prosthetics that use motors and switches. (para starting line 60)

3. _____ An amputee's nerves can still carry signals from the brain. (para starting line 67)

4. _____ The point where a metal wire enters the body may also allow germs to come in, causing an infection. (para starting line 67)

5. _____ It's startling to watch Amanda make a sandwich. (para starting line 137)

6. _____ One day Kitts will be able to feel sensations through her prosthetic fingers. (para starting line 163)

7. _____ One prosthetic arm that Kitts has experimented with allows her to tell the difference between rough surfaces and smooth surfaces. (para starting line 174)

8. _____ In the future, amputees will be able to pick up small items such as coins. (para starting line 182)

9. _____ If people who have spinal-cord injuries can feed themselves, and no one notices they have been injured, that is the definition of success. (para starting line 205)

C. Critical Thinking. Discuss these questions with a partner.

1. In your own words, explain the advantages and disadvantages of bionic arms.

2. Do you think the author is mainly optimistic or pessimistic about future developments in prosthetics? What information in the passage supports your choice?

3. Which recent developments in other fields of technology or engineering might be described as "a major leap forward"?

Vocabulary Practice

A. Completion. Complete the information by circling the most appropriate word in each pair.

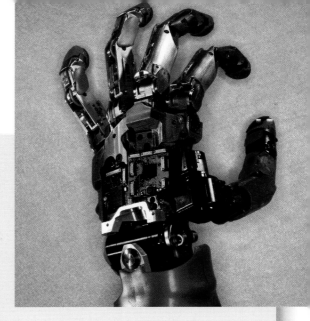

▲ Modern bionic hands allow for a sophisticated range of movement.

Bionics are being used with increasing frequency and more **1.** reliability / sensation to improve the lives of people who have suffered from the loss of hearing, sight, **2.** impulse / sensation, or movement.

For instance, about 250 people have been treated with an experimental technique to restore hand movement lost due to paralysis. A patient can **3.** salvage / vibrate some degree of movement, such as being able to pick up a knife or fork, by means of a sophisticated and **4.** intricate / reasonable piece of equipment placed in their chest.

Another bionic success has restored partial hearing to nearly 200,000 people around the world during the past 30 years. In this **5.** complicated / valid procedure, 22 electrodes are planted in the part of the inner ear that normally detects sound **6.** vibrations / complications. A microphone picks up sounds and sends signals to the electrodes; these then transmit electronic **7.** impulses / sensations directly to the nerves, allowing some degree of hearing to be restored.

Researchers are even beginning to **8.** assign / salvage the power of bionics to the brain itself. Scientists are experimenting to allow patients to move remote objects with their minds. In one experiment, test subjects were able to send signals from their brain to move a cursor around a computer screen. Researchers believe there is a **9.** reasonable / reliable chance that one day bionics may even allow us to reactivate the brain area that stores memories in people with memory loss.

B. Words in Context. Complete each sentence with the best answer.

1. A valid argument or idea is based on _____ reasoning.
   a. complex   b. sensible

2. If you manage to salvage a difficult situation, you are able to get something _____ from it.
   a. unusual   b. useful

3. People or things that are reliable can be _____ to work well.
   a. changed   b. trusted

4. If you think that someone is reasonable, you think they are _____.
   a. fair and sensible   b. extremely intelligent

5. Something that has many _____ can be described as intricate.
   a. parts   b. purposes

6. Sensation refers to your ability to _____ things physically.
   a. feel   b. see

7. If you do something on impulse, you _____ decide to do it.
   a. suddenly   b. reluctantly

Word Link

The root **sens** has the meaning of *feeling*, e.g., **sens**ation, **sens**eless, **sens**itive, **sens**itize, de**sens**itize, **sens**itivity, **sens**e, **sens**or, **sens**ory.

Bionic Mountaineer

A. Preview. You will hear these words and phrases in the video. What do you think they mean? Match each word or phrase to its meaning.

1. Some [other climbers] accused me of cheating, which was music to my ears, . . . that meant that they fully accepted [me] . . .

2. We're at the brink of a new age. I can imagine in the coming years . . .

3. [Hugh's ideas] could represent a revolution in the field of prosthetics.

a. _____ a big change

b. _____ the edge, or the moment before something begins

c. _____ a very good and pleasing thing

B. Summarize. Watch the video, *Bionic Mountaineer*. Then complete the summary below using the correct form of words in the box. Two words are extra.

compromise	discipline	implement	institute
intricate	manipulate	orientation	salvage
sensation	valid		

▲ Double amputee and MIT professor Hugh Herr demonstrates the use of his bionic legs.

In 1982, Hugh Herr and a friend set out on a climbing expedition in New Hampshire, but partway through the hike they found themselves in the middle of a fierce blizzard. They soon lost their **1.** _____ in the storm, and ended up wandering through the woods for three days and nights. Exposed to the elements, the climbers became weak and gradually began to lose **2.** _____ in their limbs.

Hugh and his friend were eventually rescued and taken to safety, but doctors were unable to **3.** _____ Hugh's legs. Hugh had to replace his legs with a pair of prosthetics. It took many **4.** _____ surgeries before Hugh could even walk on his prosthetic limbs. But still Hugh wanted to climb. So, he constructed a number of prosthetic legs specially adapted for climbing. Instead of **5.** _____ his ability to climb, Hugh's new legs gave him some advantages over other climbers.

Hugh had discovered a new passion. He earned his PhD in biophysics and now designs advanced prosthetics at the Massachusetts **6.** _____ of Technology, where he is developing ways to allow the brain to directly **7.** _____ a prosthesis. If Hugh's ideas are **8.** _____ successfully, they could represent a revolution in the field of prosthetics.

C. Think About It.

1. In the video, Hugh says, "I could imagine that people with biological legs will choose to get their legs amputated so they can achieve the same performance advantage." Do you agree? Why or why not?

2. Do you know any other examples of survival in the wild? What happened to the person, and why do you think he/she was able to survive?

To learn more about the human body, visit elt.heinle.com/explorer

UNIT 8

Social Behavior

WARM UP

Discuss these questions with a partner.

1. What aspects of social behavior are unique to humans?

2. Which animals do you think are closest to us in terms of social behavior?

3. In what ways is the behavior of insects similar to, and different from, our own?

▲ A group of chimps demonstrates a variety of emotions at the Chimfunshi Wildlife Orphange, Zambia.

8A Strength in Numbers

▲ Photographer Bobby Haas took this once-in-a-lifetime photo of a group of flamingos aligned in a remarkable formation in a lagoon along the Gulf of Mexico.

☐ Before You Read

A. Discussion/Quiz. Answer the questions below, then check your ideas with a partner.

1. English has many terms for describing groups of animals. Can you match each term with the correct animal(s)? (One of the animals can match with more than one term.)

   a. ants   **b.** bees   **c.** birds   **d.** elephants   **e.** fish   **f.** lions   **g.** monkeys   **h.** wolves

   a swarm of _____   a herd of _____   a pride of _____   a school of _____

   a flock of _____   a troop of _____   a pack of _____   a colony of _____

2. What do you think are the advantages and disadvantages for animals of living in large groups?

B. Skim and Predict. Briefly skim the passage on pages 139–142. What two animals does the article mainly focus on? How has studying the behavior of those animals influenced human activity? Note your answers below. Then read through the article again to check your ideas.

Animal: **Study of its behavior has influenced:**

1. _____   _____

2. _____   _____

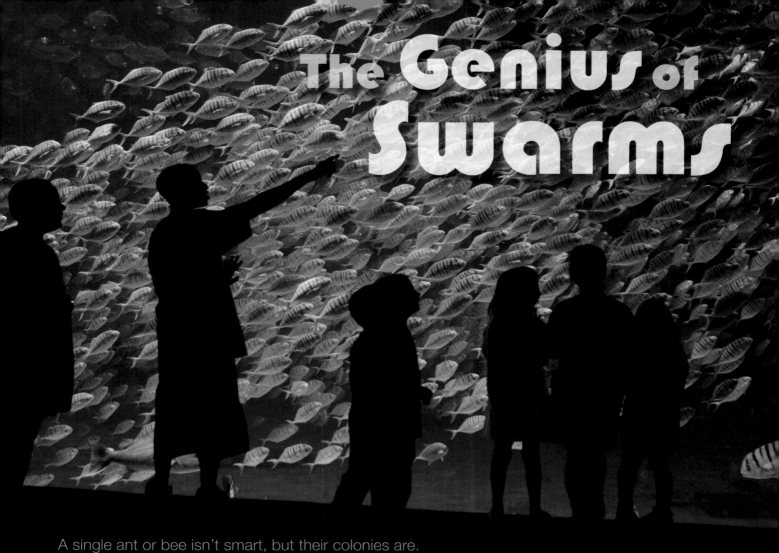

The Genius of Swarms

A single ant or bee isn't smart, but their colonies are.
The reason, as writer Peter Miller discovers, is something called swarm intelligence.

▲ Like insect swarms, schools of fish live in tight groups, often acting as a single entity.

1 I USED TO THINK ANTS knew what they were doing. The ones marching across my kitchen counter looked so confident, I just figured they had a coherent plan, knew where they were going and
5 what needed to be done. How else could ants create highways, build elaborate nests, organize epic[1] raids, and do all the other things ants do?

Turns out I was wrong. Ants aren't clever little engineers, architects, or warriors after all—at least
10 not as individuals. When it comes to deciding what to do next, most ants don't have a clue. "If you watch an ant try to accomplish something, you'll be impressed by how inept[2] it is," says Deborah M. Gordon, a biologist at Stanford University.

15 How do we explain, then, the success of Earth's 12,000 or so known ant species? They must have learned something in 140 million years.

"Ants aren't smart," Gordon says. "Ant colonies are." A colony can solve problems unthinkable for
20 individual ants, such as finding the shortest path to the best food source, allocating workers to different tasks, or defending a territory from neighbors. They do it with something called swarm intelligence.

25 Where this intelligence comes from raises a fundamental question in nature: How do the simple actions of individuals add up to the complex behavior of a group?

[1] If something is **epic**, it is very large or grand.
[2] If someone is **inept**, they are awkward, clumsy, or unable to do things.

On Barro Colorado Island, in Panama, army ants build a bridge of ant workers to move food. A single colony of army ants can consist of as many as 700,000 members.

ONE KEY TO AN ANT COLONY is that no one's in charge. No generals command ant warriors. No managers boss ant workers. The queen plays no role except to lay eggs. Even with half a million ants, a colony operates as a single entity without any management at all—at least none that we would recognize. Scientists describe such a system as self-organizing. It relies upon countless interactions between individual ants, each of which is following simple rules.

That's how swarm intelligence works: simple creatures following simple protocols, each one acting on local information. No ant sees the big picture, or tells any other ant what to do. Some ant species may go about this with more sophistication than others. (*Temnothorax albipennis*, for example, can rate the quality of a potential nest site using multiple criteria.) But in each case, says Iain Couzin, a biologist at Oxford and Princeton Universities, no leadership is required. "Even complex behavior may be coordinated by relatively simple interactions," he says.

Inspired by this idea, computer scientists have been using swarm behavior to create mathematical procedures for resolving complex human problems, such as routing trucks and scheduling airlines.

In Houston, for example, a company named American Air Liquide has been using ant-based guidelines to manage a complex business problem. The company produces industrial and medical gases at about a hundred locations in the United States and delivers them to 6,000 sites, using pipelines, railcars, and 400 trucks. Air Liquide developed a computer model inspired by the foraging[3] behavior of Argentine ants (*Linepithema humile*), a species that deposits chemical substances called pheromones.

"When these ants bring food back to the nest, they lay a pheromone trail that tells other ants to go get more food," says Charles N. Harper, who oversees the supply system at Air Liquide. "The pheromone trail gets reinforced every time an ant goes out and comes back, kind of like when you wear a trail in the forest to collect wood. So we developed a program that sends out billions of software ants to find out where the pheromone trails are strongest for our truck routes."

Air Liquide used the ant approach to consider every permutation[4] of plant scheduling, weather, and truck routing—millions of possible decisions and outcomes a day. Every night, forecasts of customer demand and manufacturing costs are fed into the model. "It takes four hours to run, even with the biggest computers we have," Harper says. "But at six o'clock every morning we get a solution that says how we're going to manage our day."

[3] **Foraging** is the act of getting something, usually food, by searching for it.
[4] A **permutation** is one of the ways in which a number of things can be ordered or arranged.

▼ Inspired by the foraging of ant colonies, delivery companies are able to send their trucks along the most efficient routes.

Other companies have also profited by imitating ants. In Italy and Switzerland, fleets of trucks now use ant-foraging rules to find the best routes for bulk deliveries. In England and France, telephone companies improved their network speed by having messages deposit virtual pheromones at switching stations, just as ants leave signals for other ants to show them the best trails.

BUT ANTS ARE NOT THE ONLY insects with something useful to teach us. On a small island off the southern coast of Maine, Thomas Seeley, a biologist at Cornell University, has been studying how colonies of honeybees (*Apis mellifera*) choose a new home. In late spring, when a hive gets too crowded, a colony normally splits, and the queen, some drones,[5] and about half the workers migrate a short distance to cluster on a tree branch. Meanwhile a small number of scouts go searching for a new site for the colony.

To find out how, Seeley's team put out five nest boxes—four that weren't quite big enough and one that was just about perfect—and released a colony of bees. Scout bees soon appeared at all five boxes. When they returned to the main group, each scout performed a waggle dance urging other scouts to go have a look. (These dances include a code giving directions to a box's location.) The strength of each dance reflected the scout's enthusiasm for the site.

The decisive moment didn't take place in the main cluster of bees, but out at the boxes, where scouts were building up. As soon as the number of scouts visible near the entrance to a box reached about 15—a threshold confirmed by other experiments—the bees at that box sensed that a quorum[6] had been reached, and they returned to the swarm with the news.

"It was a race," Seeley says. "Which site was going to build up 15 bees first?"

Scouts from the chosen box then spread through the swarm, signaling that it was time to move. Once all the bees had warmed up, they lifted off to secure their new home, which, to no one's surprise, turned out to be the best of the five boxes.

The bees' rules for decision-making—seek a diversity of options, encourage a free competition among ideas, and use an effective mechanism to narrow choices—so impressed Seeley that he now uses them at Cornell as chairman of his department.

"I've applied what I've learned from the bees to run faculty meetings," he says. To avoid going into a meeting with his mind made up, hearing only what he wants to hear, and pressuring people to conform, Seeley asks his group to identify all the possibilities, discuss their ideas for a while, then vote by secret ballot.[7] "It's exactly what the swarm bees do, which gives a group time to let the best ideas emerge and win."

▼ According to swarm theory, any crowd is capable of smart decision-making, as long as each member is independent-minded.

▲ Honeybees deciding on a new nest site perform waggle dances to express their enthusiasm for a potential site, in a simple yet ingenious system of bug balloting.

[5] A **drone** is a male bee that does not work but can fertilize the queen. The term can also be used to describe one who performs menial or tedious work.
[6] A **quorum** is the minimum number of members required to be present in a meeting or assembly before any business can be transacted.
[7] A **ballot** occurs when people select a representative or course of action by voting.

▲ On Appledore Island, Maine, biologists study swarming bee behavior as their subjects buzz around them.

IN FACT, ALMOST ANY GROUP that follows the bees' rules will make itself smarter, says James Surowiecki, author of *The Wisdom of Crowds*. "The analogy is really quite powerful. The bees are predicting which nest site will be best, and humans can do the same thing, even in the face of exceptionally complex decisions." Investors in the stock market, scientists on a research project, even kids at a county fair guessing the number of beans in a jar can be smart groups, he says. That is, if their members are diverse, independent-minded, and use a mechanism such as voting, auctioning, or averaging to reach a collective, aggregate decision.

That's the wonderful appeal of swarm intelligence. Whether we're talking about ants, bees, or humans, the ingredients of smart group behavior—decentralized control, response to local cues, simple rules of thumb—add up to an effective strategy to cope with complexity.

Consider the way an Internet search engine like Google uses group smarts to find what you're looking for. When you type in a search query, the engine surveys billions of Web pages on its index servers to identify the most relevant ones. It then ranks them by the number of pages that link to them, counting links as votes (the most popular sites get weighted votes,[8] since they're more likely to be reliable). The pages that receive the most votes are listed first in the search results.

With free collaborative encyclopedias available to anyone online, "it's now possible for huge numbers of people to think together in ways we never imagined a few decades ago," says Thomas Malone of MIT's new Center for Collective Intelligence. "No single person knows everything that's needed to deal with problems we face as a society, such as health care or climate change, but collectively we know far more than we've been able to tap[9] so far."

Such thoughts underline an important truth about collective intelligence: Crowds are wise only if individual members act responsibly and make their own decisions. A group won't be smart if its members imitate one another, unthinkingly follow fads, or wait for someone to tell them what to do. When a group is being intelligent, whether it's made up of ants or attorneys,[10] it relies on its members to do their own part. For those of us who sometimes wonder if it's really worth recycling that extra bottle to lighten our impact on the planet, the fact is that our actions matter, even if we don't see how.

"It's now possible for huge numbers of people to think together in ways we never imagined a few decades ago."

"A honeybee never sees the big picture any more than you or I do," says Thomas Seeley, the bee expert. "None of us knows what society as a whole needs, but we look around and say, oh, they need someone to volunteer at school, or mow the church lawn, or help in a political campaign."

If you're looking for a role model in a world of complexity, you could do worse than to imitate an ant or a bee.

---

[8] **Weighted voting** systems are voting systems based on the idea that not all voters are equal.
[9] When we **tap** something, like a resource, we access and use it.
[10] **Attorneys** are lawyers.

☐ Reading Comprehension

A. Multiple Choice. Choose the best answer for each question.

Main Idea

1. Which of the following is the main idea of the article?
   a. Although colonies of ants display intelligence, they are not as smart as colonies of bees.
   b. Insects such as ants and bees can teach humans lessons about collective decision-making.
   c. Individual ants and bees are far more intelligent than other types of insects.
   d. A group of humans that uses bees' methods of decision-making will be smarter than one that doesn't.

Inference

2. In the first paragraph, the author implies that he _____.
   a. has changed his mind about the behavior of ants
   b. has performed research on ants himself
   c. was not really interested in ants until he wrote this article
   d. now believes that ants can make coherent plans

Rhetorical Purpose

3. Why does the author quote Deborah M. Gordon in paragraph 4 (from line 18)?
   a. to present an idea that supports his own point of view
   b. to support the idea that individual ants are not intelligent
   c. to show how much ants have learned in 140 million years
   d. to contradict the idea that ant colonies are truly intelligent

Reference

4. The word *it* in line 23 refers to _____.
   a. the shortest path   c. solving difficult problems
   b. an ant colony   d. the best food source

Detail

5. According to the information in paragraph 6 (from line 29), what is the primary role of queen ants?
   a. They manage the worker ants.
   b. They create more members of the colony.
   c. They command warrior ants on raids.
   d. They allow the colony to operate as a single entity.

Rhetorical Purpose

6. How does Charles N. Harper explain the concept of a pheromone trail in paragraph 10 (from line 72)?
   a. by contrasting it with a computer program
   b. by explaining the chemical composition of pheromones
   c. by comparing it with a similar human activity
   d. by giving examples of several types of pheromone trails

Inference

7. In paragraph 14 (from line 113), the author implies that _____.
   a. scouts communicate information to the swarm by dancing
   b. the researchers had no idea which home the bees would choose
   c. the scouts moved as a group and visited each box in turn
   d. some scouts stayed at the new home while others informed the swarm

Main Idea

8. What is the main idea of paragraph 24 (from line 201)?
   a. A crowd is intelligent only if its members make their own decisions.
   b. Individual acts like recycling usually have little impact on the environment.
   c. Most crowds are not intelligent because members usually act irresponsibly.
   d. Even when people follow fads, the aggregate decision is usually the right one.

Graphic organizers such as a chart, a table, or a diagram can help you more clearly understand the content and the structure of a reading. Venn diagrams (see Unit 5B) are particularly useful for showing how two or more concepts have characteristics that are distinct from each other, as well as characteristics that are shared. For example, in this article, the writer discusses characteristics of behavior that relate to ants and bees.

B. Classification. Put the characteristics (**A–J**) in the correct spaces in the Venn diagram.

A. Individual members of the colony are not very intelligent, but the colony as a whole is.

B. Leadership is required for decision-making.

C. Collectively, they are clever engineers that build roads, and warriors that raid other groups.

D. Their system of collective decision-making can be useful to human groups.

E. They communicate by elaborate dances.

F. They use pheromones to mark pathways.

G. They require 15 scouts to choose a new home.

H. Decentralized control, response to local cues, and a set of simple rules help them make complex decisions.

I. Individuals are able to see the "big picture."

J. They use collective decision-making to evaluate the suitability of potential homes.

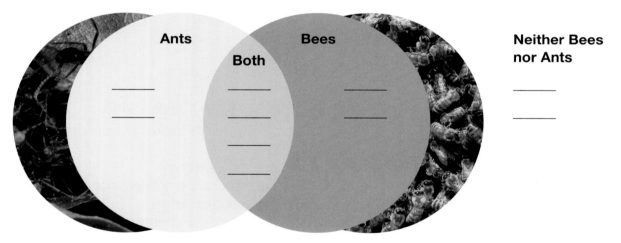

C. Critical Thinking. Discuss these questions with a partner.

1. Using information from the article, explain in your own words the difference between collective intelligence and individual intelligence in both insects and humans.

2. Thomas Malone is quoted as saying that with online technology, "it's now possible for huge numbers of people to think together in ways we never imagined a few decades ago." What benefits has the Internet brought to the way people think and make decisions? Are there any disadvantages?

3. Imagine that you and several of your friends are going to form a study group and prepare for an important exam together. How could you use collective intelligence to help you?

Vocabulary Practice

A. Completion. Complete the information by circling the most appropriate word in each pair.

▲ Herds of caribou, such as this one crossing the grasslands of Manitoba, Canada, can cover thousands of kilometers during their epic migration.

For animals in the wild, traveling in large groups offers several advantages: it increases their chances of detecting predators, **1.** imitating / securing territory, finding food, and gaining protection from predators.

Wildlife biologist Karsten Heuer has spent many years observing the annual migration of caribou, one of the longest massed movements in the natural world. Once, he spotted a wolf creeping up to a caribou herd. As soon as the wolf got within a certain distance of the herd, the nearest caribou turned and ran. This sent a **2.** code / quality to the rest of the herd that resulted in **3.** imitation / index by other caribou. Eventually the entire herd was running. Animals closest to the wolf demonstrated every variation of flight, running in all directions and confusing the wolf. In the end, the herd escaped, and the wolf was left exhausted.

Each individual caribou was engaged in its own life or death struggle, and yet the **4.** aggregate / secure behavior of the herd was characterized by precision, not fright. Every caribou knew the **5.** criteria / relevance that determined when to run and in which direction to go, even if it didn't know exactly why. No leader was responsible for coordinating the herd. Instead swarm intelligence ensured that each animal followed simple **6.** faculties / protocols evolved over thousands of years of wolf attacks.

B. Definitions. Match the correct form of words in red from **A** with the correct definition.

1. how good or bad something is _____

2. the teaching staff at a university or college _____

3. copy behavior _____

4. alphabetical list of items used for reference _____

5. obtain something after a lot of effort _____

6. made up of smaller amounts added together _____

7. important or significant to that situation _____

8. factors used to judge or decide something _____

Usage

Code and protocol

These words have similar meanings. A **code** is a set of rules about how people should behave or about how something must be done. A **protocol** is also a set of rules or guidelines about correct conduct, but it is usually used in a formal context, e.g., *He understood the proper **protocol** for declining a job offer.*

8B Cooperation and Conflict

▲ A pair of Japanese snow monkeys groom (clean) each other whilst bathing in a natural hot spring. Unselfish, or altruistic, behavior has been observed in many species, not only primates. But how did it evolve?

☐ Before You Read

A. Matching. The following nature-related words appear in the reading passage. Match each word with its definition.

a. ecosystem   **b.** habitation   **c.** organism   **d.** scavenger   **e.** specialization   **f.** vertebrate

1. _____ an animal or plant, usually one that is very small
2. _____ an animal that feeds on dead or decaying matter
3. _____ an animal with a backbone, such as a fish, reptile, bird, or mammal
4. _____ the activity of living somewhere
5. _____ the adaptation of an animal or plant to a specific function or environment
6. _____ the complex relationship between the plants and animals in a particular area

B. Skim and Predict. The passage on pages 147–150 is an interview with the American biologist, researcher, and author, Edward O. Wilson. Skim the interview, reading only the interviewer's questions. Check (✓) the topics you think the interview will cover. Read the whole passage to check your ideas.

☐ how Wilson became a naturalist
☐ how unselfish behavior developed among animals
☐ human impact on animals today

☐ similarities between ants and humans
☐ Wilson's plans for future expeditions
☐ Wilson's opinions on young people today

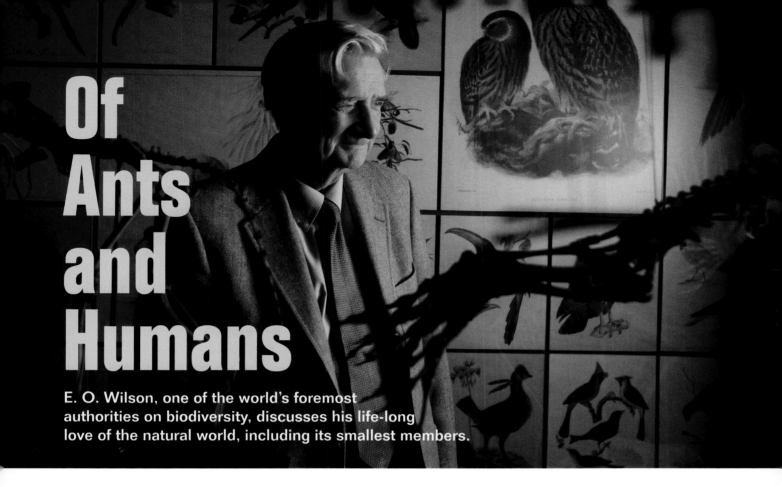

Of Ants and Humans

E. O. Wilson, one of the world's foremost authorities on biodiversity, discusses his life-long love of the natural world, including its smallest members.

1 **How did you develop a passion for nature?**
When I was nine years old and living in Washington, D.C., I somehow got excited about the idea of expeditions to far-off jungles to collect
5 the sorts of things you saw in *National Geographic*. So I decided I would do some expeditions to Rock Creek Park,[1] and I got bottles and everything, and I started collecting there. I would go on my own and wander for hours. Then I went to the National
10 Zoo, which was paradise on Earth for me. How could you avoid becoming a naturalist in that kind of environment?

Is that kind of exploration a rarer experience for kids today?
15 I worry about that. I have no data, but it appears to me that many of our young people are staying at home or being influenced by an increasingly stimulating 'artifactual' world. Fake nature, sci-fi movies, videos, being drawn into lives that are
20 pursued in front of a computer. That's a trend that would take young people away from a naturalist's experience. But there are counterinfluences. More people go to zoos in the U.S. than attend professional sports, did you know that? There's a
25 strong pull remaining that I think is primal.

Darwin loved beetles. What was it about ants for you?
Originally I was going to work on flies, because I felt that was a wide-open area to do exploration,
30 but I couldn't get the special insect pins to collect them. It was 1946, just after the Second World War, and those pins were not available. So I turned to ants, because I could collect them in bottles of alcohol.

35 **Do some say that this isn't serious science, it's just collecting?**
Well, when people say that sort of thing, you can respond quickly that you're not going to get anywhere until you do this science, and
40 furthermore, you're going to make all sorts of new discoveries while you're doing it. You never know when someone is going to be looking for some kind of lead in this growing body of information from mapping life on Earth. For instance, someone
45 might say, "What I need for my work is an ant that hunts underwater and walks around submarine fashion and then comes out and goes back to a dry nest. Does any such thing exist?" It turns out, yes!

[1] **Rock Creek Park** is an urban park in Washington, D.C.

A bulldog ant worker presents her egg to the queen.

A submarine ant?

50 Yes, in Malaysia, on the pitcher plant *Nepenthes*. This plant collects water in which insects fall and drown, and there are substances in the water that help digest the insects. *Nepenthes* gets organic material from the insects it captures. There is this

55 ant that lives on *Nepenthes*, and the workers walk in, right down into the mouth of hell. They just walk right in submarine-like and pick up insects that have fallen to the bottom.

Are you doing any field trips these days?

60 I get together with younger ant specialists—they all seem younger to me, these days—and we go into the field. It's a joyous activity. On a recent trip to the Dominican Republic we went to 8,000 feet (2.4 km). Most people don't know the Dominican

65 Republic has mountains. We were all the way up in cold pine forests, discovering new species at every mountain site.

There's no feeling that the world has been conquered now?

70 Oh, no. That's the point—we're just beginning exploration. For animals, we probably know as few as ten percent of the species. Even in a fairly familiar group like ants, we're discovering them right and left. I estimate that maybe half the ants in

75 the world remain undiscovered.

How well did Darwin know his ants?

Darwin knew his ants very well. He spent a lot of time watching ants. And part of the reason was that ants exemplified a peculiarity that he said might

80 have proved fatal to his theory of evolution. And that potential flaw was that worker ants are so completely different from queen ants, yet they are sterile. So how would you explain that by natural selection? If worker ants couldn't have offspring,[2]

85 how are their traits developed and passed on?

▲ Carrying leaf pieces that can weigh up to twenty times their own weight, these leafcutter ants consume almost 20 percent of the annual vegetation growth of the Central American rainforests.

[2] A person or animal's **offspring** are their children.

The problem was how this kind of self-sacrifice—tending the queen while giving up reproduction—evolved?

Yes, and Darwin solved the problem: What counts is the group, and that worker ants are just part of the colony, just an extension of the queen. Her heredity is what matters. If she is producing separate organisms that serve her purpose, then all together, these colonies can prevail over solitary individuals. That was the solution. And actually that isn't too far from the way we see it today. The most recent theories [are] spelled out in a forthcoming book that Bert Hölldobler and I are writing called *The Superorganism*.[3]

Why that title?

The colony is the next level of biological organization. The colony, by group selection, has developed traits that could not be possible otherwise—communication, the "caste" system,[4] cooperative behavior. It's a unit of activity and of evolution. One colony against another is what's being selected. This happens to be close to Darwin's idea but in modern genetic terms.

How does this kind of social behavior get started?

It has to do with defense against enemies. Naturalists have discovered more and more groups that have altruistic[5] workers and soldiers—ants, termites, certain beetles, shrimp, and even a mammal, the naked mole rat. What's consistently the case is that these animals have a resource, usually a place to live with food, that's very valuable. If you're a solitary individual and you build a chamber like that, somebody could chuck[6] you out. The idea is that these lines are going to find it advantageous to develop sterile castes for maintaining and protecting the colony.

So this is a story about community and home.

I've learned my lesson about jumping from ants or sponges to humans! But it does, in my opinion, call for another look at human origins. Anthropologists[7] now pretty much agree that a major factor in human origins was having a habitation, a campsite, which allowed for some specialization, where some stayed and looked after the site and the young and so on, while others ventured out to bring food back. And the pressures from predators must have been pretty intense.

But we don't have sterile castes.

No, we have a division of labor. That is very true. And that's a fundamental difference between us and insects and these other creatures, and that's why we have to be very careful about drawing analogies. Because human beings are so flexible and intelligent, we can divide labor without physical castes.

That system has worked pretty well for ants.

They dominate ecosystems. In tropical forests, from one study, ants alone make up four times the weight of all the land vertebrates put together—amphibians, reptiles, birds, mammals. The weight of all the ants in the world is roughly the weight of all the humans, to the nearest order of magnitude.[8] They are the principal predators of small animals, the principal scavengers in much of the world, and the principal turners of the soil.

In his 1859 book *On the Origin of Species*, the English naturalist Charles Darwin (1809–1882) theorized that all species of life have descended over time from common ancestors through a process of evolution he called natural selection. ▲

[3] Bert Hölldobler and Edward Wilson, **The Superorganism**: *The Beauty, Elegance, and Strangeness of Insect Societies*, W.W. Norton & Company, 2008.
[4] A **caste system** is a rigid hereditary system of social ranking.
[5] Someone who is **altruistic** is unselfish and does things out of concern for the welfare of others.
[6] When you **chuck** something out, you throw it out.
[7] **Anthropologists** are people who study human origins, institutions, and beliefs.
[8] An **order of magnitude** is an estimate of size or magnitude expressed as a power of ten.

◀ **Tongue Twister:** A red-headed woodpecker and a yellow-shafted northern flicker engage in aerial combat. Fighting may be commonplace in the natural world, but only humans, ants, and other highly evolved societies are known to fight against each other in large groups.

It's interesting that ants and humans are both social and that both dominate their environment.

165 Sure enough, we're the one highly social vertebrate[9] with altruism and high levels of division of labor, though not sterility. We're the one species that has reached this level, and we dominate.

170 **We also have a tremendous effect on other species.**

More than any kind of ant. But I'm always at risk of having it said, "That nut[10] wants to compare ants and humans." Well, obviously not. Beyond 175 the fact that we both reached high levels of social behavior based on altruism and division of labor, the resemblance between humans and ants pretty much comes to an end. For example, they communicate almost 180 entirely by taste and smell. They live in a sensory world that's totally different from humans. It's like ants are from another planet. And ants are constantly at war. Well, so are we! But they are the most warlike of animals.

185 **It makes you wonder whether war and complex societies go together.**

It may turn out that highly evolved societies with this level of altruism tend strongly to divide into groups that then fight against each other. We 190 humans are constantly at war and have been since prehistory. I know a lot of people would like to believe that this is just a nasty habit we developed, just a cultural anomaly,[11] and all we have to do is get enlightened[12] and drop it. I hope that's true.

195 **Do the ants offer any lessons?**

At least not any we would care to put in practice. Ant colonies are all female; males are tolerated only part of the year. Slavery and cannibalism[13] are commonplace. There is one lesson we have already 200 learned, however: ants keep themselves fanatically clean, so epidemics[14] are rare.

But now ants and many other creatures are threatened with extinction. Are you hopeful that we can save enough in time?

205 Actually, I am. The best funded global conservation organizations are now scoring successes in

The weight of all the ants in the world is roughly the weight of all the humans.

persuading developing countries to set up sustainable reserves—sustainable meaning they provide an actual increase in the quality of life for 210 people living in and around them. That doesn't take as much money as some have thought. It can be achieved in many of these countries where the greatest destruction is occurring because incomes may be just a few hundred dollars a year. There 215 are reasons to believe that where most of the biodiversity occurs—the tropical forest, grasslands, and shallow marine areas—a lot can be saved.

[9] A **vertebrate** is an animal with a backbone, e.g., a bird or mammal.
[10] The term "**nut**" is sometimes used to describe someone who is crazy.
[11] Something that is an **anomaly** is peculiar, or difficult to classify.
[12] An **enlightened** person is someone who has great understanding and is therefore tolerant and unprejudiced.
[13] **Cannibalism** is the eating of an animal by an animal of its own kind.
[14] **Epidemics** are widespread occurrences of a disease.

☐ Reading Comprehension

A. Multiple Choice. Choose the best answer for each question.

Detail **1.** Why did E. O. Wilson study ants and not flies?
   a. He found ants much more interesting than flies.
   b. He couldn't find the equipment he needed to study flies.
   c. He was ordered by the military to study ants.
   d. He liked the idea that the study of ants was wide open.

Detail **2.** What are *Nepenthes*?
   a. plants that grow underwater
   b. insects that are digested by certain plants
   c. submarine ants from Malaysia
   d. plants that capture insects

Detail **3.** According to Wilson, what would many people find surprising about the Dominican Republic?
   a. that it has cold pine forests
   b. that it has many species of ants
   c. that it is located in the Caribbean
   d. that it has mountainous areas

Detail **4.** What is the topic of the book *The Superorganism*?
   a. newly-discovered species of insects and their importance
   b. the idea that worker insects were once fertile
   c. species of animals that were researched by Darwin
   d. theories about the role of colonies in the evolution of species

Reference **5.** In paragraph 12, the word *some* (line 130) refers to some _____.
   a. anthropologists
   b. ancient humans
   c. predators
   d. ants or sponges

Rhetorical Purpose **6.** Wilson mentions the statistics in paragraph 14 (from line 142) to _____.
   a. present the results of some research that he recently completed
   b. show that there are more types of ants than of any other animals
   c. indicate that ants are one of the world's most dominant species
   d. compare the number of ants in the tropics with the number of ants elsewhere

Main Idea **7.** According to Wilson's responses on pages 149–150, how are humans unique?
   a. We are by far the most warlike of all the creatures on the earth.
   b. We have a high-level division of labor but no biological castes.
   c. We have a strong effect on other species with which we share territory.
   d. We are the only social creatures that do not form colonies.

Vocabulary **8.** The word *scoring* in line 206 is closest in meaning to _____.
   a. beating   c. persuading
   b. achieving   d. hoping for

We scan to find specific information that we need from an article. For example, we might scan to locate key information like dates, names, amounts, or places, as well as to identify specific points or ideas that the author is making. In some cases the specific information we are scanning for may not be mentioned in the passage. (See also Unit 3B page 47).

B. Scanning/Classification. Scan the article "Of Ants and Humans" and then mark the following items **T** (True), **F** (False), or **NG** (Not Given). Try to locate the information you need as quickly as possible.

1. _____ Wilson first became interested in natural science during a visit to the National Zoo in Washington, D.C.
2. _____ According to Wilson, there are more people visiting zoos in the United States each year than attending professional sporting events.
3. _____ The insects that fall to the bottom of the water inside the Malaysian pitcher plant are mostly ants.
4. _____ Wilson feels older than most of the other ant specialists he works with now.
5. _____ Darwin spent more time studying ants than he did studying beetles.
6. _____ The naked mole rat is given in the passage as a type of mammal that has altruistic workers and warriors.
7. _____ Solitary animals find it more difficult to maintain and defend a nest than colonial animals.
8. _____ The number of ants in the world is about the same as the number of humans.
9. _____ Ants communicate by taste and smell because they have very poor vision and hearing.
10. _____ Female ants are usually not found in ant colonies.
11. _____ Ants keep themselves so clean that epidemics seldom occur in ant colonies.
12. _____ According to Wilson, setting up sustainable reserves in developing countries is not as expensive as some people predicted.

C. Critical Thinking. Discuss these questions with a partner.

1. Do you think the author of the previous reading "The Genius of Swarms" would generally agree or disagree with E. O. Wilson? Why do you think so?

2. What does Wilson say about war in paragraph 17 (from line 185)? Do you think there may be evolutionary reasons why humans go to war? What other reasons might explain it?

3. Imagine that you are interviewing E. O. Wilson. What other questions would you ask him?

Vocabulary Practice

A. Completion. Complete the information using the correct form of words in the box.
Two words are extra.

consistent	exemplify	fake	fatal	organic
persuade	solitary	sterile	tolerate	traits

Warriors on the Move

When it comes to the art of war, army ant colonies
1. _____ an extreme fighting spirit.

With their tough bodies and powerful jaws, army ants are able to kill prey vastly larger than themselves. Although a(n) **2.** _____ ant can do no real damage, a swarm of several hundred thousand can inflict **3.** _____ attacks on tens of thousands of insects and small animals within a matter of hours.

Over the years, certain insects have developed strategies to avoid becoming ant prey. One of an army ant's **4.** _____, for example, is poor vision. So a stick insect will attempt to **5.** _____ its appearance by imitating a piece of vegetation; it will also keep completely motionless, hoping not to send any vibration that will reveal its location. In general, however, army ants **6.** _____ nothing in their path, not even lizards, snakes, and frogs, which they kill, but do not eat.

Although violent, attacks by army ants benefit the forest by helping maintain biodiversity. The ants turn the soil, move nutrients and **7.** _____ matter, and help to disperse seeds. The devastation left by an ant raid also creates opportunities for new species to enter the habitat. Environmentalists therefore feel it is important to **8.** _____ governments to protect their army ant communities because of their long-term benefit to the environment.

NORTH AMERICA

SOUTH AMERICA

Colonies of the army ant *Eciton burchelli* can be found in many parts of Central and South America.

B. Definitions. Match words from the box in **A** with the correct definition.

1. not true; pretending to be something else _____

2. particular characteristics _____

3. put up with something even though it is difficult _____

4. spending a lot of time alone _____

5. produced or found in living things _____

6. demonstrate a typical example _____

7. unable to reproduce _____

8. always behaving in the same way _____

9. resulting in death _____

10. make someone do something by giving good reasons for it _____

Word Partnership

Use *fatal* with:
(*n.*) fatal **accident**, fatal **illness**, fatal **shooting**, fatal **blow**; (*adj.*) fatally **wounded**; fatally **shot**

Monarch Migration

A. Preview. Look at the map and read the caption. Where do monarch butterflies travel from and to? Why do you think they migrate? Do you know any other animals that travel long distances when they migrate?

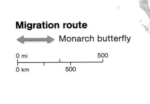

Migration route

⟷ Monarch butterfly

0 mi _____ 500
0 km _____ 500

◀ Every year, monarch butterflies travel ▶ south to their winter roosts in Mexico.

Monarch Butterfly
Biosphere Reserve

B. Summarize. Watch the video, *Monarch Migration*. Then complete the summary below using the correct form of words in the box. Two words are extra.

consistent	fatal	fragile	implement	index
persuade	relevant	secure	suspect	tolerate

Every year, millions of monarch butterflies fly south, covering over 3,000 kilometers on their way to their wintering grounds in Mexico.

But these beautiful creatures are also very **1.** _____ animals, and are often unable to **2.** _____ sudden changes to their environment. In fact, such environmental changes can prove **3.** _____ for these very delicate creatures. For example, in 2002, a rainstorm and freezing temperatures killed almost 80 percent of the monarch population in the "El Rosario" butterfly sanctuary.

Mike Quinn, a Texas biologist with the organization Monarch Watch, **4.** _____ illegal logging may have destroyed sections of the forest which serve as the butterflies' habitat. Usually, the thick forests protect the monarchs, keeping the temperature and environment around them largely **5.** _____ during the winter months. But logging opens up the forest and lets in the cold air, freezing the places where the monarchs rest.

The Mexican government, along with the World Wildlife Fund, has tried to **6.** _____ laws that will help **7.** _____ the butterflies' future, for instance, offering payments to landowners to **8.** _____ them not to cut down trees. The hope is these measures will enable millions of monarchs to continue to take flight each year.

C. Think About It.

1. The monarch migration is described as "one of the great spectacles of nature." What other great natural spectacles have you seen, or heard about?

2. The video mentions paying money to persuade loggers not to cut down trees. But would fines work better, or some other incentive? What do you think?

To learn more about the social behavior of animals, visit elt.heinle.com/explorer

UNIT 9
Creativity

◀ Painted in about 1490, **Portrait of Cecilia Gallerani** (*Lady with an Ermine*) is one of only 15 or so surviving paintings that can be attributed solely to the Renaissance painter Leonardo da Vinci. Looted from a gallery in Poland by the Nazis at the start of World War II, it was later returned to the Muzeum Narodowe in Cracow, where it can be seen today.

WARM UP

Discuss these questions with a partner.

1. Who are the most creative artists, writers, or designers today?
2. Who do you think were the most creative people in the past?
3. To what extent is creativity something that people are born with?

9A Portrait of a Genius

Recent analysis by researchers and scientists has revealed some of the secrets of the *Mona Lisa*, Leonardo da Vinci's most famous masterpiece.

The *Mona Lisa*'s famous smile, which seems to disappear if you look directly at it, "is an illusion that [results from] the way the human eye processes images," says Harvard professor Margaret Livingstone. Leonardo used "shadows that we see best with our peripheral [indirect] vision. This is why we have to look her in the eyes or somewhere else in the painting to see her smile."

According to Italian researcher Dr. Vito Franco, the *Mona Lisa* shows clear signs of a build-up of fatty acids under her skin, caused by too much cholesterol. There also seems to be a lipoma, or benign fatty-tissue tumor, near her right eye.

What happened to the *Mona Lisa*'s eyebrows? According to French engineer Pascal Cotte, they were probably removed during an attempt to clean the painting years ago. Using a ultra-high resolution scan, he was able to find the brushstroke of a single eyebrow hair—perhaps the only one that remains.

Cotte's multi-spectrum analysis also revealed why the *Mona Lisa*'s wrist rests so high on her stomach. "If you look deeply in the infrared you understand that she holds a cover with her wrist," Cotte says. The hidden cover, or blanket, has almost completely disappeared.

The sky behind the *Mona Lisa* was once a glowing blue, far different from today's gray-green shades, says Cotte, who says the darkened coloring is the result of 500 years of aging.

In 2010, researcher Philippe Walter revealed that Leonardo applied up to 30 layers of paint over several years to create his transitions from light to dark, a technique known as *sfumato*. The layers add up to about half the thickness of a human hair—"an amazing achievement even by today's standards," says Walter.

Was the *Mona Lisa* pregnant? Beneath its surface layer, the painting has traces of a veil around the woman's shoulders, of a type that "was typical of the kind worn in early 16th century Italy by women who were pregnant or who had just given birth," says researcher Bruno Mottin.

Close examination reveals a small patch of damaged paint next to the woman's left elbow, caused when an enraged man threw a rock at the painting in 1956. The painting is now kept in the Louvre behind bulletproof glass.

Before You Read

A. Labeling. Read the information about the *Mona Lisa* above and match each description with a number (**1–8**).

B. Scan. Quickly look through the reading on pages 157–160. Which of Leonardo da Vinci's works of art does the author discuss? Note them below.

_____

_____

Decoding Leonardo

▲ Despite over 500 years of chipping wall and flaking paint, the brilliance of Leonardo da Vinci's masterpiece, *The Last Supper*, still shines through.

1　ACCORDING TO LEGEND, in the year 1505 near the Tuscan town of Fiesole, a great bird rose from Monte Ceceri (Swan Mountain) and took to the air. No witness testimony remains of the event.

5　But if anyone was present on that hillside, the most likely candidate is Leonardo da Vinci, a man whose ambition for many years had been to fly like a bird. Some 50 years later, an acquaintance, Girolamo Dardano, wrote: "Leonardo da

10　Vinci . . . attempted to fly, but failed. He was an excellent painter."

To call Leonardo an excellent painter is like labeling Shakespeare a clever wordsmith.[1] He was a true genius, recognized in his own time

15　and idolized in ours. His paintings are as secret and seductive as himself, done with the hand of an angel, the intellect of a scientist, and the soul of a romantic. His drawings are among the most beautiful ever made; his most treasured painting,

20　the *Mona Lisa*, is undoubtedly the most famous in the world.

His love of painting notwithstanding, it was knowledge itself that was Leonardo's great love—knowledge, and the experience from which it

25　may be drawn. To acquire it, Leonardo turned to a diverse array of fields: mathematics, geometry, optics, astronomy, geology, botany, zoology, hydraulics, mechanics, anatomy, as well as painting and drawing. As an engineer, he could think in

30　four dimensions, visualizing not only the shapes of mechanical parts but also their interrelated motions.

Among his designs for flight, Leonardo imagined parachutes, landing equipment, even an aerial

35　screw that acted like the blades of a helicopter. But, like so much else in his life, Leonardo's attempts to actually create a workable flying machine are a mystery. There remains only one enigmatic[2] reference, in a notebook characteristically filled

40　with phrases and sketches, in which he proclaims that his great bird "will bring eternal glory to the nest where it was born . . ."

[1] A **wordsmith** is someone who is good with words and language.
[2] A person, thing, or situation that is **enigmatic** is mysterious or puzzling.

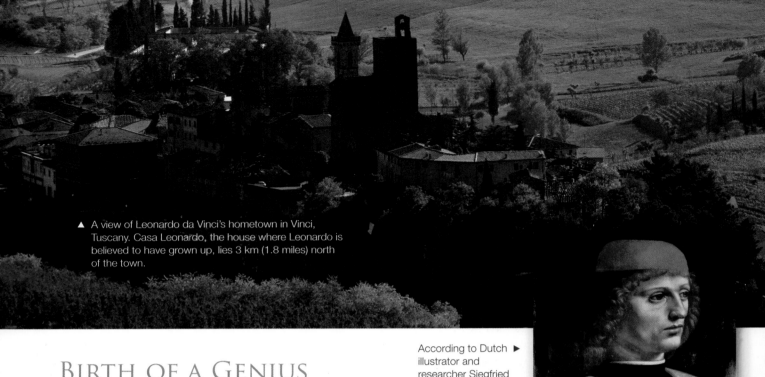

▲ A view of Leonardo da Vinci's hometown in Vinci, Tuscany. Casa Leonardo, the house where Leonardo is believed to have grown up, lies 3 km (1.8 miles) north of the town.

BIRTH OF A GENIUS

Leonardo da Vinci was born in 1452, the
45 illegitimate child of a peasant girl named Caterina and respected notary[3] Piero da Vinci. Leonardo lived at first with his mother in a three-room stone house on a hill just outside the village of Vinci, some 20 km (12 miles) west of Florence. In that
50 idyllic Tuscan countryside began the youngster's lifelong love of nature—a love that would remain implicit in all his later works.

Around 1469 Leonardo's father took him to Florence, where the statesman Lorenzo de Medici
55 had established an academy where all arts were honored. For years, art had been an instrument of religious expression, and the parameters of what was ideologically acceptable had been decided by the Church. But in the more tolerant atmosphere
60 of Florence, painters represented things as they saw them, rather than as the Church said they must be. It was a society well suited to the ever-questioning country boy.

Leonardo commenced an apprenticeship at the
65 studio of Andrea del Verrocchio, with whom he studied for at least six years. The boy mastered every medium and continued his studies of nature, discovering so much so fast that it seemed to him that everything must eventually be revealed to
70 his searching. In painting he not only outshone his more mature colleagues but also his teacher.

According to Dutch ▶ illustrator and researcher Siegfried Woldhek, Leonardo's *Portrait of a Musician*, painted when the artist was about 33, is really a self-portrait. Many art historians, however, believe Leonardo never painted himself.

Assigned to paint the figure of an angel, he gave it a whole new dimension that drew the viewer directly into the painting, in a way that
75 Verrocchio's inhibited style could never do. Some say that Verrocchio never painted again.

EARLY MASTERWORKS

Leonardo left Florence in 1482 at the age of 30. He stayed away for 18 years. The young Florentine
80 hoped to find the glory he sought in the court of Lodovico Sforza, ruler of Milan. A practical city, Milan cared more for knowledge than for the arts. It housed no great artists but counted many learned men. Leonardo came as a musician, but
85 presented himself as an engineer, describing in a long boastful letter his inventiveness in the field of weapons. Almost as an afterthought he assured Sforza that, " . . . also I can do in painting whatever may be done, as well as any other, whoever he
90 may be."

[3] A **notary** is a clerk licensed to prepare legal documents.

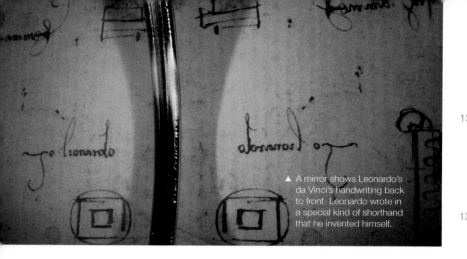

It was as an artist that Leonardo was accepted. He established an art factory much like Verrocchio's shop in Florence and at once accepted assignments.
These included a portrait of Sforza's beautiful and
95 learned mistress, Cecilia Gallerani (see page 155, *Lady with an Ermine*), a portrait of a musician that some scholars believe is really a self-portrait (page 158), and a brilliant early version of *Virgin of the Rocks*, begun in 1483 and now in the Louvre.

100 Around 1485 he began his notebooks. These are detailed, cryptic[4] compilations of material on a seemingly arbitrary range of topics, from geology and geometry to anatomy and astronomy, all interwoven and superimposed as one burning
105 interest gave way to the next. His notes are written left-handed from right to left, and there are sketches everywhere that complement his text. His discussions were addressed to himself, leaving us an extraordinary record of the movements of
110 his mind.

BRONZE HORSE AND LAST SUPPER

Along with his varied duties at court, which ranged from painting to plumbing, two great
115 works mark Leonardo's years with Sforza. One was to be a bronze statue of the duke's late father as a conquering hero riding a horse. The other, ordered by Sforza for his favorite church, was a "Last Supper." The themes were not unlike other
120 commissions of the time, but if the subjects lacked originality, their treatment did not.

The horse was to be colossal, in a pose full of motion and life. The concept was so bold, so ambitious, that it finally brought the artist the
125 praise he sought. His contemporaries thought it

could not be created, but Leonardo devised workable plans. Sadly, he was denied the chance to complete his project. War broke out and the bronze
130 was used for cannon instead.

The Last Supper, too, was presented as never before. Leonardo arranged the 13 figures in a brilliant composition reflecting the terrible moment following
135 Christ's words, "One of you shall betray me." He gave the figures deep emotions, varying according to their natures, perfectly illustrating the intention of each subject's soul.

140 Unfortunately Leonardo's brilliance was not matched by his planning. He hated deadlines and fixed schedules; painting fresco (that is, on freshly prepared plaster) imposed both. So he worked with oil mixtures, which could be applied whenever the
145 mood struck him. The technique suited the artist, but not the wall. The paint soon blistered and began to peel away from the damp surface.

With his doomed masterworks behind him, and with the French army of Louis XII approaching the
150 city, Leonardo left Milan, and in the spring of 1500 he was back in Florence.

BATTLE OF THE GIANTS

Leonardo came home a famous man. No one knew or cared much about his science and his
155 inventions, but everyone had heard of his horse and his *Last Supper*.

▼ A workman at the Louvre holds the *Mona Lisa* as a colleague cleans the glass of the painting's frame.

[4] Something that is **cryptic** is mysterious in meaning, puzzling, or ambiguous.

Many of his competitors had either died or gone to Rome. His most serious rival was Michelangelo Buonarroti, 23 years his junior, surly,[5] ambitious, and a great painter. The two Florentines hated each other wholeheartedly.

Once again, two great works drew his artistic effort. One was a huge mural for the Council Chamber depicting the Battle of Anghiari, an important political victory for Florence. The other was a life-size portrait of a middle-class woman. He worked on the paintings concurrently, the portrait offering him pleasant relief from the subject of the battle.

Some say the subject of the portrait is Lisa, wife of Florentine merchant Francesco del Giocondo, while others suggest different identities. Known today as *Mona Lisa*, it hangs in the Louvre, glass shrouded and guarded. Its colors have suffered a strange change, as if bathed in undersea light, but the lady still glows with an inner radiance, both troubling and serene.

The battle scene thrust Leonardo into an artistic rivalry with Michelangelo, who was to paint another wall of the same chamber. The rivals did their preliminary sketches in separate quarters. Both were magnificent in their own way: the younger man's picture of male bathers interrupted by a call to arms was as dynamic as Leonardo's cavalry[6] confrontation. Benvenuto Cellini, who saw them both while they were still intact, wrote that "they were the school of the world."

Michelangelo never transferred his draft to the Council Chamber wall. Leonardo did, or at least, he began to. Forgetting the fate of his *Last Supper* (or perhaps not yet aware of it), he again used an oil paint for greater freedom and brighter colors. The paint soon began to flake and run. The work

▲ Even today, Leonardo's inventions excite and inspire. Here, a man flies an air machine, using a design inspired by Leonardo's drawings.

"The great bird will take its first flight upon the back of the Great [Swan], filling the whole world with amazement and filling all records with its fame."

– Leonardo da Vinci, Turin Codex, 1505

was doomed, another masterpiece lost—at least until its traces were rediscovered in the 1970s.

A LIFE UNFINISHED

Leonardo now turned from art to his old love: flight. By this time, his knowledge went far beyond the limits of his age and was approaching the understanding that much later gave men wings. But his efforts, including his legendary attempt on Monte Ceceri, brought him no satisfaction, only the certainty that he himself would never fly or witness manned flight.

In 1513, Leonardo journeyed south to Rome to work for the new pope, Leo X; three years later, he set out once again, this time for France, on the last journey of his homeless life. France's young new king, Francis I, regarded Leonardo as the wisest of men, and wanted him nearby whether he painted or not. Thus he lived the three remaining years of his life in a small chateau among the peaceful landscape of the river Loire.

In his heart Leonardo felt defeat. His greatest works crumbling, his great knowledge undisclosed, Leonardo grieved for what might have been, for all the wondrous, unfinished projects that forever filled his extraordinary mind. He had no way to know that the few magnificent works he did complete would alone make his name immortal. And so the universal man—symbol of his time and anticipator[7] of ours—passed into eternal fame.

Reading Comprehension

A. Multiple Choice. Choose the best answer for each question.

Detail **1.** Which of these questions can definitely be answered by the information in paragraph 1?
    a. Was the "great bird" actually one of Leonardo's flying machines?
    b. Did Leonardo see the "great bird" take off from Monte Ceceri?
    c. Is Swan Mountain named for the legend of the "great bird"?
    d. Did Dardano believe Leonardo tried to build a flying machine?

Detail **2.** What does the author say about Leonardo in paragraph 2?
    a. Today he is considered much more talented than Shakespeare.
    b. He was known in his own era and is greatly respected today.
    c. His drawings are thought to be more beautiful than his paintings.
    d. The painting *Mona Lisa* was not well known when he first painted it.

Reference **3.** The word *it* in line 24 refers to _____.
    a. love   b. experience   c. knowledge   d. painting

Inference **4.** What does the author imply about the painter Verrochio in paragraph 7 (from line 64)?
    a. He was not able to teach Leonardo much because he was not a very good painter.
    b. His painting of an angel was a great inspiration for his apprentice Leonardo.
    c. He taught Leonardo more about nature than he did about the art of painting.
    d. He stopped painting because he was not as skillful as Leonardo.

Detail **5.** What happened to the metal that was going to be used for the bronze horse sculpture?
    a. It was used to create other works of art.
    b. It was stolen by the enemies of Milan.
    c. It was used to make weapons of war.
    d. It was used for plumbing in the Duke's palace.

Detail **6.** What was the problem with the oil paints Leonardo used?
    a. They had to be applied to surfaces quickly.
    b. They were not as colorful as the paints used for frescos.
    c. They did not last long without peeling and flaking.
    d. They were expensive and difficult to find.

Inference **7.** The section title "Battle of the Giants" refers to _____.
    a. Cellini's criticism of Michelangelo and Leonardo
    b. Florence's victory at the battle of Anghiari
    c. the dispute about the identity of the subject of *Mona Lisa*
    d. the competition between Leonardo and Michelangelo

Paraphrase **8.** What does the author mean when he says, "He had no way to know that the few magnificent works he did complete would alone make his name immortal" (lines 243–245)?
    a. Leonardo could not predict that the few great works he finished would be enough to make him famous for years to come.
    b. Leonardo could not decide which of the works he produced were best and would make him famous after his death.
    c. At the end of his career as an artist, Leonardo had no way to be certain how many of the great works he created were still in existence.
    d. Although he produced many great works of art, Leonardo would be surprised to know that only a few of them are still famous.

In an article that mentions a number of dates and place names, you will have a clearer understanding of the sequence of events if you follow the flow of the article on a map.

B. Labeling. Write either the missing place name or the year in which Leonardo arrived in each place (**1–6**). Then draw arrows on the map to show Leonardo's key movements over the course of his life.

① Place: _____
From: 1452

② Place: Florence
From: _____

③ Place: _____
From: 1482

④ Place: _____
From: 1500

⑤ Place: Rome
From: _____

⑥ Place: _____
From: _____

C. Critical Thinking. Discuss these questions with a partner.

1. According to the author, how did Leonardo feel toward the end of his life? Why? What language does the author use to express Leonardo's feelings?

2. The term "Renaissance man" is sometimes used to describe a person who can do many things well rather than specializing in only one field. Using information from the article, write a list of the fields in which Leonardo worked and one or more of his accomplishments in those fields.

3. Do you think it would be possible today to work successfully in as many fields as Leonardo did? Why or why not?

Vocabulary Practice

A. Completion. Complete the information using the correct form of the words in the box. Two words are extra.

academy	arbitrary	commission
concurrent	deny	draft
ideology	implicit	parameter
preliminary		

Leonardo da Vinci was perhaps the greatest multi-tasker of all time, a genius who could work
1. _____ as an artist, sculptor, inventor, engineer, and architect. During his career as an artist, Leonardo received numerous
2. _____ from some of the wealthiest and most powerful people in Italy. Yet his artworks represent just a fraction of what he wanted to achieve. The pages of his codices, or notebooks, are filled with scientific sketches and notes on a seemingly
3. _____ range of topics. However, only a few of Leonardo's original artworks survive, and very few practical examples of his designs. Most of these are kept in museums and, until recently, **4.** _____ to a wider international audience.

Now a traveling exhibition, *Da Vinci—The Genius*, has opened Leonardo's life to the world. The show features reproductions of Leonardo's most famous paintings—from detailed early
5. _____ to finished works—and a range of full-scale models, including
6. _____ designs for a glider, a parachute, and a submarine. These have all been carefully constructed using the detailed **7.** _____ set down in Leonardo's drawings. The exhibition also includes a section devoted to French engineer Pascal Cotte's analysis of the *Mona Lisa*, which reveals the sophisticated ideas **8.** _____ in Leonardo's most famous work of art.

▲ Leonardo's drawings included this 1503 design for an early type of armored tank, reproduced five centuries later for the exhibition *Da Vinci—The Genius*.

B. Definitions. Match words from the box in **A** with the correct definition.

1. beginning, introductory _____

2. institution for teaching and learning _____

3. limit, guideline _____

4. refuse access _____

5. early version _____

6. expressed in an indirect way _____

7. happening at the same time _____

8. not based on any system or plan _____

9. piece of work that is requested and paid for _____

10. set of beliefs on which actions are based _____

Word Partnership

Use **deny** with:
(*n.*) deny a **charge**, deny **access**, deny **entry**, deny **a request**, deny **the chance**;
(*v.*) **confirm or** deny

9B From Tablets to E-mail

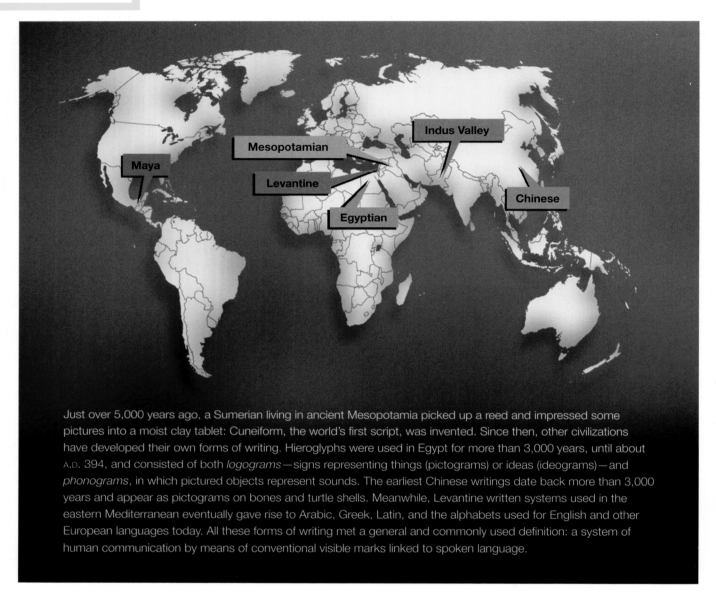

Maya

Mesopotamian

Levantine

Egyptian

Indus Valley

Chinese

Just over 5,000 years ago, a Sumerian living in ancient Mesopotamia picked up a reed and impressed some pictures into a moist clay tablet: Cuneiform, the world's first script, was invented. Since then, other civilizations have developed their own forms of writing. Hieroglyphs were used in Egypt for more than 3,000 years, until about A.D. 394, and consisted of both *logograms*—signs representing things (pictograms) or ideas (ideograms)—and *phonograms*, in which pictured objects represent sounds. The earliest Chinese writings date back more than 3,000 years and appear as pictograms on bones and turtle shells. Meanwhile, Levantine written systems used in the eastern Mediterranean eventually gave rise to Arabic, Greek, Latin, and the alphabets used for English and other European languages today. All these forms of writing met a general and commonly used definition: a system of human communication by means of conventional visible marks linked to spoken language.

☐ Before You Read

A. Discussion. How did your native language develop? What language(s) is it most similar to? In what ways is it similar to, and different from, English?

B. Skim and Predict. Quickly look at the title, captions, and first two paragraphs of the article on pages 165–168. What topics do you think the author will cover? Note them below. Then read the rest of the article to check your predictions.

_____

_____

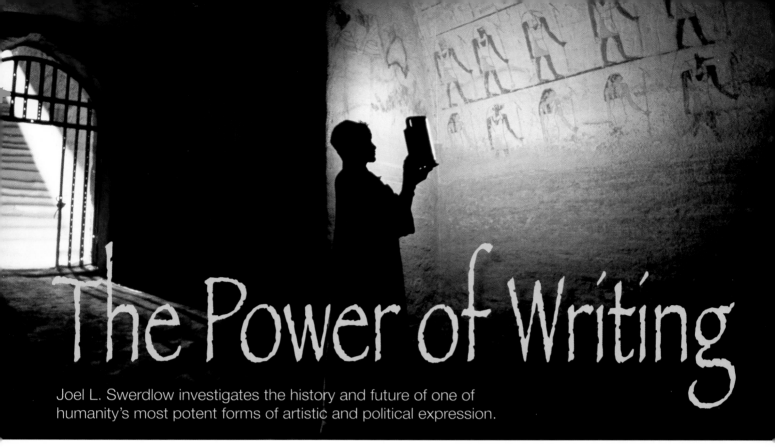

The Power of Writing

Joel L. Swerdlow investigates the history and future of one of humanity's most potent forms of artistic and political expression.

1 NO OTHER INVENTION—perhaps only the wheel comes close—has had a longer and greater impact on humanity's development than writing. Written words have overthrown governments and changed
5 the course of history. So powerful is writing that the beginnings of civilization and history are most often defined as the moment cultures develop it. The transformation of language into written words has immortalized passion, genius, art, and science.

10 Much of writing's power comes from its flexibility. Ever since the Sumerians[1] began keeping records by carving signs on clay tablets 5,000 years ago, humans have searched for the ideal tool to portray words. They have carved symbols in stone and
15 bone and written on leaves, bark, silk, papyrus, parchment, paper, and electronic screens. This skill, once known only to a few professional scribes, grew into mass literacy: More than five billion people— about 85 percent of the world's population—can
20 now read and write.

TO UNDERSTAND HOW WRITING EVOLVED, I visited Sarabit el Khadim, a flat-topped, wind-eroded mountain of reddish sandstone in the southwestern Sinai Peninsula of Egypt. Here, in a turquoise mine
25 dug by Egyptians almost 3,500 years ago, is one of the earliest examples of a phonetic alphabet.

▲ In Al Kurru, Sudan, the burial site of the Nubian Kings, a man illuminates hieroglyphics on a tomb wall, revealing writing, and knowledge, preserved for thousands of years.

"What do you think?" asked Avner Goren as we stooped to enter a dark hole. Goren, an archaeologist who supervised excavations in the
30 Sinai for 15 years, was pointing to a wall just ahead of us. Carved into the stone were crude sketches of a fish, ox head, and square. The simplicity of the marks belied[2] their significance. The people who made them were among the first to use characters
35 that denote sounds—an alphabet. The alphabetic symbols each represented the initial sound of an object. The picture of the square—a house—thus stood for the *b* sound because the word for house was *beit*.

40 The signs were remarkably different from the Egyptian hieroglyphs found elsewhere at the site. If these ancient writers were not Egyptians, who were they? Most researchers now believe that this alphabet was invented in Canaan, a region between
45 the Jordan River and the Mediterranean Sea. Most likely, Canaanites who were brought in to work the mines left these messages.

[1] The **Sumerians** were an ancient people in southern Mesopotamia, modern Iraq. See also *Explore More*, page 172.
[2] If one thing **belies** another, it hides it and gives it a false impression.

▲ Because many words in Japanese are homophones—having the same sound but different meaning—
an exchange of business cards is often necessary to know the spelling of a person's name.

Egyptian scribes had to master hundreds of
symbols. I asked Goren if alphabetic writing must
50 have seemed attractive to those scribes. "Probably
not," he says. "About 30 of the symbols in
Egyptian hieroglyphs represent single sounds, just
like the alphabet. They knew about using symbols
to represent sounds. To the Egyptians the Semitic
55 writing may have looked too primitive to
be significant."

Goren warned me against seeing an alphabet as
"superior" to pictographic writing. "If you came
from outer space and wrote a report, you'd give
60 the alphabet high marks," he says. "It's flexible
and easy to learn. But what actual effect did that
have? There was no mass literacy until after the
development of the printing press in the
mid-15th century."

65 Nevertheless, although it took hundreds of years,
alphabets would eventually change the way people
thought. From a small patch in the Middle East,
the notion of one symbol per sound gradually
became widespread around the world, taking
70 root first among the Greeks, who adapted some
characters into written vowels. The Latin alphabet
of the Romans evolved from the Greek around
the sixth century B.C. By the ninth century

A.D., Japan had integrated phonetic components
75 into its written language; Korea by the 15th.

Indeed, of the several hundred written languages
in the world today, only Chinese still relies on
a traditional writing system whereby individual
characters represent individual words. These
80 characters often mean one thing when used alone,
but something else when combined. The Chinese
character for "sincerity," for example, shows the
character for "man" alongside the one for "word,"
literally a man standing by his word.

85 SINCE ITS BEGINNING as a means for keeping records,
writing has evolved into one of humanity's most
powerful forms of self-expression. People have
used writing to counter loneliness and to establish
a sense of self. In the fourth century B.C., Aristotle[3]
90 saw writing as a way to express "affections of the
soul." Recent studies have shown that writing
about feelings can alleviate[4] depression, boost the
immune system, and lower blood pressure.

And yet, of the more than 10,000 languages ever
95 spoken, most had no written form. How, then,
do people in societies without writing
express themselves?

[3] **Aristotle** (384 B.C.–322 B.C.) was a Greek philosopher and scientist.
[4] When you **alleviate** something, usually someone's pain or suffering,
you lessen it.

▲ Donny Edenshaw is a member of the Haida Nation, whose oral histories go back hundreds of generations.

"We talk to each other, listen, visit, and trust the spoken word," says Guujaaw, a leader of the Haida Nation. "Writing is not essential to living. Expressing yourself without writing is natural."

The Haida have lived on the Queen Charlotte Islands off the coast of British Columbia for more than 10,000 years. I suggest to Guujaaw that things get distorted when people repeat them to one another, especially over a long duration of time.

"Things get distorted in writing as well," he says. "People with writing are a brief chapter in our history. Oral histories from our people go back thousands of years. They are a living history. They provide a link between storyteller and listeners that written stories cannot. In fact, human intimacy and community can best come through oral communication."

Plato, Aristotle's teacher, would probably agree. Living at a time when writing began to challenge Greece's oral-based culture, he warned that writing would make people "trust to the external written characters and not remember of themselves . . . They will be hearers of many things and will have learned nothing."

But Plato lived in the fifth century B.C., when reading was physically difficult. Books were papyrus scrolls often more than 15 meters (50 feet) long; the idea of pages only emerged in Europe in the second century A.D. Space between words did not become standard in Western society until the seventh century. Long after Plato's time, writing served mostly as an aid to memory, something to stimulate the spoken word.

The transition from the spoken to the written word occurred because writing meets certain needs so much more effectively. Writing permits analysis, precision, and communication with both current and future generations in a way that is much more powerful than the spoken word.

THOUSANDS OF YEARS AGO, China's rulers learned the value of a uniform written language, recognizing that it has the power to unite people. In the third century B.C., Chinese people spoke at least eight languages and countless dialects, but with the establishment of a unified empire and a standard writing system around 200 B.C., everyone could read the same characters.

Today, the extra work needed to manually enter Chinese into a computer—up to five keystrokes for one Chinese character—raises an important issue. China could become the wealthiest country in the world; it already is a major factor in the international economy. As this economy relies more on computers, does the Chinese writing system act as a constraint on its development?

Perhaps not. Usama Fayyad, a senior researcher at Microsoft Corporation, whose job is to think about the long-term future of computers and data storage, says technology will eventually offer efficient and economical ways to bypass[5] keyboards. Technology that incorporates voice and handwriting recognition, he claims, could make it irrelevant which writing system is used.

Fayyad also says that the distinction between an alphabet and Chinese characters does not matter in terms of how a computer operates. He explains that when you hit a letter on the keyboard, the computer enters that action into its memory as a number. Each letter is a different number, and a sentence inside the computer is a string of numbers. It's up to the computer program to interpret how the string of numbers corresponds to an instruction.

[5] If you **bypass** something, you go or get around it, trying to avoid it.

▲ The ability to exchange written messages by cell phone represents one of the latest stages in the evolution of written communication.

Overall, computers are great at bookkeeping,[6] Fayyad says, "but not yet great at recording impromptu[7] ideas, thoughts, feelings. For that,
175 paper is still far superior. You can hold it, fold it, put it in your pocket, look at it again later when it's convenient."

Fayyad's praise of paper leads me to Joseph Jacobson, a professor of
180 physics at the Massachusetts Institute of Technology. He helped found a company, E-Ink, whose technology is transforming ink from a permanent medium to a format that can change
185 electronically.

"Paper is fantastic," Jacobson tells me as we tour E-Ink offices in Cambridge, Massachusetts. "If books or newspapers on paper had not
190 already been invented, if we lived in a world only with computer screens, then paper would be a breathtaking breakthrough. But the way we use paper is incredibly wasteful."

195 Jacobson illustrates to me the E-Ink technology he hopes will someday supplement ink on paper. It prints electronic letters on squares of plastic that can be erased and reused.

200 I ask Jacobson why he uses plastic. "Paper tears too easily," he replies. "We're working on a plastic substance that looks and feels like paper. You could photocopy it, even underline on it with a special pen."

205 "Isn't that a lot of trouble to solve a problem that doesn't exist?"

"A problem does exist," Jacobson says. "Paper needs to be taken into the digital age. We need writing that changes on paper. Think about all the
210 information people download from the Internet. They don't want to read it on a computer screen, so they print it on paper. The demand for paper is soaring. Think of all the savings in cost and the pollution prevented if you needed less paper."

215 As I watch the E-Ink letters blink, I feel as if I'm back in the cave at Sarabit el Khadim—looking at a piece of the future.

6 **Bookkeeping** is the activity of keeping an accurate record of the money spent and received by a business or organization.
7 If something is done **impromptu**, it is done suddenly, without preparation.

▲ Since its early days as a means of keeping records, writing has evolved into one of our most powerful and versatile forms of expression.

Reading Comprehension

A. Multiple Choice. Choose the best answer for each question.

Detail **1.** According to the passage, what percentage of people in the world today cannot read or write?

    a. 5 percent   b. 15 percent   c. 50 percent   d. 85 percent

Vocabulary **2.** The phrase *crude sketches* in line 31 is closest in meaning to _____.

    a. rough drawings   c. old statues
    b. faded pictures   d. mysterious signs

Detail **3.** What was the probable occupation of the Canaanites who wrote the inscriptions in stone in the Sinai?

    a. supervisors   b. scholars   c. farmers   d. miners

Detail **4.** According to Avner Goren, how did Egyptian scribes probably feel about the Canaanite alphabet?

    a. It was too complicated because it had so many letters.
    b. It was confusing because it used symbols to represent sounds.
    c. It was not as sophisticated as their own writing system.
    d. It was not easy to understand because it was based on pictures.

Reference **5.** The word *it* in paragraph 8 (line 65) refers to _____.

    a. the creation of the Roman alphabet   c. the spread of alphabets to other places
    b. the development of the printing press   d. a small section of the Middle East

Inference **6.** Which of these people would probably agree that a written language is not of great importance?

    a. Aristotle and Plato   c. Plato and Guujaaw
    b. the author and Avner Goren   d. Guujaaw and Aristotle

Inference **7.** Which of these opinions would Usama Fayyad most likely agree with?

    a. A new type of keyboard now under development will soon make it easier to enter information on computers.
    b. The Chinese should develop a special writing system that can be used more easily with computers.
    c. In China, computers may one day soon be replaced with a new generation of technology.
    d. New technology will allow us to enter data on computers in various languages, without using a keyboard.

Paraphrase **8.** Which of the following is closest in meaning to this sentence from lines 188–193?
"If books or newspapers on paper had not already been invented, if we lived in a world only with computer screens, then paper would be a breathtaking breakthrough."

    a. If newspapers and books had never been invented, then the development of computers would have been considered a breathtaking achievement.
    b. There were no computers at the time when newspapers and books were first printed, so the development of paper was very important.
    c. The invention of paper would be an amazing innovation in a world without printed materials, where information could only be viewed on monitors.
    d. Certainly the invention of digital technology has been extremely important, but not nearly as important as the development of newspapers and books.

To understand an article that describes the development of an idea, it is often useful to create a timeline to identify the chronological sequence of events that relate to that idea. The article *The Power of Writing* highlights some of the milestones in the development of writing. Some of the important events and the eras in which these stages occurred can be seen in the sequence chart below.

B. Sequencing. Using information from the article, complete the chart by writing either the event or situation that occurred at that time, or the correct time period.

Time Period	Event
5,000 years ago	
	Canaanite people carved alphabetic symbols into stone in a mine in Sinai.
6th century B.C.	
	In Plato's time, writing began to challenge the Greek oral-based tradition.
	Aristotle recognized the emotional benefits of writing.
3rd century B.C.	
200 B.C.	
	The concept of pages appeared in Europe.
7th century A.D.	
9th century A.D.	
	The Korean language included phonetic elements in its written language.
mid-15th century A.D.	

C. Critical Thinking. Discuss these questions with a partner.

1. Using information from the article, explain some of the differences between pictographic alphabets such as Chinese and phonetic alphabets such as the Roman alphabet.

2. In line 207, the author quotes Jacobson: "A problem does exist." What problem does Jacobson refer to? What is his solution?

3. What advantages does a culture with writing have over one that has only an oral tradition? Can you think of any disadvantages?

Vocabulary Practice

A. Completion. Complete the information by circling the most appropriate word in each pair.

400-Year-Old Letter Reveals Evidence of "Lost" Language

On the back of a letter pulled from the ruins of a Peruvian church in 2008, archaeologists have discovered words written 400 years ago in a previously unknown language. The unknown Spanish author **1.** incorporated / unified

▲ The newfound native language may have shared elements with Quechua, still spoken by indigenous peoples of Peru.

a series of written numbers in the letter, **2.** corresponded / formatted as a list with two columns. The left column contained Spanish numbers—*uno, dos, tres*, etc.—**3.** constrained / supplemented with numerals (4, 5, etc); in the right column these were translated into a mysterious language never seen before by modern scholars. The translated numbers **4.** correspond / unify to a decimal system which suggests the language may have **5.** constrained / integrated elements of other decimal-based Incan languages such as Quechua, a language still spoken by millions of people across the Andes.

The fragment was just one of hundreds of historic papers trapped inside a ruined church for almost four centuries. Despite the long **6.** duration / format, the extremely dry climate allowed the papers to remain in good condition. This has enabled archaeologists to learn more about a significant **7.** chapter / manual in South America's history, when various indigenous peoples were adjusting to the arrival of invading Europeans.

B. Words in Context. Complete each sentence with the best answer.

1. Literacy is usually _____ as the ability to read and write.
   a. defined
   b. integrated

2. Ancient civilizations often found that a shared writing system _____ the different groups in an empire.
   a. supplemented
   b. unified

3. Over a long _____, such as centuries, a written message is more reliable than a spoken one.
   a. duration
   b. format

4. Most languages _____ the sounds of the language into their written language.
   a. correspond
   b. incorporate

5. Some scholars argue that the complex system of Chinese writing may be a _____ on the nation's future development.
   a. chapter
   b. constraint

6. Writing is a short _____ in human history compared to oral communication.
   a. chapter
   b. format

7. Languages with characters, instead of letters, require additional time for _____ entry into a computer.
   a. unified
   b. manual

Word Link

Use the root **cor** with: **cor**relate, **cor**relation, **cor**respond, **cor**respondence, **cor**respondent, **cor**roborate

The Birthplace of Writing

A. Preview. A pictogram is a form of writing in which a picture is used to represent a physical object. The first written system to use pictograms developed in Mesopotamia (present-day Iraq) and is known as cuneiform. What do you think these cuneiform pictograms mean? (Answers are below.)

1.  _____

2.  _____

3.  _____

4.  _____

▲ This life-size bronze head was unearthed in Nineveh, Iraq, and is thought to represent Sargon, a ruler who united the northern and southern parts of the Tigris-Euphrates basin more than 4,000 years ago.

B. Summarize. Watch the video, *The Birthplace of Writing*. Then complete the summary below using the correct form of words in the box. Two words are extra.

channel	chapter	constraint	correspond
duration	format	implicit	incorporate
supplement	versatile		

Meaning "land between the rivers," Mesopotamia is widely considered to be the cradle of civilization. It was here, in 5000 B.C., that people settled into an agricultural lifestyle by the mighty Tigris and Euphrates rivers. Because there was little rain, the people depended on these rivers for their survival. The Mesopotamians created **1.** _____ to distribute the flood waters that flowed for a short **2.** _____ each year to their crops. The efficiency of their irrigation systems allowed their society to flourish, enabling them to create the world's first towns and cities. At the center of each town stood a temple complex with food stores, a treasury, and living spaces, all **3.** _____ into the overall design. Over time, these towns evolved into city-states, eventually becoming an empire.

Soon there arose a need to keep reliable records of commodities traded, and out of this need, writing was born. The first **4.** _____ that writing took was a code of symbols which **5.** _____ to various items and numbers. These were carved into soft clay and were known as cuneiform. This system proved to be very **6.** _____ and quickly spread to other uses.

Although they eventually declined, the Mesopotamian civilizations left us a huge legacy of law, literature, and engineering. In fact, much of what we know of that **7.** _____ in the region's history has come from excavations of ruined cities, **8.** _____ by translations of ancient clay tablets.

C. Think About It.

1. Emoticons (symbols used in text messages and emails, such as ☺ and ☹) could be described as a return to pictogram-based writing. Do you think this trend will continue? Why or why not?

2. Human creativity can be seen in the paintings and writings of the past. How do you think humans will express themselves in the future?

To learn more about art and writing, visit elt.heinle.com/explorer

A. Answers
1. Sun 2. Fish 3. Mountain 4. Man

A. World Heritage Spotlight. Read the information about the historical sites of Iraq on pages 174–175 and answer the questions (**1–3**).

1. Matching. Match each person with a description (**a–h**). One name is extra.

____ Abu al-Kindi		**a.** created an institute for international learning
____ Donny George		**b.** has worked at Baghdad's National Museum
____ Harun al-Rashid		**c.** his regime's fall led to widespread looting
____ Ibn al-Haytham		**d.** noticed the difference between two similar diseases
____ Jabir ibn Hayyan		**e.** ruled a major city more than 2,500 years ago
____ Muhammad al-Khwarizmi		**f.** studied the smallest parts of the natural world
____ Muhammad al-Razi		**g.** was a pioneer in the study of optics
____ Nebuchadnezzar II		**h.** wrote an early study of the environment
____ Saddam Hussein		

2. Vocabulary from Context. Find words or phrases on page 175 that are closest in meaning to the following (**a–h**).

a. _____ comes or originates from

b. _____ desire to know about something

c. _____ eventually resulted in

d. _____ had an idea for and created (something)

e. _____ having many skills

f. _____ small parts of something that survive after the main part has disappeared

g. _____ something that lives on after a particular event or period of history

h. _____ thought to be responsible for (e.g., an achievement)

3. Discussion. What challenges have archaeologists faced in trying to preserve Iraq's heritage? Can you think of other parts of the world that face similar problems?

B. A Global View. Read the information on pages 176–177 and discuss the following questions with a partner.

1. What are some benefits and challenges for developing countries investing in education?

2. Why are Tanzania and Mongolia mentioned in connection with school enrollment?

3. What is the purpose of the "Light for Eve" program? How does it work?

4. Roughly how many adults in your country are unable to read and write? Do you think the percentage is rising or falling? Why?

5. Compare the maps for literacy and female primary education enrollment. In what ways are they similar, and different?

6. Why are some people concerned about language extinction? Do you agree with David Harrison that it is a global "crisis"?

Iraq's Fragile Heritage

Sites: **Historical sites of Iraq**

Location: **Iraq**

Category: **Cultural**

Status: **World Heritage Site since 1985** (Hatra)

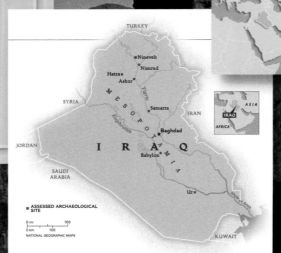

Iraq has been home to some of the world's greatest ancient civilizations—the Sumerians, the Assyrians, the Babylonians—and is the source of some of its most amazing treasures. Over the years, tens of thousands of important discoveries have been made in Iraq, from tiny clay tablets inscribed with the world's oldest writing to remnants of some of the world's earliest cities. Each find is unique and has its own story to tell. But each one is also endangered.

In the last decade of the 20th century and the first years of the 21st, many of Iraq's ancient sites and monuments fell victim to the wars that swept through the country. During the 1991 Gulf war, the ancient city of Ur—perhaps the oldest in the world—was bombed, and its great ziggurat (spiral tower) was damaged. Following the war, looting became commonplace. Sculptures disappeared from the palaces of Nimrud and Nineveh and from the temples at Hatra. Then, with the fall of Saddam Hussein's government in 2003, the situation became worse. As law and order collapsed, the National Museum in Baghdad was looted, and an estimated 15,000 pieces went missing.

Attempts by local historians and archaeologists, supported by international institutes, have helped track down many of the missing pieces, including the 5,000-year-old Warka vase, the oldest carved stone vase in the world. However, there is a profitable illegal market for stolen objects, which presents a considerable challenge to the archaeologists trying to save Iraq's rich but fragile heritage.

▲ Iraqi archaeologist Donny George stands amid the devastation of the Assyrian Gallery during the Iraq War of 2003. George was forced to leave Baghdad's National Museum at the height of the fighting: "I couldn't sleep at night," he later recalled. When he returned, he found that many of the museum's pieces had been broken, looted, or destroyed. Since the war, more than 50 percent of the missing pieces have been recovered.

Hanging Gardens Mystery

The ancient city of Babylon, located about 90 km (55 miles) south of Baghdad, is perhaps best known for its hanging gardens, one of the Seven Wonders of the Ancient World. But did they really exist?

Babylon rose to power during the reign of Nebuchadnezzar II in the sixth century B.C. According to legend, the king built the "hanging gardens" (a reference to the many balconies and terraces) for one of his wives who disliked the dry desert environment. Various archaeologists claim to have found remnants of the gardens, but not all historians agree they existed at all. Although the Babylonians left many records on clay tablets, not one of these mentions the gardens by name.

Baghdad's House of Wisdom

The House of Wisdom in Baghdad was a library and translation academy established by the Abbasid caliph (ruler) Harun al-Rashid (A.D.763–809), and continued by his son, al-Mamun. The rulers, renowned for their tolerance and intellectual curiosity, brought in scholars of various fields from around the Islamic world to share ideas in a period now referred to as an Islamic "Golden Age." Mongol invaders destroyed the institute, and much of the city, in the 13th century, but the legacy of Baghdad's Islamic scholars lives on.

The Physicist. Scientist, engineer, and astronomer Ibn **al-Haytham** (965–1040), also known as Alhazen, was the first person to give an accurate account of vision, proving that light travels in straight lines into the eye, rather than emerging from it.

The Physician. Muhammad **al-Razi** (865–925) was the first person to differentiate smallpox from measles. He is also credited with discovering medical uses for compounds including alcohol and kerosene.

The Chemist. The chemical studies of Jabir **Ibn Hayyan** (721–815), also known as Geber, ultimately led to the classification of elements used today. Often referred to as the "father of chemistry," he invented several terms now used in English, including *alkali*.

The Mathematician. Muhammad **al-Khwarizmi** (780–850) made a huge contribution to mathematics. The word "algebra" derives from al-jabr, one of the methods he devised to solve quadratic equations; "algorithm" comes from Algoritmi, the Latin form of his name.

The Philosopher. Among many achievements, the multi-talented Abu **al-Kindi** (801–873) played an important role in introducing Arabic numerals to the Islamic and Christian world. He is also credited with the world's earliest known work on environmentalism and pollution.

A researcher (top left) studies the

175

Learning and Literacy

A Global View

Goals 2 and 3 of the UN MDGs focus on education and gender equality. Specifically, the goals aim to achieve universal primary education for all school-age boys and girls, and the elimination of gender gaps at both primary and secondary levels.

Basic education is widely regarded as an investment for the long-term prosperity of a nation. Nevertheless, for many poor countries, paying for schools and teachers today is a tough challenge, especially as they may have to wait 20 years for the economic returns to those investments. Consequently, many boys and, especially, girls in low-income countries still have limited access to basic education.

However, there are encouraging signs: enrollment in primary education in developing regions reached 89 percent in 2009, up from 83 percent in 2000. Several nations have introduced new programs to increase educational enrollment. Tanzania has implemented an ambitious program of education reform, building more than 50,000 classrooms between 2002 and 2006, as well as hiring 18,000 additional teachers, while in Mongolia, mobile schools ("tent schools") now reach children in remote areas.

Other programs target female school attendance. Egypt's Girls' Education Initiative led to the creation of a thousand "girl-friendly" schools and almost 28,000 new student enrollments. In some rural communities, rewards are offered to encourage parents to let their daughters attend school. In Ethiopia, a program called Berhane Hewan ("Light for Eve") aims to boost female attendance and reduce child marriages by providing economic incentives to parents. Each schoolgirl receives a $25 sheep or two hens, for example, in return for completing at least two years of the program.

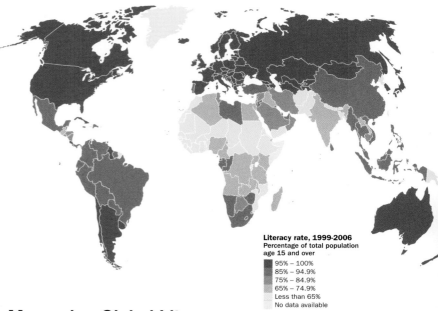

Literacy rate, 1999-2006
Percentage of total population
age 15 and over
- 95% – 100%
- 85% – 94.9%
- 75% – 84.9%
- 65% – 74.9%
- Less than 65%
- No data available

Measuring Global Literacy ▲

The United Nations estimates that globally there are about one billion adults unable to read and write. Women make up two-thirds of that total, with more than 90 percent of nonliterate people living in the developing world. There is a direct correlation between literacy and income: those able to read and write make significantly more money. But illiteracy is more than an individual issue, as less earning potential slows the economic development of countries.

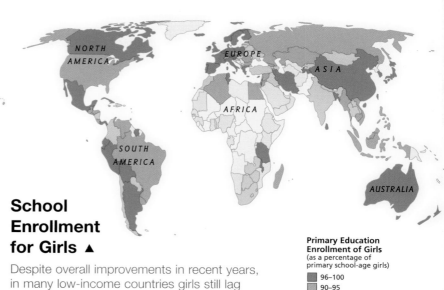

School Enrollment for Girls ▲

Despite overall improvements in recent years, in many low-income countries girls still lag behind boys in enrollment and completion of school education. In 2008, there were 96 girls for every 100 boys enrolled in primary school, and 95 girls for every 100 boys in secondary school in developing regions.

Primary Education Enrollment of Girls
(as a percentage of primary school-age girls)
- 96–100
- 90–95
- 80–89
- 60–79
- 0–59
- No data

Languages in Crisis

From Alaska to Australia, hundreds of languages are on the edge of extinction. More than 500 languages may be spoken by fewer than ten people; some are spoken only by a single person.

"Languages are undergoing a global extinction crisis that greatly exceeds the pace of species extinction," says linguistics professor David Harrison, who has traveled the world to interview the last speakers of critically endangered languages as part of the National Geographic Society's Enduring Voices Project.

When a language is lost, centuries of human thinking may be lost with it. "We're throwing away centuries' worth of knowledge and discoveries," Harrison says. The best way to ensure the survival of a language is to ensure that school children feel it is valued. "It's not really the parents who have control," says Harrison, "it's actually the children who have the power [to] affect the future of their language."

UN Millennium Development Goals

Goal 2: Achieve universal primary education

Goal 3: Promote gender equality and empower women

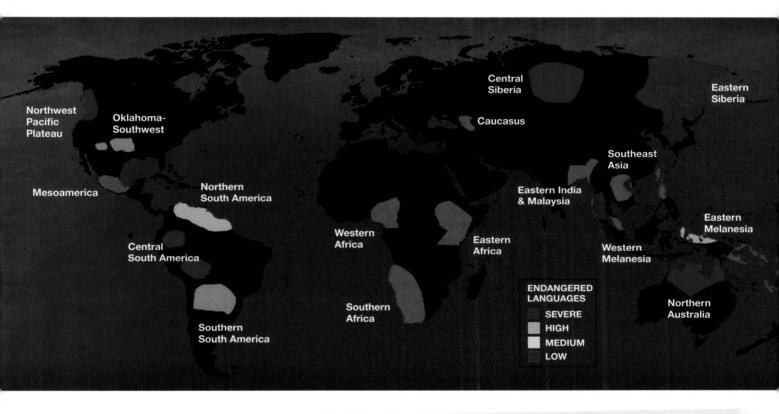

Central Siberia

Eastern Siberia

Northwest Pacific Plateau

Oklahoma-Southwest

Caucasus

Southeast Asia

Mesoamerica

Northern South America

Eastern India & Malaysia

Eastern Melanesia

Western Africa

Central South America

Eastern Africa

Western Melanesia

Southern South America

Southern Africa

Northern Australia

ENDANGERED LANGUAGES
- SEVERE
- HIGH
- MEDIUM
- LOW

"Hidden" Language Discovered

In 2008, a team of linguists with the National Geographic Society's Enduring Voices Project discovered a previously unknown language still being used by people today. The team came across the language, known as Koro, in an isolated hill tribe in northeastern India, where it is spoken by about a thousand people. However, the majority of the remaining Koro speakers are older than 20—and the language hasn't been written down—so there are fears it could soon join the list of minority languages that have gone extinct.

◀ An Indian woman who speaks the obscure regional language of Koro.

A. Word Link. Negative prefixes for adjectives include **in-**, **un-**, **il-**, **ir-**, and **im-**. Add the correct prefix to make each of the following adjectives negative. Then match an adjective to each definition.

a. _____ adequate   f. _____ consistent   k. _____ logical   p. _____ reasonable
b. _____ ambiguous   g. _____ conspicuous   l. _____ organic   q. _____ relevant
c. _____ capable   h. _____ delicate   m. _____ paralleled   r. _____ reliable
d. _____ complicated   i. _____ efficient   n. _____ possible   s. _____ tolerant
e. _____ conscious   j. _____ legal   o. _____ practical   t. _____ valid

1. _____ not difficult to understand or deal with

2. _____ cannot be depended on, or untrustworthy

3. _____ not important or significant in that situation

4. _____ not accepting of different types of people or points of view

5. _____ not always behaving or doing things in the same way

6. _____ not made of living things

7. _____ not enough

8. _____ exceptional, without equal

B. Word Forms. Complete the chart with the missing noun form. Then complete each sentence below using the correct form of the words from the chart. One word is extra.

1. A common language tends to _____ different ethnic groups within a country.

2. Tourists in Switzerland may _____ four different languages spoken in the country.

3. Minority languages may die out when another language is _____ in school and in the workplace.

Verb	Noun
align	
encounter	
endure	
enforce	
enhance	
integrate	
manipulate	
tolerate	

4. The United Nations encourages its member states to show _____ toward other ethnicities and cultural practices.

5. Strong government support is one of the reasons for the long _____ of the Irish language in Ireland, despite the widespread use of English.

6. Voters tend to _____ themselves with politicians who share their language and culture.

7. The learning of foreign languages can be _____ by the use of up-to-date methodologies and innovative technologies.

C. **Word Partnership.** Combine each word from Column **A** with a word from Column **B** to make word partnerships. Match each partnership with a definition (**1–9**).

A	B
faculty	accident
fake	design
fatal	document
intricate	draft
organic	meeting
personality	society
preliminary	test
tolerant	trait
valid	vegetable

1. _____ a collision of cars resulting in death

2. _____ a population that accepts different races and attitudes

3. _____ a characteristic related to how a person acts

4. _____ an exam that provides accurate results

5. _____ food that is grown without the aid of chemicals

6. _____ an official paper that is not real

7. _____ first version of a piece of writing

8. _____ complicated, delicate pattern

9. _____ an event at which professors come together to discuss academic issues

D. **Choosing the Right Definition.** Study the numbered definitions for *code*. Then write the number of the definition (**1–6**) that relates to each sentence below. One definition is extra.

code /koʊd/ (**codes, coding, coded**) **1** N-COUNT A **code** is set of rules about how people should behave or about how something must be done. **2** N-COUNT A **code** is a system of replacing the words in a message with other words or symbols so that it cannot be understood unless the system is known. **3** N-COUNT A **code** is a group of numbers or letters that is used to identify something, such as a mailing address or a telephone system. **4** N-COUNT The genetic **code** is the information contained in DNA, which determines the characteristics of all living things. **5** V-T To **code** something means to give it a code or to mark it with its code. **6** N-UNCOUNT Computer **code** is a system of language for expressing information and instructions in a form that can be understood by a computer.

_____ **a.** Letters and packages may not reach their intended destination if the postal **code** is incorrect.

_____ **b.** Employees in many companies must follow a dress **code** appropriate to their level of work.

_____ **c.** One of the tasks of a sales clerk is to **code** items before they are put on a shelf for sale.

_____ **d.** In my new job as a computer engineer, I have to write **code** to operate special software.

_____ **e.** Spies often use **code** to send secret messages to each other.

E. Crossword. Use the definitions below to complete the missing words.

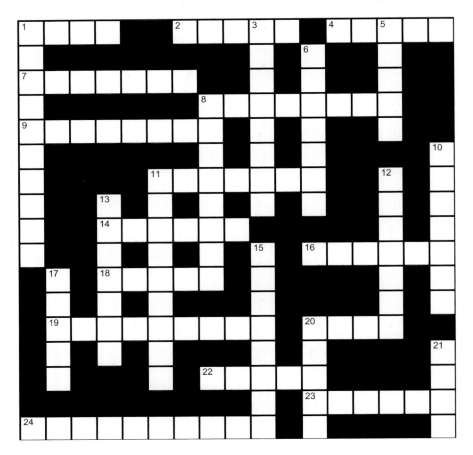

Across

1. a system of signals or symbols that have meaning
2. based on sensible reasoning; acceptable
4. to bring different things or parts together to form one thing
7. produced by natural processes, or found in living things
8. can be trusted to work well, or behave as you want it/them to
9. easy to harm or damage, needs to be handled carefully
11. completely clean and free from germs
14. involving the use of hands or physical strength
16. If you _____ something that you want or need, you obtain it.
18. a particular characteristic or quality that someone or something has
19. having many small parts or details
20. If something is _____, it may seem to be real, but is not.
22. an early version of a piece of writing, such as a letter, book, or speech
23. If you _____ work or a position to someone, you give it to them.
24. to accept something different from what you really want because of circumstances

Down

1. to organize activities or groups so that they are efficient
3. expressed in an indirect way
5. A(n) _____ is an alphabetical list of words at the back of a book.
6. a period of history; a section of a book
8. important or significant to a particular situation or person
10. a school, especially one that specializes in a particular subject
11. physical feeling
12. a sudden desire to do something; a short electrical signal
13. to copy what someone does or how they behave
15. to accept a person or situation, although you do not like them
17. to place something in a certain position in relation to something else
20. A(n) _____ action is one that causes death, or very undesirable effects.
21. to state that something is not true

UNIT 10
Chemistry of Life

WARM UP

Discuss these questions with a partner.

1. What kinds of health problems can be caused or made worse by environmental factors?

2. Do you think you live in a healthy environment? Why or why not?

3. How much sleep do you get each day? What factors can make it difficult to sleep?

A computer-enhanced model reveals a ▶ close-up view of one of the 100 billion nerve cells (neurons) inside the human brain.

10A

Hidden Hazards

At a school in Shchuchye, Russia, second grade students learn how to prepare for a chemical attack. Today, concerns about hazardous chemicals are not limited to acts of terrorism; other kinds of poisonous chemicals may be hidden in some of the most commonplace of items.

☐ Before You Read

A. Matching. The following words appear in the passage on pages 183–186. Use the words to complete the definitions (**1–7**).

compound	concentration	dose	exposure	pesticides	pollutants	toxic

1. In chemistry, a(n) _____ is a substance that consists of two or more elements.
2. If something is _____, it is poisonous.
3. _____ are chemicals that farmers put on their crops to kill insects.
4. _____ is the measure of how much of a given substance is mixed with another substance.
5. A(n) _____ of medicine or a drug is the measured amount taken at one time.
6. Examples of _____ are gases from vehicles and poisonous chemicals produced as waste by industrial processes.
7. _____ to something dangerous, such as a poison, means being in a situation where it might affect you.

B. Skim and Predict. Read the first few paragraphs of the article on page 183. What "experiment" is the author taking part in? What does he want to find out? Note your ideas below, then read the rest of the passage to check your ideas.

The Pollution Within

Modern chemistry makes life more convenient and helps save lives. But at what price? Writer David Ewing Duncan begins a journey of chemical self-discovery.

▲ An X-ray shows chips of lead paint present in the body of a child. Chemicals such as lead, if allowed to build up inside the body, can severely affect human health.

1　MY EXPERIMENT IS TAKING a disturbing turn. A Swedish chemist is on the phone, talking about flame retardants, chemicals added for safety to just about any product that can burn. Found in
5　carpets, electronic circuit boards, and automobiles, flame retardants save hundreds of lives a year in the United States alone. These, however, are where they should not be: inside my body.

Åke Bergman of Stockholm University tells me he
10　has received the results of a chemical analysis of my blood, which measured levels of flame-retarding compounds called polybrominated diphenyl ethers (PBDEs). In mice and rats, high doses of PBDEs interfere with thyroid[1] function, cause reproductive
15　problems, and slow neurological[2] development. Little is known about their impact on human health.

"I hope you are not nervous, but this concentration is very high," Bergman says with
20　a light Swedish accent. My blood level of one particularly toxic PBDE, found primarily in U.S.-made products, is 10 times the average found in a study of U.S. residents, and more than 200 times the average in Sweden. The news about another
25　PBDE variant is nearly as bad. My levels would be high even if I were a worker in a factory making the stuff, Bergman says.

In fact I'm a writer participating in a journey of chemical self-discovery. Last fall I had myself tested
30　for 320 chemicals I might have picked up from food, drink, the air I breathe, and the products that touch my skin—the secret compounds I have acquired by merely living. It includes older chemicals that I might have been exposed to
35　decades ago, such as DDT and PCBs. It also includes pollutants like lead, mercury, and dioxins; newer pesticides and plastic ingredients; plus other compounds that hide beneath the surface of modern life, making shampoos fragrant,[3] pans
40　nonstick, and fabrics water-resistant and fire-safe.

[1] The **thyroid** is a large gland in the neck that produces hormones that regulate growth and metabolism.
[2] If something, usually a medical condition or disorder, is **neurological**, it involves the nerves or the nervous system.
[3] Something that is **fragrant** has a pleasant or sweet smell.

◄ Author David Ewing Duncan cooks breakfast at home, exposed to the potentially dangerous chemicals found in plastic containers, pans, and other everyday household items.

The fee for the tests is expensive, and only a few labs have the technical expertise to detect the amounts involved. I submitted myself for them to learn what substances build up in a typical person over a lifetime, and where they might come from. Prior to the tests, I had little knowledge of what was lurking inside my body. Now I'm learning more than I really want to know.

FIRST, BERGMAN WANTS TO solve my flame-retardant mystery. Have I recently bought new furniture or rugs? No. Do I spend a lot of time around computer monitors? No, I use a titanium laptop. Do I live near a factory making flame retardants? Nope, the closest one is over a thousand miles (1,600 kilometers) away. Then I come up with an idea.

"What about airplanes?" I ask.

"Yah," he says, "do you fly a lot?"

"I flew almost 200,000 miles (300,000 kilometers) last year," I say. In fact, as I spoke to Bergman, I was sitting in an airport waiting for a flight from my hometown of San Francisco to London.

"Interesting," Bergman says. He tells me that he has long been curious about PBDE exposure inside airplanes, whose plastic and fabric interiors include flame retardants to meet safety regulations.

"I have been wanting to apply for a grant to test pilots and flight attendants for PBDEs," Bergman says. But for now the airplane connection is only a hypothesis. Where I picked up this chemical remains a mystery. And there's the bigger question: How worried should I be?

The same can be asked of other chemicals I've absorbed from air, water, the nonstick pan I used to scramble my eggs this morning, my faintly scented shampoo, my cell phone. I'm healthy, and as far as I know have no symptoms associated with chemical exposure. In large doses,[4] some of these substances can have horrific effects. But many toxicologists[5] insist that the minimal amounts of chemicals inside us are, on the whole, nothing to worry about.

"In toxicology, dose is everything," says Karl Rozman, a toxicologist at the University of Kansas Medical Center, "and these doses are too low to be dangerous." A standard unit for measuring most chemicals inside us is a ratio of one part per billion (ppb)—an amount so small it's like putting half a teaspoon (two milliliters) of dye into an Olympic-size swimming pool. Moreover, some of the most feared substances, such as mercury, normally dissipate[6] within days or weeks unless the individual is constantly re-exposed.

[4] A **dose** is a quantity of something, e.g., medicine, taken at one time.
[5] **Toxicologists** study the effects of poisons and the treatment of poisoning.
[6] When things **dissipate**, they disperse, scatter, and break up.

EVEN THOUGH MANY health statistics have improved over the past few decades, a few illnesses are rising mysteriously. From the early 1980s through the late 1990s, autism[7] increased tenfold; from the early 1970s through the mid-1990s, one type of leukemia[8] was up 62 percent, male birth defects doubled, and childhood brain cancer was up 40 percent. Some experts, albeit with little firm evidence, suspect there is a link to the man-made chemicals in our food, water, and air. Over the years, several chemicals that were thought to be harmless turned out to be otherwise once the facts were in.

The classic example is lead. In 1971 the U.S. Surgeon General declared that lead levels of 40 micrograms per deciliter[9] of blood were safe. It's now known that any detectable lead can cause neurological damage in children. From DDT to PCBs, the chemical industry has released compounds first and discovered damaging health effects later. Regulators have often allowed a standard of innocent until proven guilty. Leo Trasande, a pediatrician[10] and environmental health specialist at Mount Sinai Hospital in New York City, calls it "an uncontrolled experiment on America's children."

Each year the U.S. Environmental Protection Agency (EPA) reviews an average of 1,700 new compounds that industry is seeking to introduce. Yet the 1976 Toxic Substances Control Act legally requires that they be tested before approval only if there is evidence of potential harm—which is seldom the case for new chemicals. The agency approves about 90 percent of the new compounds without any restrictions. Only a quarter of the 82,000 chemicals in use in the U.S. have ever been tested for toxicity.

Studies by an environmental organization known as the Environmental Working Group found hundreds of chemical traces in the bodies of volunteers. Until recently, no one had measured average levels of exposure among large numbers of Americans. No regulations required it, the tests are expensive, and technology sensitive enough to measure the tiniest levels didn't exist.

SO WHY TAKE A CHANCE on these chemicals? Why not immediately ban them? In 2004, Europe did just that for penta- and octa-BDEs, which animal tests suggest are the most toxic of the compounds. California will also ban these forms by 2008, and in 2004 Chemtura, an Indiana company that is

▲ At the University of Texas, scientists test the "near-head environment" using common soaps and fragrances, to find that even natural fragrances can potentially mix with ozone in the air to form toxins.

the only U.S. maker of pentas and octas, agreed to phase them out. Currently, there are no plans to prohibit the much more prevalent deca-BDEs. They reportedly break down more quickly in the environment and in people, although their breakdown products may include toxic pentas and octas.

Nor is it clear that banning a suspect chemical is always the best option. The University of Surrey in England recently assessed the risks and benefits of flame retardants in consumer products. In its summary, the report concluded that the "benefits of many flame retardants in reducing the risk from fire outweigh the risks to human health."

[7] **Autism** spectrum disorder (ASD) is a range of complex neurodevelopmental disorders, characterized by social difficulties, communication problems, and repetitive patterns of behavior.
[8] **Leukemia** is a cancer of the blood or bone marrow.
[9] A **deciliter** is a metric unit of volume equal to one-tenth of a liter.
[10] A **pediatrician** is a doctor who specializes in treating children.

◄ At six months old, the amount of lead in Christine Larson's blood was over twice the level the government says is safe. The house where she lived had lead paint, illegal for residential use since 1978.

Except for some pollutants, every industrial chemical was created for a purpose. Even DDT, the chemical whose toxic effects helped launched
165 the modern environmental movement, was once seen as a miracle substance. It saved countless lives because it was able to kill the mosquitoes that carry malaria, yellow fever, and other diseases. Eventually it was banned in much of the world because of its
170 danger to wildlife. "Chemicals are not all bad," says Scott Phillips, a medical toxicologist in Denver. "While we have seen some cancer rates rise," he says, "we also have seen a doubling of the human life span in the past century."

175 The key is knowing more about these substances, so we are not blindsided[11] by unexpected hazards, says California State Senator Deborah Ortiz, chair of the Senate Health Committee and the author of a bill[12] to monitor chemical exposure. "We benefit
180 from these chemicals, but there are consequences, and we need to understand these consequences much better than we do now."

The European Union last year gave initial approval to a measure called REACH—Registration,
185 Evaluation, and Authorization of Chemicals— which would require companies to prove the substances they market or use are safe, or that the perceived benefits outweigh any risks. The bill, which the chemical industry and the U.S.
190 government oppose, would also encourage companies to find safer alternatives to suspect flame retardants, pesticides, solvents,[13] and other chemicals. That would give a boost to the so-called green chemistry movement, a search for
195 alternatives that is already under way in laboratories on both sides of the Atlantic.

As disturbing as my journey of chemical self-discovery was, it left out thousands of compounds, among them pesticides, plastics, and solvents. Nor
200 was I tested for chemical cocktails—mixtures of chemicals that may do little harm on their own but act together to damage human cells. Mixed together, pesticides, PCBs, phthalates, and others "might have additive effects, or they might be
205 antagonistic," says James Pirkle of the CDC, "or they may do nothing. We don't know."

Soon after I receive my results, I show them to my internist,[14] who admits that he too knows little about these chemicals, other than lead and
210 mercury. But he confirms that I am a healthy adult, as far as he can tell. He tells me not to worry. So I'll keep flying, and scrambling my eggs on Teflon, and using my scented shampoo. But I'll never feel quite the same about the chemicals that make life
215 better in so many ways.

[11] When someone is **blindsided**, they are surprised by something, usually with harmful consequences.
[12] A **bill** is a draft of a proposed law presented for approval to a legislative body, as well as the law that results from the draft.
[13] **Pesticides** are any substances or mixtures of substances intended for preventing, destroying, or repelling any pest. **Solvents** are substances, usually liquids, that are capable of dissolving another substance.
[14] An **internist** is a doctor of internal medicine, a branch of medicine that deals with the prevention, diagnosis, and treatment of adult diseases.

Reading Comprehension

A. Multiple Choice. Choose the best answer for each question.

Purpose **1.** What is the author's main purpose in writing this article?
   a. to discuss the research done by a Swedish scientist on the health dangers of flame retardants
   b. to report on an experiment he conducted on himself regarding common toxic chemicals
   c. to contrast U.S. government policies regarding chemical pollutants with European government policies
   d. to argue that dangerous chemicals such as flame retardants should be immediately banned

Paraphrase **2.** Which of the following is closest in meaning to this extract from lines 24–27?
   The news about another PBDE variant is nearly as bad. My levels would be high even if I were a worker in a factory making the stuff.
   a. The author's levels of PBDE were bad, but would be more serious if he were directly involved in its manufacture.
   b. The levels of PBDE in the author's body may be even higher than those found in PBDE factory workers.
   c. The author's PBDE levels were not as bad as he feared, and he is relieved he is not exposed to it in his work.
   d. The author suspects his high levels of PBDE may be due to work he once performed in a chemical factory.

Inference **3.** Bergman suspects that the author's PBDE levels are probably due to _____.
   a. flame retardants used on new furniture and rugs
   b. exposure to radiation from computer monitors
   c. pollution from a factory that manufactures PBDEs
   d. flame retardants used inside airplanes

Rhetorical Purpose **4.** The author provides the statistics in the paragraph starting on line 123 mainly to show that _____.
   a. an enormous number of new chemicals are introduced each year
   b. the products of the U.S. chemical industry are largely untested
   c. more and more chemicals are tested for toxicity every year
   d. chemicals in the environment are becoming increasingly toxic

Reference **5.** The word *its* in line 158 refers to _____.
   a. the flame retardant   c. a suspect chemical
   b. the best option   d. the university's report

Cohesion **6.** Where would be the best place to insert this sentence in the paragraph starting on line 155?
   After all, flaming beds and airplane seats are not an inviting prospect either.
   a. before the first sentence   c. after the second sentence
   b. after the first sentence   d. after the third sentence

Negative Detail **7.** Which of the following is NOT true about DDT?
   a. It has saved many lives.   c. It can help stop the spread of some diseases.
   b. It is dangerous to animals.   d. Its use is supported by environmentalists.

Inference/Tone **8.** Which of the following best describes the author's attitude in the final paragraph?
   a. entirely reassured   c. extremely worried
   b. somewhat uneasy   d. completely unaffected

B. Scanning/Classification. Read each statement and locate the section in the passage that it relates to. According to the information in the passage, is each statement really a fact or a theory? Check (✓) **fact** or **theory**. Underline any signal words or phrases in the passage that help you decide.

	fact	theory
1. In laboratory animals, large doses of PBDEs can cause health problems.	☐	☐
2. PBDEs also cause severe health problems in humans.	☐	☐
3. The level of PBDEs in the author's blood was much higher than the level typically found in Swedish people.	☐	☐
4. The flame retardants used in airplanes caused the high levels of PBDEs in the author's blood.	☐	☐
5. Some of the most dangerous chemicals, such as mercury, disappear from a person's body unless that person encounters the chemical again and again.	☐	☐
6. There is a link between dangerous chemicals and the rising incidence of autism, childhood brain cancer, and birth defects in male babies.	☐	☐
7. Any measurable amount of lead in a child's blood can cause damage to the child's nervous system.	☐	☐
8. Only 25 percent of the chemicals now in use in the United States have been tested to see if they are dangerous.	☐	☐
9. When certain chemicals such as pesticides and PCBs mix inside the human body, they become stronger or they interact in a negative way.	☐	☐

C. Critical Thinking. Discuss these questions with a partner.

1. Consider these two statements:
   a. Chemicals such as PBDEs and pesticides are dangerous to human health and should be banned.
   b. Chemicals that provide useful functions should be permitted.

   Find information in the article that supports each of these two points of view. Do you think the author provides enough information to completely support either one of these two positions?

2. If the tests that the author took were inexpensive and easy to get, would you have these tests done? Why or why not?

3. Imagine that a chemical factory is operating in your hometown. It provides good jobs for hundreds of citizens. However, scientists say that there is at least a 10 percent chance that the chemicals the factory produces may cause some health problems. Would you vote to close this factory? What would your decision depend on?

Vocabulary Practice

A. Completion. Complete the information using the correct form of the words in the box. Two words are extra.

albeit	approval	evaluate
grant	interfere	participate
phase out	ratio	statistics
technical		

When people think of the Arctic, they probably imagine a pure and beautiful—**1.** _____ harsh—environment. So it is an unwelcome surprise, perhaps, that the region's native animals and people are among the most chemically contaminated on Earth.

Recently, various studies were conducted to **2.** _____ the levels of toxic chemicals in the bodies of Arctic animals, as well as in the native Inuit people. The **3.** _____ are alarming. Both the animals, and the Inuit who **4.** _____ in the studies showed unusually high levels of man-made toxins.

▲ Arctic animals like polar bears have layers of fatty tissue to keep them warm. Toxins that break down slowly can collect in these tissues over several years.

These included older pollutants like dioxins and PCBs which many governments have been trying to **5.** _____ since the 1970s. Such chemicals are known to **6.** _____ with our hormones and damage the immune system. The studies also found newer compounds—ones that currently have widespread **7.** _____ for use in flame retardants—building up in the Inuits' bodies at a **8.** _____ of five to one compared to levels found in other Canadians.

Experts say the reason is diet. Whale skin and other contaminated animal fats are important foods in Inuit communities. Scientists are still researching how these animals came to be contaminated. There is now great concern that over time such chemicals will have a serious impact on the health of Inuit people.

B. Definitions. Match words from the box in **A** with the correct definition.

1. take part in something _____

2. official acceptance _____

3. involving machines, processes, and materials _____

4. an amount of money given for a specific purpose, such as research _____

5. comparison between two things, expressed in numbers _____

6. consider something in order to make a judgment about it _____

7. gradually stop using something _____

8. even though _____

9. facts obtained from analyzing information expressed in numbers _____

10. have a damaging effect on a process or activity _____

Usage

Albeit is used to introduce a fact or comment that reduces the force or significance of what has just been said, e.g., *My friend appeared on the talk-show, albeit briefly.*

10B Sleep Science

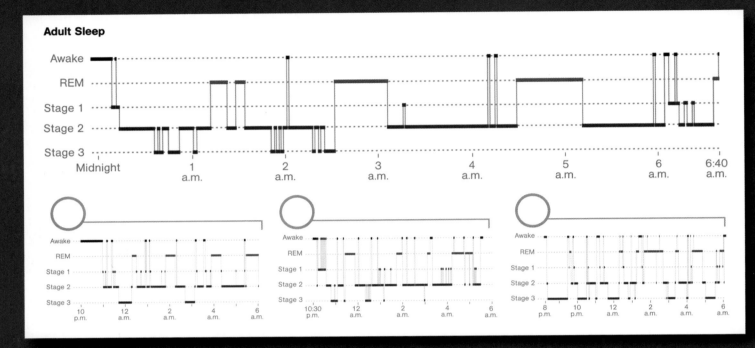

Adult Sleep

▲ Sleep is no longer thought of as merely the time we spend unconscious. It is a dynamic state characterized by shifting levels of electrical activity and the movement of chemicals between various regions of the brain. At night we cycle several times through ever deeper phases of sleep. During **stage 1** (light sleep) we move in and out of wakefulness. Brain waves slow in **stage 2**, with occasional bursts of rapid waves. **Stage 3** is deep sleep, with extremely slow brain waves. During more active periods of **REM** (rapid eye movement) sleep, heart rate, and breathing speed up and most dreams occur.

☐ Before You Read

A. Understanding Charts. Read the information above and the three captions below. Match each caption (**1–3**) with the chart it describes.

1. Electrical brain activity in a **3-year-old girl** reveals a sudden descent at bedtime into deep stage 3 sleep.

2. Brain activity of a **14-year-old girl** shows the difficulty many teenagers have of falling asleep in late evening, and of waking up early morning.

3. Brain activity of an **89-year-old female** shows frequent short awakenings during the night, and less time spent in the deep sleep of stage 3.

B. Skim and Predict. Look quickly through the information on page 191. What issues or problems is the writer investigating in this article? Note them below. Then read through the rest of the article to check your ideas.

The Secrets of Sleep

From birth, we spend a third of our lives asleep.
After decades of research, we're still not sure why.
Writer D.T. Max investigates the secret world of sleep.

▲ An office worker takes a lunch-hour nap in New York's Central Park.

1   IF WE DON'T KNOW why we can't sleep, it's in part
because we don't really know why we need to sleep
in the first place. We know we miss it if we don't
have it. And we know that no matter how much we
5   try to resist it, sleep conquers us in the end.

We know that seven to nine hours after we give
in to sleep, most of us are ready to get up again;
15 to 17 hours after that we are tired once more.
We have known for 50 years that we divide our
10   slumber between periods of deep-wave sleep and
what is called rapid eye movement (REM) sleep,
when the brain is as active as when we're awake,
but our voluntary muscles are paralyzed. We know
that all mammals and birds sleep. Fish, reptiles, and
15   insects all experience some kind of repose too.

We know all this—but still the most basic question
remains: Why? William Dement, a co-discoverer of
REM sleep and co-founder of the Stanford Sleep
Medicine Center, knows more than most about the
20   inner workings of sleep. "As far as I know," he says,
"the only reason we need to sleep that is really,
really solid is because we get sleepy."

Unfortunately, the reverse is not always true; we
don't always get sleepy when we need to sleep.
25   Insomnia is at epidemic levels in the developed
world. Fifty to 75 million Americans, roughly a
fifth of the population, complain about problems
sleeping. Fifty-six million prescriptions for sleeping
pills were written in 2008, up 54 percent over the
30   previous four years.

The social and economic costs from the
undertreatment of sleeplessness are huge. The
Institute of Medicine, an independent national
scientific advisory group, estimates nearly 20
35   percent of all serious motor vehicle accidents are
associated with driver sleepiness. It places the direct
medical cost of our collective sleep debt[1] at tens
of billions of dollars. The losses in terms of work
productivity are even higher. Then there are the
40   softer costs—the damaged or lost relationships, the
muting of enjoyment in life's pleasures.

[1] **Sleep debt** is the cumulative effect of not getting enough sleep.

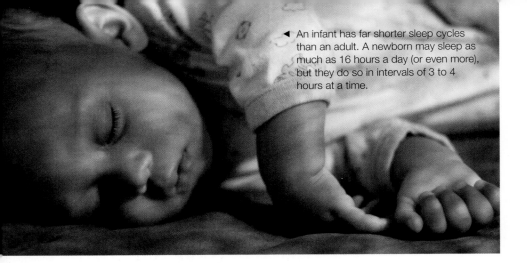

An infant has far shorter sleep cycles than an adult. A newborn may sleep as much as 16 hours a day (or even more), but they do so in intervals of 3 to 4 hours at a time.

THE SLEEP MEDICINE CENTER at Stanford, founded in 1970, was the first U.S. institute devoted to the problem of insomnia, and it remains among the most important. The sleep center sees over 10,000 patients a year and does more than 3,000 overnight quantitative and qualitative studies, in which researchers use techniques such as video taping and polygraph[2] analysis to observe participants while they are asleep.

The main diagnostic[3] tool at the clinic is the polysomnogram, which captures the electrical output from a sleeping patient's brain. As you fall asleep, your brain slows down, and its electrical signature changes from short, jagged waves to longer, rolling ones. In the brain, these gentle changes are interrupted periodically by a renewal of the sudden agitated[4] mental activity of REM sleep. For unknown reasons, REM is the time during sleep when we do nearly all our dreaming.

The polysomnogram data also records body temperature, muscle activity, eye movement, heart rhythms, and breathing. The researchers look over the input for signs that deviate from normal sleep, such as frequent wake-ups. When a person has narcolepsy, for instance, he or she goes from wakefulness into REM sleep without any intermediate steps.

Clete Kushida, the clinic director, can discriminate between her patients' different sleep problems even at the intake interview stage: There are those who cannot keep their eyes open, and those who just speak of their exhaustion but don't actually fall asleep. The former often have sleep apnea. The latter have the attributes of what Kushida calls "true insomnia."

In obstructive sleep apnea sufferers, the muscle relaxation that comes with sleep causes the soft tissue of the throat and esophagus[5] to close, shutting off the sleeper's air passage. When the brain realizes it is not getting oxygen, it sends an emergency signal to the body to wake up. The sleeper awakes, takes a breath, the brain is replenished,[6] and sleep returns. A night's sleep for an apnea sufferer is really just a hundred micro-naps.

Apnea is a serious problem, implicated in increased risk for heart attacks and stroke.[7] But it is only indirectly a sleep disease. True insomniacs—people diagnosed with what some sleep doctors call psychophysiological insomnia—are people who either can't get to sleep or can't stay asleep for no evident reason. They wake up and don't feel rested. They lie down and their brains remain active. This group makes up about 25 percent of those seen in sleep clinics, according to John Winkelman, medical director of a sleep health center in Massachusetts.

While apnea can be treated with a device that forces air down the sleeper's throat to keep the airways open, the treatment of classic insomnia is not so clear-cut.[8] First come sleeping pills. Though safer than they once were, sleeping pills can lead to psychological addiction. Many users complain that their sleeping-pill sleep seems different, and they feel hungover[9] when they wake up.

[2] A **polygraph** is an instrument that measures and records several physiological signs such as blood pressure and respiration.
[3] If a test is **diagnostic**, it is used for the identification of something, usually an illness or problem.
[4] If something is **agitated**, it is excited or disturbed.
[5] The **esophagus** is the muscular tube through which food passes from the pharynx (the throat) to the stomach.
[6] When something is **replenished**, it is made full or complete again by supplying what has been used up.
[7] A **stroke** occurs when blood supply to part of the brain is disrupted.
[8] Something that is **clear-cut** is clear and certain.
[9] If someone is feeling **hungover**, they are experiencing the aftereffects of drinking too much alcohol, usually consisting of headache and sometimes nausea.

The second step in treating true insomniacs is usually cognitive behavioral therapy (CBT). In CBT, a specialized psychologist teaches the insomniac to think about his or her sleep problems as manageable—that's the cognitive part—and to practice good "sleep hygiene." Good sleep hygiene mostly consists of common sense advice: sleep in a dark room, go to bed only when you are sleepy, don't exercise before bed. Studies have shown that CBT is more effective than sleeping pills at treating long-term insomnia.

John Winkelman thinks CBT is more appropriate for helping some kinds of insomniacs than others. Insomnia covers a multitude of conditions. Some insomniacs suffer from restless legs syndrome (RLS), an intense discomfort in their limbs that prevents falling asleep, or periodic limb movement disorder (PLMD), which produces involuntary kicking during sleep. Narcoleptics often have difficulty both staying asleep and staying awake. Then there are people who can't sleep because of depression, and people who are depressed because they can't sleep. Age and gender are also factors: older people in general sleep less well than young, and an individual's sex may also play a role (women are twice as likely to have insomnia as men). Of all these non-sleepers, patients with insomnia derived from physical internal causes—probably excesses or scarcities of various neurotransmitters—are usually least able to respond to CBT treatment. For most other conditions, CBT is a potential cure.

IF WE'RE NOT ABLE TO SLEEP, perhaps it's also because we've forgotten how to. In premodern times people slept differently, going to bed at sunset and rising with the dawn. In winter months, with so long to rest, our ancestors may have broken sleep up into chunks. In developing countries people still often sleep this way. They bed down in groups and get up from time to time during the night. Some sleep outside, where it is cooler and the effect of sunlight on our circadian rhythm[10] is more direct.

The publication in 2002 of a survey conducted by Carol Worthman and Melissa Melby of Emory University revealed how people sleep in a variety of cultures. They found that among foraging groups,

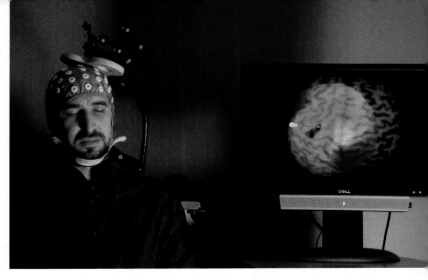

▲ Scientists at the University of Wisconsin discovered how to stimulate brain waves that characterize the deepest stage of sleep by sending magnetic signals into the brain.

"the boundaries of sleep and waking are very fluid." There is no fixed bedtime, and no one tells anyone else to go to sleep.

No one in developed nations sleeps this way today, at least not on purpose. We go to bed near a fixed time, and sleep on soft cushions covered with sheets and blankets. We sleep on average about an hour and a half less a night than we did just a century ago. We also refuse to pay attention to our biology. The natural sleep rhythms of teenagers call for a late-morning wake-up—but most teens start high school at 8 a.m. The night shift worker who sleeps in the morning is fighting ancient body rhythms that require him or her awake to hunt or forage during daylight hours.

▲ Scientists study the effect of sleep deprivation on driving using a simulator. According to the United States National Highway Traffic Safety Administration, drowsy driving is a factor in more than 100,000 crashes nationwide, resulting in 1,550 deaths and 40,000 injuries annually.

[10] **Circadian rhythms** are physical, mental, and behavioral changes that follow a roughly 24-hour cycle, responding primarily to light and darkness in the environment.

In many cultures, particularly in warm climates, it is traditional to take a siesta, or afternoon nap. However, as the pace of life around the globe quickens, opportunities for rest are becoming increasingly scarce.

We ignore these natural cycles at our peril.[11] In February 2009 a U.S. jet on a domestic flight from Newark to Buffalo crashed, killing all 49 aboard and one on the ground. The copilot, and
180 probably the pilot, had only sporadic[12] amounts of sleep the day leading up to the crash. This sort of news enrages Harvard's Charles Czeisler. He notes that going without sleep for 24 hours or getting only five hours of sleep a night for a week is the
185 equivalent of a blood alcohol level of 0.1 percent. Yet modern business ethic celebrates such feats. As Czeisler says, "We would never say, 'This person is a great worker! He's drunk all the time!'"

Starting in 2004, Czeisler published a series of
190 reports in medical journals based on a study of 2,700 first-year medical residents. The participants were young men and women who worked shifts as long as 30 hours twice a week. Czeisler's research revealed the remarkable public health risk caused
195 by this sleep debt.

"We know that one out of five first-year residents admits to making a fatigue[13]-related mistake that resulted in injury to a patient," he told me in the spring of 2009. "One in 20 admits to making a
200 fatigue-related mistake that resulted in the death of a patient." He is doubtful anything much will change until U.S. employers get serious about insomnia and sleepiness.

IN 2008 I ATTENDED A MEETING of a Spanish
205 government commission that was investigating the impact of sleep deprivation on productivity. Spain is famous for its siesta, yet the government has become increasingly concerned about the amount of sleep Spanish
210 people are getting. The speakers at the meeting spoke of accidents by tired workers, women exhausted by long work hours and household duties, and small children deprived
215 of their proper ten to twelve hours of sleep.

The organizers attempted to keep the speeches short and the meeting moving. But the lights were low and the room warm. In the audience a few
220 participants' heads began to fall to their chests, then pop back up as they resisted, then their eyes closed more fully, their conference programs lowering to their laps, as they began to pay back their nation's sleep debt.

▲ Travelers take the opportunity for a nap at a bus terminal in New York City, 1949.

[11] If we do something **at our peril**, we do it despite knowing that there is a risk we could get hurt, sick, or in trouble.
[12] If something is **sporadic**, it happens only at irregular intervals, once in a while.
[13] **Fatigue** is another word for tiredness.

Reading Comprehension

A. Multiple Choice. Choose the best answer for each question.

Gist
1. Most of this article deals with _____.
   a. promising new treatments for sleep problems
   b. sleep disorders and their treatment
   c. the social problems caused by insomnia
   d. the sleeping habits of early humans

Detail
2. According to the information in paragraph 4 (from line 23), what percentage of people in the United States suffer from sleep problems?
   a. 5 percent   b. 20 percent   c. 50 percent   d. 75 percent

Vocabulary/Inference
3. When the author mentions "softer costs" in line 40, he probably means costs that are _____.
   a. less serious   c. harder to measure
   b. more obvious   d. easier to explain

Detail
4. What does the author say about REM sleep?
   a. People usually move from wakefulness directly into REM sleep.
   b. REM sleep appears on polysomnogram read-outs as long, rolling lines.
   c. Most, but not all, dreaming occurs during REM sleep.
   d. REM sleep is frequently interrupted by wake-ups.

Detail
5. Which of the following is a true statement about "true insomnia" but not sleep apnea?
   a. Its symptoms have no obvious cause.
   b. It causes the sleeper's oxygen supply to be cut off.
   c. It often leads to health problems such as heart attacks.
   d. It causes the sleeper to constantly wake up and go back to sleep.

Negative Detail
6. Which of the following would be LEAST likely to respond to cognitive behavioral therapy (CBT)?
   a. people with restless leg syndrome (RLS)
   b. people with periodic limb movement disorder (PLMD)
   c. people with imbalances of certain neurotransmitters
   d. people suffering from narcolepsy

Inference
7. From the information in paragraph 17 (from line 164), it can be inferred that the author believes that _____.
   a. people would sleep better if they kept to a fixed bedtime
   b. high school students should start school at a later time
   c. night-shift workers require more sleep than day-shift workers
   d. people generally sleep more naturally today than 100 years ago

Rhetorical Purpose
8. Charles Czeisler shows the dangers of not getting enough sleep by _____.
   a. showing how insomnia can change the chemistry of the blood
   b. pointing out that the pilot of the commuter jet had fallen asleep
   c. indicating that businesses today are trying to solve this problem
   d. comparing the effects of sleeplessness with those of drinking alcohol

Strategy Focus: Understanding Subordinate Clauses

Authors often use connecting words or phrases to join short, simple sentences into more complex sentences. One way to do this is to use subordinate conjunctions.

I couldn't fall asleep. I was nervous. → *I couldn't fall asleep **because** I was nervous.*

The first part of the sentence (*I couldn't fall asleep*) is the main clause; the second part (*because I was nervous*) is called a subordinate clause. The word *because* is a subordinate conjunction. Subordinate clauses can come before the main clause or after it:

Because I was nervous, I couldn't fall asleep.

Use	Subordinate conjunction	Examples
Cause	because, since, as	*Because I was nervous, I couldn't fall asleep.* *Since I didn't sleep well last night, I took a nap this afternoon.*
Condition	if	*If I had a firmer mattress, I would sleep better.*
Time	when, as, while, until, before, after, once	*While Marie was sleeping, I was doing my homework.* *I never wake up until my alarm goes off.*
Concession/contrast	although, though, even though, while	*Although I was tired, I couldn't get to sleep.*

B. Comparing sentences. Look at the sentences below. Does the first sentence (which contains a subordinate clause and is taken from the article) have the same meaning as the second sentence, or a different meaning? Circle S (Same) or D (Different).

S D **1.** a. Seven to nine hours after we give in to sleep, most of us are ready to get up again.
 b. Once we sleep for seven to nine hours, most of us are ready to wake up.

S D **2.** a. As you fall asleep, your brain slows down, and its electrical signature changes from short, jagged waves to longer, rolling ones.
 b. The brain's electrical signals change their wavelength during the period when you are falling asleep.

S D **3.** a. When the brain realizes it is not getting oxygen, it sends an emergency signal to the body to wake up.
 b. The brain knows it is suffering from lack of oxygen as soon as an electrical signal causes the body to wake up.

S D **4.** a. Then there are people who can't sleep because they are depressed, and people who are depressed because they can't sleep.
 b. Some people are depressed and therefore can't sleep; some people can't sleep and so they are depressed.

S D **5.** a. If we're not able to sleep, perhaps it's also because we've forgotten how to.
 b. Not being able to sleep can cause us to become forgetful.

S D **6.** a. He is doubtful anything much will change until U.S. employers get serious about insomnia and sleepiness.
 b. He doubts there will be major changes unless U.S. employers take insomnia and sleepiness seriously.

C. Critical Thinking. Discuss these questions with a partner.

1. The author says, "The social and economic costs from the undertreatment of sleeplessness are huge." Explain in your own words what some of those costs are. Can you think of any other costs of sleeplessness besides the ones that the author gives?

2. The author compares the way people in the past slept with the way people today sleep. Explain in your own words how these are different.

3. The author suggests that people in different cultures take different approaches to going to sleep. How do people in your own culture try to get to sleep if they have problems sleeping?

Vocabulary Practice

A. Definitions. Read the information below and match each word in red with its definition.

High ▬▬▬ ▬▬▬▬ Low

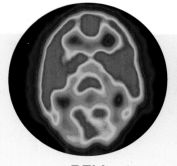 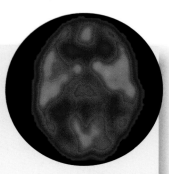

REM   Non-REM

▲ A brain experiencing REM sleep shows activity similar to that during waking hours.

Much has been written in research publications about the sleep stage known as REM, which is crucial for complex thinking, making connections, and discriminating between points of view. During REM sleep, the brain deviates from common expectations and comes up with creative solutions.

However, scientists are now discovering the benefits of Stage 2 non-REM sleep. In a recent study, young adults of both sexes were asked to perform certain learning tasks. One group was then asked to take a 90-minute nap. The other group stayed awake. Afterward, both groups were given more tasks, which revealed the output of the non-nappers' minds to be much lower than that of the nappers'. Measuring the electrical activity of the nappers' brains revealed that their brains "cleared" during stage 2 non-REM sleep, preparing them to learn more.

Now scientists may have figured out how this happens. During stage 2 non-REM sleep, information locked in short-term storage migrates into the longer-term database in the brain. This action not only helps the brain process new information, it also clears out space in the brain for us to input new experiences.

Unfortunately, naps are not for everyone. Some nappers tend to wake from this intermediate sleep stage feeling tired and confused. In some cases, however, it is possible to get similar memory benefits simply by taking a short mental rest.

1. related to the process of thinking _____
2. something that is produced _____
3. does something different from the norm _____
4. between beginning and advanced _____
5. recognizing differences _____
6. books or journals _____
7. two groups, male and female _____
8. to enter into a database or storage system _____

Word Link

The root *ment* has the meaning of *mind*:
e.g., de**ment**ed, **ment**al, **ment**ality, **ment**ally

B. Words in Context. Read the information below and circle the most appropriate word in each pair.

One of the main tools for diagnosing sleep disorders is the polysomnogram. Firstly, for
1. ethical / mental reasons, participants must officially agree to be studied while they are sleeping.
A machine then records the electrical 2. output / input from the brain of a sleeping patient, including
the increased 3. intermediate / mental activity characteristic of REM sleep. Then technicians check
the 4. published / taped data for any signs of 5. deviation / discrimination from normal sleep, and doctors
provide follow-up treatment which allows them to 6. discriminate / input between various sleep problems.

Sigmund Freud

A. Preview. Match the words in blue to the definitions.

According to Freud's theories of psychoanalysis, a patient is able to gain a deeper understanding of their own unconscious thoughts and drives, as a result of therapy.

1. an approach to psychology and patient treatment invented by Freud which concentrates on bringing forward supressed thoughts and feelings

_____

2. a part of the human mind where we keep thoughts that we are not aware of, and that we don't want _____

3. the treatment of physical, mental, or social disorders or disease

_____

4. motives or interests, such as hunger _____

▲ Sigmund Freud (1856–1939) had a major influence on the science of psychology.

B. Summarize. Watch the video, *Sigmund Freud*. Then complete the summary below using the correct form of words in the box. Two words are extra.

approve	deviate	evaluate	grant	intermediate
mental	publication	statistics	suppress	thesis

Sigmund Freud is often considered the founder of the science of psychology. He began studying neurology after receiving his medical degree in 1881 in Vienna. But Freud's interests quickly **1.** _____ from the technical workings of the human brain, which most of his contemporaries were studying. Instead, he was much more interested in **2.** _____ and understanding the **3.** _____ states of people.

In the 1890s, Freud began developing the theories behind the practice he named "psychoanalysis." He believed that all humans have an unconscious portion of the mind. In this portion, according to Freud's **4.** _____, strong drives struggled against the mind's attempts to **5.** _____ them. Freud also believed that our dreams can give us insights about our deepest desires and fears. The **6.** _____ of his book, *The Interpretation of Dreams*, in 1900 introduced to the world the theory of psychoanalytic therapy. The book's content was controversial, and there were many people who did not **7.** _____ of Freud's work. In 1938, the Nazis, who had already burned Freud's books in Germany, invaded Austria. Freud fled to England; he died soon after, on September 23, 1939.

Today, **8.** _____ suggest fewer than 5,000 patients in the U.S. are treated with Freud's method of psychoanalysis. Nevertheless, as a theorist, Freud's work endures, and still has a major influence on how we understand the human mind.

C. Think About It.

1. According to Freud, dreams are symbolic, containing both obvious, surface meanings as well as underlying, unconscious thoughts. Do you agree? Have you had dreams that you think have an unconscious meaning?

2. What was the most surprising thing you learned about sleep or dreams in this unit?

To learn more about the human mind, visit elt.heinle.com/explorer

Islam and the West

Discuss these questions with a partner.

1. Who is the most respected leader in your country's history? Why is that person admired?

2. What have been the most significant turning points in your country's history? What impact did those events have?

3. Which are the most important religious or cultural places in your country today? Why are they important?

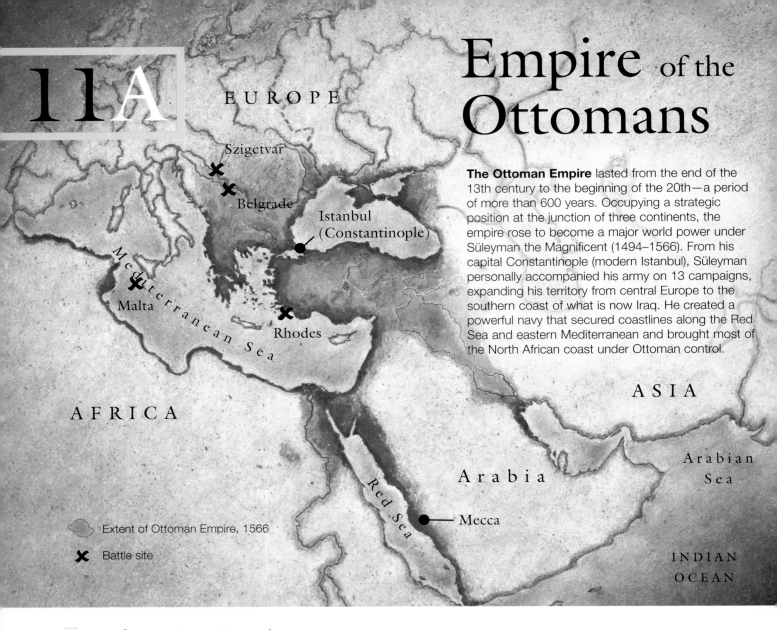

11A Empire of the Ottomans

EUROPE

Szigetvar ✗

Belgrade ✗

Istanbul (Constantinople) ●

✗ Malta

Mediterranean Sea

✗ Rhodes

AFRICA

ASIA

Arabia

Arabian Sea

Red Sea

Mecca ●

INDIAN OCEAN

⬟ Extent of Ottoman Empire, 1566

✗ Battle site

The Ottoman Empire lasted from the end of the 13th century to the beginning of the 20th—a period of more than 600 years. Occupying a strategic position at the junction of three continents, the empire rose to become a major world power under Süleyman the Magnificent (1494–1566). From his capital Constantinople (modern Istanbul), Süleyman personally accompanied his army on 13 campaigns, expanding his territory from central Europe to the southern coast of what is now Iraq. He created a powerful navy that secured coastlines along the Red Sea and eastern Mediterranean and brought most of the North African coast under Ottoman control.

☐ Before You Read

A. Discussion. Look at the map and information above and answer the questions.

1. Which modern-day countries did the Ottoman Empire include at the height of its power?
2. Who was Süleyman the Magnificent? When did he live and why was he important?
3. Where was the Ottoman capital? How is it known today? What advantages did its location offer?

B. Skim and Predict. Briefly skim the passage on pages 201–205. What do you think each section will be about? Note your predictions. Then read the passage to check your ideas.

The Lord of Lords _____

The Lamb and the Lion _____

An Audience with Süleyman _____

The Secret Sultan _____

The End of the Dream _____

The World of Süleyman the Magnificent

Writer Merle Severy examines the legacy of one of the giant historical figures of the 16th century—a ruler who stood at the crossroads of East and West.

▲ Built for Süleyman I, the Magnificent, (1494–1566), the Süleymaniye Mosque is the largest work of the renowned Ottoman architect Sinan. The graves of Süleyman and his wife, Roxelana, are located in the garden behind the mosque.

1 NEAR THE HUNGARIAN town of Szigetvar, a road sign caught my eye: "Szulimán." It was a dying village, the young having moved away, the old hanging on.

"It was named for a sultan who came long ago,"
5 a man in his garden told me.

"What did he do here?"

"I heard that he died here," a woman said, the lines of many years etching[1] her face. "The old folks would know. But they are all dead now."

10 My curiosity led me finally to a churchyard amid cornfields in the nearby countryside. A church without a village must mark some special spot. I went through the gate, past a large crucifix,[2] and on the church facade saw an Ottoman Turkish inscription.
15 A crescent stood by the wall, bathed in the light of the setting sun.

It was at this site, I read, that was buried the heart of Sultan Süleyman.

The Lord of Lords

20 The 16th century was an age notable for the overlapping reigns of giant historical figures: Spanish Emperor Charles V, protector of the Christian Church; his rival Francis I, King of France; Henry VIII of England; Ivan the Terrible, all-powerful ruler
25 of the Russian empire.

Yet, even among this hierarchy of great leaders, one ruler arguably stood taller than the rest: Süleyman, Commander of the Faithful, Shadow of God on Earth, Protector of the Holy Cities of Mecca,
30 Medina, and Jerusalem, Lord of the Lords of the World, East and West. Revered by his people as "Kanuni," the Lawgiver, and feared and admired by the West as "the Magnificent," Süleyman brought the Ottoman Empire to the peak of its power.

[1] If lines are **etched** on a surface, they are cut or carved into that surface.
[2] A **crucifix** is a symbol of Christianity, a model cross with a figure of Christ on it, most commonly associated with the Catholic Church.

▲ Süleyman I shook the world of the 16th century as he raised the Ottoman Empire to the height of its glory.

35 Süleyman was born at a time of world war, of East against West, with two superpowers locked in mortal conflict on the lands and seas of three continents. Time and again, Christian and Muslim forces clashed in the seas around the Indian Ocean, the Red Sea,
40 and the Mediterranean, and on land in Europe from Turkey to Austria.

Away from what the Ottomans called the Realm of War, the frontier against their unholy enemies, was the Realm of Peace, where races and religions
45 coexisted with the sultan acting as a great mediator of peoples. At its heart was Constantinople (present-day Istanbul), a cosmopolitan crossroads of continents that grew so large no other European capital overtook it until the start of the 19th century.

50 It was Süleyman's great-grandfather, Mehmed the Conqueror, who turned Constantinople into the greatest of all European cities. Mehmed was a descendant of nomadic tribesmen from central Asia who became followers of Osman, the first Ottoman
55 sultan, in the 13th century. From these humble origins, Mehmed rose in power, carrying the banner[3] of Islam in a series of conquests through Serbia,

Greece, and Eastern Europe; only his death in 1481 prevented him from pressing the conquest of Italy
60 and taking Rhodes, the last Christian stronghold in the east.

Mehmed's dream of achieving Alexander the Great's ambition—of building a world empire that brought together East and West—would eventually
65 be taken up by his great-grandson, Süleyman. As a young man, the future sultan was educated in a river valley near the Aegean Sea where he had been assigned as governor. Well read in history, the Koran, politics, science, astrology, and poetry, and skilled
70 in horsemanship and archery, Süleyman had been carefully prepared for his role as a future world leader.

On hearing of his father Selim's death in 1520, Süleyman rode for three days until he arrived in Constantinople. As he approached, Süleyman looked
75 with fresh eyes at the city that would become his capital: the fortress with its great cannons; the dome of the magnificent Hagia Sophia, a church that had been converted to Muslim worship; the wooden houses sheltering immigrant families. In this crowded
80 city, Spanish Moors and Jews expelled by Ferdinand and Isabella[4] joined with Turks, Greeks, and Armenians in the shops and stalls that filled the city's covered bazaar.[5]

On September 30, eight days after Selim's death,
85 Süleyman took up the sword of Osman in an elaborate ceremony and was declared sultan. From that time on, he held absolute power over the welfare of his people, with the right of instant death over any subject. But as he first rode from his palace, his
90 people gathered to raise their voice in a ritual warning to a new monarch: "Be not proud, my sultan. God is greater than you!"

The Lamb and the Lion

Süleyman's first official acts were to order a tomb,
95 mosque, and school built in honor of his father; freeing 1,500 Egyptian and Iranian captives; and paying back merchants for goods that Selim had taken from them. These won him popular approval for piety, magnanimity,[6] and justice. "It seemed to all
100 men," one observer commented, "that a gentle lamb had succeeded a fierce lion."

[3] Someone **carrying the banner** of a specific cause or idea stands for that idea.
[4] **Ferdinand** of Aragon (1452–1516) **and Isabella** of Castile (1451–1504) were rulers of Spain. See Unit 11B, *When the Moors Ruled Spain*.
[5] A **bazaar** is a market area, usually a street of small stalls.
[6] **Piety** is dutiful devotion, usually with reference to a particular theology (religion); **magnanimity** is generosity in forgiving an insult or injury.

But the lamb proved a lion in disguise. A revolt in Syria was put down savagely. Then Süleyman set out to achieve what Mehmed the Conqueror had failed to do. In his first European campaign,[7] the city of Belgrade—the key to Christian defenses in the Balkans—fell after weeks of massed attacks.

The next summer, in 1522, he besieged[8] the Christian stronghold of Rhodes, which stood between his capital and the ports of Egypt and Arabia, including the Islamic holy city of Mecca. The siege began on July 29 and lasted 145 bloody days, until the knights'[9] desperate defense ended.

Having brought into submission the strongest fortified city in Christendom, Süleyman offered generous terms. Knights and mercenaries could leave freely within 12 days; citizens could depart at any time within three years. Again he won admiration for his magnanimity. Little did he realize the price he would pay later for letting the knights go.

As success followed success in his campaigns, contemporaries wrote with awe of the glories of the sultan's empire. "I know of no State which is happier than this one," reported the Venetian ambassador in 1525; "it is furnished with all God's gifts. It controls war and peace with all; it is rich in gold, in people, in ships, and in obedience; no State can be compared with it. May God long preserve the most just of all Emperors."

An Audience with Süleyman

The Venetian ambassador's glowing, and no doubt somewhat biased, description is perhaps understandable considering the spectacular show that was put on to welcome visitors to the Ottoman capital. A foreign ambassador's reception was carefully designed to show Ottoman grandeur and power at its most impressive.

On approaching the Sultan's Topkapi Palace, the envoy first saw the heads of executed traitors hanging from the Imperial Gate. Passing the executioner's chambers, the envoy entered a shining portico.[10] There he was met on the Sultan's behalf by the monarch's vizier, or grand advisor, who, on special occasions, led the envoy past 2,000 bowing officials and heaps of silver coins. The visitor was then offered a "hundred dishes or there about, most boiled and roasted."

Then on to the sacred inner precincts.[11] Visitors spoke of the silence—the "silence of death itself." The ambassador was robed in gold cloth while his royal presents were inspected, since the sultan was "not to be approached without gifts." At the door of the throne room two officials held the visitor firmly by the arms; at no time would they let go. The visitor was led across the room, then forced to subordinate himself by kneeling down and kissing the sultan's foot. He was then raised to deliver his message.

▲ In Mohacs, Hungary, the site of one of Süleyman's greatest victories, a modern sculpture depicts the sultan holding the heads of his enemies.

[7] A **campaign** is a series of coordinated activities designed to achieve a goal, such as a military objective.
[8] If soldiers **besiege** a place, they surround it in order to stop the people inside resisting.
[9] In medieval times, a **knight** was a man of noble birth who fought for his king or lord.
[10] A **portico** is a porch or covered walkway with columns supporting the roof.
[11] **Precincts** are districts, as of a city, or the parts or regions immediately surrounding or within a place.

▲ A fresco portrays the 1565 Turkish siege of Malta, where Jean Parisot de la Valette and the Knights of Malta stood firm against Süleyman's formidable army.

The sultan, heavy with silk, gold and silver threads, sat on a jewel-studded throne. Süleyman might make
160 a comment or indicate with a nod that the audience was over. The ambassador was then led backwards out of the room, never turning his back on the sultan. The sultan's response might come much later, usually via the grand vizier.

165 The envoys who met Süleyman in this way would scan his features for signs of his health and character. From their descriptions we know something of how the great sultan looked, how he acted. But we know very little of his thoughts, of what really was in the
170 mind of the Lord of Lords.

The Secret Sultan

What sort of man was Süleyman? Of his private life— his attitudes and his thoughts—we can infer very little. His campaign diaries are written in the third
175 person, without emotion. For example, from his third campaign: "The Emperor, seated on a golden throne, receives [his] viziers . . . ; massacre of 2,000 prisoners; the rain falls in torrents."

Glimpses[12] of humanity are rare, but revealing. After
180 the siege of Rhodes, Süleyman consoles the knights' leader for his loss, praises his brave defense, then confides to a follower: "It is not without regret that I force this brave man from his home in his old age."

We know that Süleyman showed wisdom as a
185 lawgiver, creating a new code of laws and giving legal protection to minorities. He was also pious, consulting theologians on crucial decisions; just, allowing no corruption or injustice to go unpunished; and, usually, fair.

190 Ironically, it was an act of generosity that led, years later, to his greatest defeat. As a young man, Jean Parisot de la Valette fought against Süleyman in the siege of Rhodes, but was later released. Just over four decades later, la Valette led the defense of the great
195 Christian stronghold of Malta. The surprise defeat at the hands of the Christian knights marked the beginning of the end of Ottoman domination in the Mediterranean.

As the siege of Malta ended, Süleyman was entering
200 his 73rd year, making him the longest-reigning of all Ottoman monarchs. During his reign he had extended his Islamic empire through southeastern Europe, across much of the Middle East, and in north Africa as far west as Algeria. His code of laws, known
205 as the *kanun-i Osmani* ("Ottoman Laws"), was to last more than 300 years. And he presided over some of the greatest architectural achievements in the Islamic world.

Despite these
210 achievements, Süleyman's mood became increasingly dark. To wipe out the disappointment
215 of Malta, he set out on May 1, 1566, to capture Vienna. The journey was painfully slow.
220 The sultan could no longer sit on a horse but had to ride in a carriage. Suddenly,
225 word came that a Hungarian count[13] had executed one of Süleyman's governors and
230 was now hiding in Szigetvár. In a fury, Süleyman diverted his entire army to avenge the injustice.

▲ Housed in the Tokapi Palace Museum, Istanbul, this painting depicts the circumstances under which Süleyman the Magnificent rode to his last battle in Hungary.

---

[12] **Glimpses** are brief views or vague indications.
[13] A **count** is a nobleman in European countries.

Even with only 2,500 defenders, Szigetvár
235 held up the Ottomans for a month,
until the fortress was finally shattered by
explosives. Holding up his jeweled sword
in surrender, the count came out with his
survivors. But there was no sultan to greet
240 him. Süleyman had died in the night in
his tent.

The End of the Dream

Following Süleyman's death, the Ottoman
empire was squeezed by Russian expansion
245 in the east and European domination of
southern Asia. Ottoman possessions in
the Mediterranean lost their strategic role.
Western technology overtook Ottoman
military might, and—
250 with no new lands,
taxes, or manpower—
imperial decline set
in. During the 19th
century, the empire
255 became known as
the "Sick Man of Europe." Nevertheless, when more
than a dozen nations emerged from its umbrella in
the early 20th century, their languages, religions, and
cultures had been largely preserved—a legacy, in part,
260 of Süleyman's tolerance of minorities.

Three weeks after the emperor's death, the sultan's
successor was announced, and Selim, the son of
Süleyman and his queen Roxelana (see below),
became the new Sultan Selim II. According to
265 Ottoman custom, Süleyman's heart was buried where
he died, and the rest of his embalmed[14] remains

▲ The small town of Szulimán, in Hungary, is named after Süleyman I who died at a
site near the town in 1566. According to custom, Süleyman's heart was buried at
the site where he died.

The people think of wealth and power as the greatest fate,
But in this world a spell of health is the best state.
What men call sovereignty is a worldly strife and constant war;
Worship of God is the highest throne, the happiest of all estates.

- Süleyman the Magnificent

began the long journey home. When the sultan's
body reached the capital, the army fell silent, as did
the people who followed behind in a long procession.
270 Their leader all their lives, he raised their sacred
empire to its golden age. Their descendants would
look back on it with pride and nostalgia.[15] But they
would never see his like again.

[14] A dead body that is **embalmed** is preserved by the use
of chemicals and oils.
[15] **Nostalgia** is an affectionate feeling you have for the past,
especially a particularly happy time.

The Slave Who Became Queen

Süleyman was strongly influenced by two slaves he raised to power: Ibrahim, whom he
promoted to grand vizier, and Hürrem—"laughing one"—a captive Russian known to the
West as Roxelana, who became his wife.

To gain influence over Süleyman, Roxelana first set out to remove Ibrahim, who had served
as grand vizier for 13 years. With prompting from Roxelana, Süleyman began to suspect
Ibrahim was acting as if he were the sultan. One evening, Ibrahim was invited to dine with
Süleyman. The next morning he was found strangled.

Next, in order to strengthen the position of her own sons, Roxelana needed to remove
Mustafa, Süleyman's firstborn son. He, too, was found strangled in his father's tent.
Eventually, one of Roxelana's sons, Selim, succeeded Süleyman to the throne. Rising from
slavery to royalty, this strong-willed woman played a man's game with great skill for the
highest stakes.

Reading Comprehension

A. Multiple Choice. Choose the best answer for each question.

1. The phrase *overlapping reigns* in line 21 indicates that the leaders mentioned in this paragraph _____.
a. were more powerful than kings in previous centuries
b. ruled their lands during some of the same years
c. lived longer lives than previous monarchs
d. reigned during a time of war and trouble

2. Which of the following is NOT true about Constantinople at the time of Selim's death in 1520?
a. It contained diverse groups of people.
b. It was where Süleyman was living.
c. It was located in the "Realm of Peace."
d. It was the heart of the Ottoman Empire.

3. Which of the following leaders made Constantinople a more important city than any in Europe?
a. Süleyman   c. Mehmed
b. Osman   d. Selim

4. Which of the following is closest in meaning to this sentence from line 102?
But the lamb proved a lion in disguise.
a. Süleyman was not interested in warfare, only in peaceful pursuits.
b. Süleyman proved to his people that it was better to be powerful than kind.
c. Süleyman revealed himself to be much fiercer than people first believed.
d. Süleyman pretended to be strong, but was actually very gentle.

5. What does the author imply in the paragraph starting on line 114?
a. The "generous" terms offered by Süleyman were not really very generous.
b. Although Rhodes was believed to be very strong, it fell to Süleyman easily.
c. The knights and mercenaries were allowed to become citizens of Rhodes.
d. Süleyman would later be sorry that he had treated the knights so liberally.

6. Why does the author of the article quote from Süleyman's campaign diaries in the paragraph starting on line 172?
a. to support the idea that the third campaign was his most important
b. to demonstrate that he was not only a military genius but also a skillful writer
c. to point out the impact of bad weather on military operations
d. to show that his writing revealed very little about his true personality

7. What does the author say about the siege of Malta?
a. It was considered Süleyman's most brilliant campaign.
b. It was the final battle in which Süleyman fought.
c. The siege did not last as long as Süleyman had predicted.
d. Jean Parisot de la Valette's victory there was unexpected.

8. Which of the following questions can be answered with the information in the paragraph starting on line 234?
a. How was the fortress at Szigetvár destroyed?
b. Was Count Szigetvár freed after the battle?
c. What was the cause of Süleyman's death?
d. How many Ottoman soldiers fought against Szigetvár?

We scan to find specific information that we need from an article, for example, key details like dates, names, amounts, or places (see also Units 3A and 8B). To scan, you must have a clear idea of the kind of information you are looking for. If possible, have one or two key words in mind. Then, read through the material quickly looking for these words or related words. When you find the relevant word(s), read the surrounding context to check how the information relates to the rest of the text.

B. Scanning/Completion. Use content words (names, places, etc.) in each sentence (**1–12**) to help you quickly locate the section(s) of the article it relates to. Use the information in that section to complete the sentence. Note the line number(s) where you find the missing information.

1. On his way to attack Vienna in 1566, Süleyman traveled by _____.	line(s) _____
2. Mehmed was Süleyman's _____.	line(s) _____
3. Important visitors to the Topkapi Palace were offered food, which was usually _____ and _____.	line(s) _____
4. After capturing Rhodes, Süleyman permitted citizens to leave peacefully within a period of _____ _____.	line(s) _____
5. After Süleyman died, the Ottoman Empire clashed with _____ in the east and with Europeans in _____ _____.	line(s) _____
6. Ottomans referred to Süleyman as "Kanuni," which means _____.	line(s) _____
7. Süleyman's first military victory in Europe was the capture of the strategic city of _____.	line(s) _____
8. After becoming sultan, Süleyman ordered that _____ prisoners from Iran and Egypt should be freed.	line(s) _____
9. In the 19th century, the Ottoman Empire was called the "_____ of Europe."	line(s) _____
10. Only Süleyman's _____ was buried in the town of Szigetvár.	line(s) _____
11. Mehmed's ancestors came from _____ _____.	line(s) _____
12. The siege of Rhodes took place _____ decades before the siege of Malta.	line(s) _____

C. Critical Thinking. Discuss the questions with a partner.

1. The author frequently emphasizes the power and wealth of Süleyman. List five ways in which he supports the idea that Süleyman was a rich and powerful leader, and note in which lines you found this information.

2. The author also points out that Süleyman could be a merciful ruler. List three ways in which the author supports the idea that Süleyman was sometimes a generous leader, and note in which lines you found this information.

3. In what ways do you think Süleyman's leadership is similar to, and different from, that of world leaders today?

Vocabulary Practice

A. Definitions. Complete the information using the correct forms of the words in the box. Two words are extra.

biased	confide	console
consult	hierarchy	infer
justify	mediate	subordinate
successor		

During the 12th century, Saladin—known to his many loyal
1. _____ as Al-Malik An-Nasir Salah al-Din—was a great war leader. At the height of his power, he ruled over the lands of Egypt, Syria, Mesopotamia, and Yemen, defending his homeland against European invaders.

Saladin began his life as a soldier under his uncle, an army commander, and quickly rose up the military
2. _____. After taking control of Egypt in 1171, he seized power in Syria following the death of its king. Some saw this as an act of treason against the king's son, who was also the king's intended **3.** _____, but Saladin felt his actions were
4. _____ by his mission—to unite the Muslim lands and defend them from the Christian crusaders arriving from Europe.

▲ Saladin, leader of the Muslim forces during the Third Crusade

While historical accounts of the Crusades are frequently **5.** _____ and somewhat unreliable, contemporary accounts of Saladin's actions—from both sides—allow us to
6. _____ that he was in fact a fair and generous ruler, despite the ruthlessness he showed in battle. For example, he **7.** _____ truces between other Muslim leaders, frequently **8.** _____ with his councils, and also showed mercy to many of his prisoners.

B. Definitions. Match words from the box in **A** with the correct definition.

1. system of organizing people into different levels of importance _____

2. person who replaces someone else _____

3. show or prove that an action is reasonable or necessary _____

4. ask for advice _____

5. discuss inner thoughts or secrets _____

6. lessen the feeling of loss, comfort _____

7. behaving unfairly towards one group _____

8. someone in a lower position _____

9. decide that something is true based on partial information _____

10. try to solve a problem between two groups _____

> ### Word Link
> The prefix **bi-** has the meaning of *two*: e.g., **bi**ennial, **bi**monthly, **bi**ased, **bi**cycle, **bi**noculars, **bi**lingual, **bi**national.

Cultural Encounters

▲ A girl in a red dress stands among a crowd of Muslim worshippers attending prayers at a mosque in Surabaya, Indonesia. The most populous Muslim country, Indonesia marks the eastern edge of the Islamic world today. The first Arab Muslim traders probably arrived there in the 8th century. At about the same time, 12,000 kilometers away, the first Muslims known as Moors—arrived on the southern coast of Spain. Known as Moors, their arrival marked the beginning of an Islamic age in Spain that would last for almost 800 years.

Before You Read

A. Matching. The following words appear in the reading passage. Match each word with its definition.

a. cathedral   **b.** clergy   **c.** creed   **d.** mosque   **e.** prayer   **f.** prophet   **g.** shrine

1. _____ a set of beliefs, or principles, that strongly influence the way a person lives and works

2. _____ a person who is believed to speak for a divine authority

3. _____ a building where Muslims go to worship

4. _____ a place of worship associated with a particular holy person or object

5. _____ the activity of speaking to God

6. _____ the official leaders of the religious activities of a group of believers

7. _____ a very large and important church which has a bishop in charge

B. Skim and Predict. Look quickly through the article on pages 210–214. Check (✓) the topics you think the author discusses. Then read through the passage to check your ideas.

☐ origins of the Moors   ☐ Moorish poetry

☐ how the Moors came to Spain   ☐ Moorish paintings

☐ Moorish architecture   ☐ how the Moorish era ended

WHEN THE MOORS RULED SPAIN

From the Rock of Gibraltar, writer Thomas J. Abercrombie set out to explore a forgotten corner of Europe's past.

▲ The narrow Strait of Gibraltar, which passes between Morocco's Jabal Musa (in the distance) and the Rock of Gibraltar, separates Africa from Europe by just 15 kilometers.

1 "PERFECT WEATHER FOR a morning's sail—or an intercontinental passage," said my Spanish shipmate, Rafa, as I scanned the rising mists ahead. Suddenly a silhouette of our destination appeared above the haze
5 ahead: Gibraltar.

"Wow, what a beauty!" Rafa exclaimed.

A beacon for mariners since the dawn of seafaring, the famous Rock of Gibraltar was one of the Pillars of Hercules (Jabal Musa, behind us on the northern
10 coast of Africa, formed the other). For ancient Romans and Greeks, the pillars marked the boundary of the known world. For me, the stronghold marked the first stop on a journey into a neglected corner of Europe's history, a distant time when Muslims
15 ruled Spain, and Islam had a powerful influence on the West.

"Only recently have the Spanish begun to approach their Islamic past," Rafa told me. In recent years, Rafa had presided over a Madrid-based institute that
20 promotes cultural exchange between Spain and its Muslim neighbors. "We are finding that much of what we think of as 'pure Spanish,' our architecture, our temperament,[1] our poetry and music—even our language—is a blend from a long Arabic heritage."

25 Rafa and I were sailing in the wake of Tariq ibn Ziyad, a Muslim general. With soldiers and horses in four boats, he crossed from Ceuta on the African side—as did we—and set up his beachhead on the narrow ledge below, where the town of Gibraltar sits
30 today. In the spring of 711, he marched northward with 12,000 Muslims. At the Rio Barbate, south of Cadiz, the invaders met the hastily assembled forces of Spain's Visigoth[2] king, Roderic.

"Before us is the enemy; behind us, the sea," shouted
35 Tariq, drawing his scimitar[3] and invoking Allah for his blessing and support. "We have only one choice: to win!"

The battle of Barbate proved a mortal wound for the weak Visigoth ruler. King Roderic was slain; his body
40 was never recovered. Whole battalions of soldiers fled, and the Christian army collapsed. The Islamic conquest of Spain had begun.

[1] Your **temperament** is your basic nature, such as how you react to situations.
[2] The **Visigoths** were a tribe who settled in France and Spain in the 4th century A.D.
[3] A **scimitar** is a sword with a curved blade.

THE CREED OF ISLAM had been revealed to the seventh-century prophet-statesman Muhammad in distant
45 Arabia. It spread swiftly, embracing the entire desert peninsula⁴ by the time of his death in 632. Six years later, Syria and Palestine fell to the Muslims. From their new capital in Damascus, Muslim armies spread eastward through Mesopotamia to India and Central
50 Asia, westward to the Nile and across North Africa. A century after the birth of Islam, its call to prayer rang from minarets⁵ all the way from the Atlantic to the outskirts of China, an empire larger than Rome's at its height.

55 History named the Muslim conquerors of Spain "Moors," probably because they arrived by way of Morocco. The
60 Moors themselves never used the term. They were Arabs, from Damascus and Medina, leading armies of North African Berber
65 converts. Most married into Spanish and Visigoth families or took fair-skinned Galician⁶ slaves as wives. From this mix of
70 race and culture sprang a civilization that would have a major influence on Spain, including its language: the name Gibraltar descends
75 from *Jabal Tariq*, Arabic for "Tariq's mountain."

From Gibraltar, I followed Tariq's footsteps northward. After the victory at the Rio Barbate he moved swiftly, with Spanish cities
80 falling to him in quick succession. Early in 712, his soldiers rode through the gates of the Visigoth capital, Toledo. The remaining Christian armies were forced to retreat to the northernmost mountains of Spain.

85 The Moors' hold of Toledo was temporary, however. In 1085, it fell to Alfonso VI of Castile and Leon, who thereby initiated the *Reconquista*—the reconquest of Spain by the Christians. For several centuries after Toledo's recapture, the city remained
90 liberal, tolerant, and bilingual. Alfonso X supported an important 13th-century translation school where Christian, Muslim, and Jewish scholars collaborated to translate manuscripts into Latin—works by the Greek scholars Aristotle and Ptolemy; empirical
95 studies of algebra and mathematics by al-Khwārizmī;⁷ and the Canon of Ibn Sina (Avicenna), which remained Europe's standard medical textbook for 500 years.

Today, the whole city of Toledo has been declared
100 a national monument. It remains the country's religious capital. Mosques and synagogues have been restored and splendid palaces opened to the public—museums to display Toledo's abundant cultural heritage.

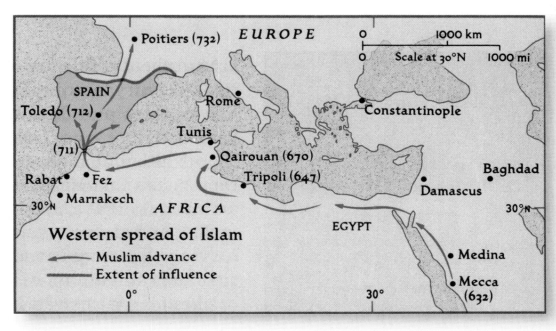

▲ In a mere hundred years, the Prophet Muhammad's followers spread the word of Islam westward from Mecca through Northern Africa to Spain and France, where their advance was halted in 732.

105 But there is a dark side, too, to the region's history. In 1469, Prince Ferdinand of Aragon wed Princess Isabella of Castile, uniting Christian Spain under their rule. They waged war against Moorish rulers to the south and persecuted Muslims and Jews in their
110 own lands.

⁴ A **peninsula** is a narrow strip of land projecting from the mainland into a sea or lake.
⁵ **Minarets** are tall towers attached to mosques. They have projecting balconies from which people are called to prayer.
⁶ **Galicians** were a race of people who lived in the kingdom of Galicia, in northwest Spain.
⁷ **Muhammad ibn Mūsā al-Khwārizmī** was a Muslim scholar who studied at the House of Wisdom in Baghdad (see page 175).

▲ This astrolabe was used by the Moors to locate and predict the positions of the sun, moon, planets, and stars. It thus served as a tool for navigation, surveying, and timekeeping.

stretches of paved, lamp-lighted streets. The largest city in western Europe, Córdoba rivaled Baghdad and Constantinople as the greatest cultural center of the world.

135 The highlight for most visitors to Córdoba is its Mezquita, or mosque, which in 1986 celebrated its 1,200th anniversary. Begun by the first Abd-al-Rahman, it has a shrine that rivals in size Islam's holiest in Mecca, and still today retains its status
140 as the crown jewel of Moorish architecture. As my eyes grew accustomed to the darkness, I wandered through a forest of more than 800 columns and Moorish arches. My footsteps led me to the mosque's domed *mihrab*, or prayer area. Arabic calligraphy
145 decorated the walls, declaring ". . . praise to Allah who led us to this place."

In the dim vastness I hardly noticed the cathedral. After the Christian Reconquest, Catholics began using the Mezquita as a church and for 300 years
150 held services there. Then the clergy persuaded Emperor Charles V to raise a cathedral in its midst, despite strong protests from city leaders who felt that amending the building in this way would violate its sanctity.[9] Later, when he inspected the rather
155 banal addition to the extraordinary mosque, Charles confessed disappointment: "By installing something that is commonplace," he declared, "you have destroyed what was once unique."

WHEN CÓRDOBA FELL to the Christian Reconquest
160 in 1236, and Seville 12 years later, the Moors found themselves confined to a 320-kilometer (200-mile) strip along Spain's southeast coast, curving from Gibraltar to Almeria. Here sultans of the Nasrid dynasty ruled from their stronghold at Granada.
165 From 1248 to 1354 they raised their masterpiece, a clay-red palace-fortress known as the Alhambra. I climbed the hill leading to the Alhambra with Professor Miguel José Hagerty, a lecturer on Arabic poetry at the University of Granada.

170 "Arab Spain nurtured scores of poets. Many of its rulers—Abd-al-Rahman I, for instance—were poets in their own right," Professor Hagerty said. Strict Islamic tradition discourages the making of "graven images," so painting and sculpture never flourished

In 1480 they established the Spanish Inquisition.[8] Before it was over, three centuries later, thousands of Muslims and Jews had died and an estimated three million people had been driven into exile. Having
115 lost many of its leading businessmen, artists, and scientists, Spain found itself victim of its own cruelty.

FROM TOLEDO, A TRAIN RIDE south brought me to Andalucia. It was here that Islamic culture sank its
120 deepest roots. Perhaps it is not surprising. Southern Spain, with its warm, gentle landscape of grape vines and olive and citrus trees, is almost a mirror of parts of Morocco and the eastern Mediterranean. Here the Arabs felt at home.

125 In 756, Prince Abd-al-Rahman, whose dynasty had been overthrown in Syria, planted his capital at Córdoba in Andalucia's heartland. Under his successors, Córdoba blossomed into a city of half a million people, with more than 20 suburbs, 500
130 mosques, 300 public baths, 70 libraries, and long

---

[8] The **Spanish Inquisition** was a religious tribunal established by Catholic monarchs Ferdinand of Aragon and Isabella of Castile.

[9] If you talk about the **sanctity** of something, you mean that it is very important and should be treated with respect.

▲ Moorish arches dominate the inside of the Great Mosque of Córdoba. Built in A.D. 786, the mosque has been described as the ultimate achievement in Moorish architecture.

175 among the Moors. Instead they channeled creative energy into language. With its wealth of vocabulary, its distinctive sounds, its flowing calligraphy, Arabic is well suited to the task.

"Little has been translated," he said, but he quoted
180 some lines that survived the journey into Spanish and English. From Ibn al-Sabuni:

I present you a precious mirror,

Behold there the beauty that consumes me

O furtive love, your reflection is more yielding

185 *And better keeps its promises, . . .*

The Nasrid rulers' mansions of the Alhambra make up the most visited site in Spain. It is a miracle that they survived the centuries. They have been abused by squatters,[10] eroded by neglect, and suffered various
190 appendages, including a massive addition built during the Renaissance by Charles V. The integrity of the Alhambra endures nonetheless, a sublime Moorish mix of artifact and nature.

Here the walls themselves speak—if you know Arabic.
195 We found quotations and poems in the calligraphy of the walls, archways, and fountains. One marble

fountain declared:

No greater mansions I see than mine

No equal in East or West.

200 I had to agree. Even in the oil-rich Arab countries of today, architects with unlimited budgets have yet to match the Alhambra.

THE MARRIAGE OF FERDINAND and Isabella sealed the fate of the weakening Granada sultans. In 1492,
205 the same year they launched Christopher Columbus on his historic voyage across the Atlantic, the king and queen rode into Granada to preside over the abdication[11] of the last Moorish ruler, Muhammad Abu-Abdullah—Boabdil, as the Spanish call him.

210 On the way out of Córdoba, I paused at a pass above the city called *Suspiro del Moro*, the Sigh of the Moor. It was here Boabdil stopped to look back and shed a tear over his lost kingdom. According to legend his domineering mother, Aisha, berated[12] him for
215 passively allowing his kingdom to fall: "Fitting you cry like a woman over what you could not defend like a man."

[10] **Squatters** are people who live in unused buildings without having a legal right to do so.
[11] An **abdication** occurs when a person gives up being king or queen.
[12] When someone is **berated**, they are scolded angrily.

The remote villages of the Alpujarras, halfway up the southern slopes of
220 Mulhacen, Spain's highest peak, were the last domains of the Moors in Spain until they were finally driven into exile in 1609. Many towns still wear their Arabic names, as does Mount Mulhacen—and
225 the Alpujarras itself. I descended from the mountains via a series of sharp turns, to a very different world: Spain's Costa del Sol—tropical, cosmopolitan, and booming.

"Last year 50 million visitors came to
230 Spain," Costa del Sol Tourist Board promotion manager Diego Franco told me, "one for every Spaniard and then some. It's an invasion—but a peaceful one."

All over the coastal region are signs
235 that modern-day Moors have joined the "peaceful invasion"; signs in Arabic script point you to the Lebanese Delicatessen, the Banco Saudi-Espanol, to Arab doctors, a Muslim cemetery . . .

Near the Andalucia Plaza Casino, I drank coffee
240 with Mokhles "George" El-Khoury, a Christian Arab who moved here from Beirut to run a building-management firm.

"[Andalucia] reminds me of Lebanon—without the wars and politics," George said. "You have the
245 mountains, the sea, the fine climate of olives and palm trees. The Spanish are a warm people, not stiff and formal like many Europeans. The food is much like ours, so is the shape of the houses and the towns. To an Arab—well, Andalucia feels like home."

▲ Residents of Villena parade through the streets in period costumes, reenacting the *Reconquista*. Every year, almost 150 celebrations of "Moors and Christians" take place across Spain.

250 NOWHERE IS THIS MORE TRUE than in the old Muslim capital of Córdoba, where I spent my last Spanish days. I was awakened there early one morning by the noise of workmen at the Mezquita across the street. No other artifact more richly evokes the golden age
255 of the Moors, a stormy millennium that brought together two faiths, two cultures, two continents. Throughout, while king and sultan fought bitterly for the hand of Spain, ordinary life prospered as people of different backgrounds worked together to create the
260 brilliant civilization that helped lead Europe out of the Dark Ages.[13]

Ultimately the Moors themselves faded into history, leaving behind their scattered dreams. But Spain and the West stand forever in their debt.

[13] The **Dark Ages** refers to a period of cultural and economic decline in Western Europe following the end of the Roman Empire.

FLAMENCO
265

Arabic poetry was crafted, above all, for recital and song. In Morocco and Spain, the soul-stirring music of *cante jondo*, the deep song of Gypsy flamenco, is still played and sung by descendants of ethnic minorities who survived the Inquisition centuries ago.

270 Throughout Spain the art of flamenco is threatened by its commercialization in shows called *tablaos*, characterized by dramatic lighting and loud amplifiers. Sacrificed in the process is flamenco's most distinctive aspect, its *duende*: soul. But after midnight, it is still possible to sample flamenco *puro* ("pure Flamenco") in the bars of
275 Granada's Albaicin area, when Gypsies gather to recall the moods and rhythms of a lost age.

◀ Spanish flamenco is a mix of Moorish, Arab, Jewish, and Gypsy influences. The Gypsy influence on Spain began when the Roma people reached Andalucia through North Africa in the early 15th century. This photograph of a woman in traditional Gypsy clothing was taken in 1929.

Reading Comprehension

A. Multiple Choice. Choose the best answer for each question.

Inference/Tone   **1.** The author's general attitude toward the Moors is best described as _____.
a. questioning
b. respectful
c. neutral
d. bitter

Detail   **2.** What does the author say about the word *Moors*?
a. It was applied only to the North African Berber soldiers.
b. It was used because the invaders came to Spain from Morocco.
c. It was what the Muslim conquerors called themselves.
d. It was originally applied to the Visigoth conquerors of Spain.

Detail   **3.** The name *Gibraltar* comes from the name of a _____.
a. Visigoth ruler
b. Moorish war leader
c. Christian king
d. Galician slave

Inference   **4.** From the information in the paragraph starting on line 85, we can infer that _____.
a. at least some of Toledo's scholars could understand Latin
b. Alfonso X was the Spanish leader who recaptured Toledo from the Moors
c. Ibn Sina helped translate his medical textbook from Arabic to Spanish
d. speaking or writing in Arabic in Toledo after 1085 was forbidden

Reference   **5.** The word *their* in line 107 refers to _____.
a. Muslims and Jews
b. Moorish rulers to the south
c. Ferdinand and Isabella
d. Spanish Christians

Vocabulary   **6.** The word *banal* in line 155 is closest in meaning to _____.
a. ordinary and unexciting
b. small and inconspicuous
c. strange and unlikely
d. unholy and insulting

Negative Detail   **7.** According to the article, the Moors had the LEAST impact on Spanish culture through their _____.
a. poetry
b. architecture
c. painting
d. music

Detail   **8.** The last remnants of Moorish rule in Spain were in _____.
a. the city of Córdoba
b. the northernmost mountains
c. the strip of coast from Gibraltar to Almeria
d. villages on the slopes of Mulhacen

B. Scanning/Inferring. Find the discussion of the topics listed below in the article. Decide if the author's attitude towards the topic is positive or negative, and note words or phrases that signal the author's attitude.

Topic	Author's attitude (+ or -)	Words/phrases that indicate the author's attitude
Toledo in the two centuries after its reconquest		
the rule of Ferdinand and Isabella		
Andalucia		
Córdoba		
the cathedral inside the Mezquita		
Arabic language and poetry		
changes to the Alhambra since its construction		
tablaos shows		

C. Critical Thinking. Discuss these questions with a partner.

1. How does the author use metaphoric language to make an analogy (comparison) between the Moor's cultivation of land and Moorish culture? What other words or expressions could the author have used?

2. Why do you think the author describes his own trip in this article about the history of the Moors in Spain? Do you think including his personal experiences makes the article stronger? Why or why not?

3. Think of a nation or culture that has been influenced by being conquered, ruled, or occupied by another culture. In what ways was the original culture changed? How does its experience compare with the conquest of Spain by the Moors as described in this article?

Vocabulary Practice

A. Completion. Complete the information using the correct forms of the words in the box. Three words are extra.

amend	appendage	empirical	initiate
integrity	invoke	liberal	persecute
temporary	violate		

▲ El Greco's *View of Toledo* is considered among the best known depictions of the sky in Western art, and a masterpiece of the Spanish Renaissance.

Ruled in turn by the Romans, Moors, and Christians, the city of Toledo in Spain stands as a living showcase of Spanish history, an enduring meeting place of cultures and peoples.

From A.D. 712, under the rule of the Moorish Caliphate of Córdoba, Toledo enjoyed the benefits of a
1. _____ society in which Muslims, Jews, and Christians co-existed. But Moorish rule was only
2. _____ . On May 25, 1085, Alfonso VI of Castile officially reclaimed Toledo for Christian Spain.

During his rule, Christian, Muslim, and Jewish scholars continued to collaborate, translating Arabic and Hebrew documents into Spanish and Latin, and **3.** _____ advancements in education that lasted over several centuries. These included **4.** _____ studies in science and mathematics. However, in the 1400s, intolerance flamed in Toledo. Muslims and Jews were
5. _____ and their religious freedoms were **6.** _____ .
Many were expelled from Spain. It was a dark time that continued well into the 1800s.

In 1941, the city of Toledo was declared a national monument and laws were set up to protect the
7. _____ of Toledo's surviving buildings and monuments.

B. Words in Context. Complete each sentence with words in the box in **A**.

1. When something is attached to a larger object, it can be called a(n)_____.
2. When you _____ something, you disturb it, damage it, or treat it with disrespect.
3. Someone who is _____ believes people should have a lot of freedom in deciding how to think or act.
4. When you _____ something, you start it, or cause it to happen.
5. Something that is _____ lasts only for a limited time.
6. _____ evidence or studies rely on practical experience rather than on theories.
7. If you _____ someone, you treat them cruelly and unfairly because of their race or beliefs.
8. The _____ of something is its quality of being preserved as whole or united.
9. If you _____ something that has been written or said, you change it.
10. If you _____ something, like a famous person, you refer to them to support your argument.

Word Partnership

Use *violate* with: (n.) violate **an agreement**, violate **the law**, violate **rights**, violate **rules**, violate **someone's privacy**, violate **(religious) freedom**.

EXPLORE MORE

Heritage of Spain

A. Preview. Flamenco, a dance and music style that originated in Spain, is the product of Moorish, Jewish, Christian, and Gypsy influences. Do you know any other art forms, customs, or traditions that are the product of more than one culture? How did they develop? Discuss with a partner.

B. Summarize. Watch the video, *Heritage of Spain*. Then complete the summary below using the correct form of words in the box. Two words are extra.

commission	discipline	dynamic	exemplify
facet	encounter	ideology	initiate
impede	successor		

The cities of Spain are among the most vibrant in the world, each displaying various **1.** _____ of Spanish life in their architecture.

In the city of Barcelona, visitors are treated to the colorful artwork of Antoni Gaudi, including his final and most important **2.** _____, Sagrada Familia. Work on the cathedral was **3.** _____ in 1883. However, over the years, its progress has been **4.** _____ by not only Gaudi's death in 1926, but also periods of war, and the lack of funding for the project. The massive building remains uncompleted until today.

In the streets, people gather for "tapas" and the famous rhythms of flamenco music. The art of flamenco is a **5.** _____ mix of three **6.** _____—singing, guitar-playing, and dance—and can be traced back to various cultural roots.

In addition to influencing its music, Spain's rich multi-cultural heritage can be seen in many of its most spectacular buildings. For instance, the Alhambra, in Granada, is a palace and fortress built by Moorish rulers of the past. Similarly, the architectural styles displayed in Córdoba **7.** _____ the mixed cultural heritage of the region, especially its years under the control of the Umayyad Muslims.

Wherever you turn, in Spain you're sure to **8.** _____ that unique mix of cultures and peoples, located at this crossroads of continents.

▲ The varied influences that make up Spanish culture come together in the art of flamenco.

C. Think About It.

1. Which art forms, customs, or traditions do you think are the most representative of your country's culture?

2. Do you think cultures will, in general, become more mixed in future? Why or why not?

 To learn more about Islamic heritage, visit elt.heinle.com/explorer

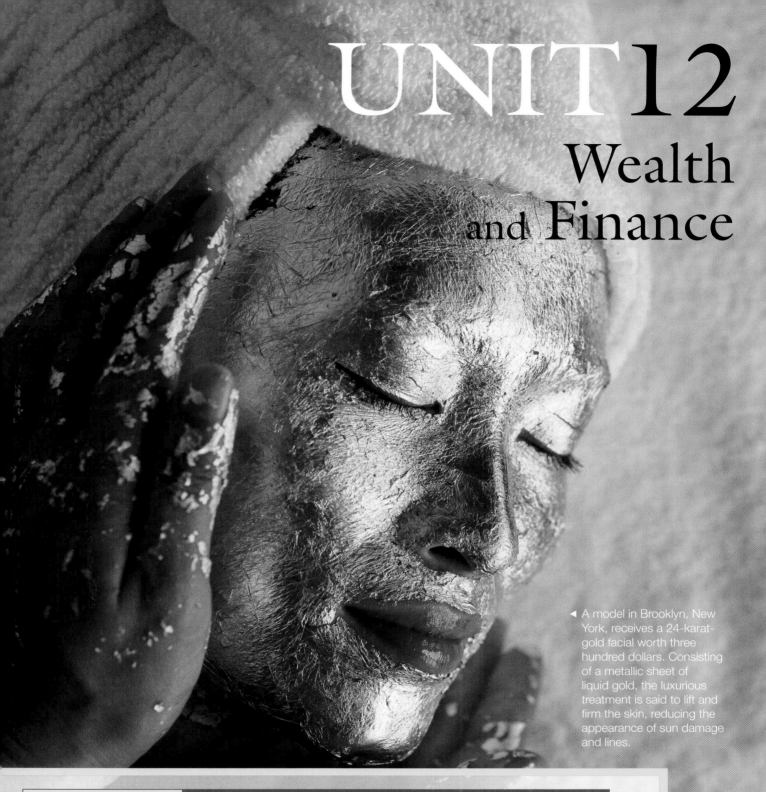

UNIT 12
Wealth
and Finance

◀ A model in Brooklyn, New York, receives a 24-karat-gold facial worth three hundred dollars. Consisting of a metallic sheet of liquid gold, the luxurious treatment is said to lift and firm the skin, reducing the appearance of sun damage and lines.

Discuss these questions with a partner.

1. How would you define "price"? How does it compare with the "value" of something?

2. How many different methods of payment do you use for buying items? What are the pros and cons of each one?

3. What social and economic role does gold play in your country?

12A
The World of Money

Before You Read

▲ Dollar bills and other ritual offerings rain down on a statue of Saint Anthony during a Catholic festival in Boston, USA.

A. Matching. The following money-related words appear in the passage on pages 221–225. Use the words to complete the definitions (**1–8**).

balance	bill	exchange rate	inflation	interest	mint	reserve	treasury

1. The _____ in your bank account is the amount of money you have in it.
2. _____ is a general increase in the prices of goods and services in a country.
3. The _____ is the place where the official coins of a country are made.
4. A(n) _____ is a supply of something, such as money, that is available for use when it is needed.
5. The revenues or funds of a government may be referred to as the _____.
6. A(n) _____ is a written statement of money that you owe for goods or services.
7. The _____ of a country's unit of currency is the amount of another country's currency that you can get for it.
8. _____ is extra money you receive if you have invested a sum of money; it is also the extra money you pay if you have borrowed money or are buying something on credit.

B. Skim and Predict. Skim the following passage, focusing on the captions and headings. Number the topics (**1–5**) in the order you think they appear. Then read the passage to check your predictions.

☐ the causes and dangers of inflation
☐ life without coins and paper money
☐ the origins of coins and paper money
☐ how banking and foreign exchanges developed
☐ traditional attitudes to money in a modern-day society

From Clams

TO CREDIT CARDS

Writer Peter T. White traces the history of one of humanity's oldest creations: from the beginnings of coinage in antiquity to the emergence of a cashless society.

▲ A shopper pays a vendor at the Pettah market in Colombo, Sri Lanka, continuing the never-ending circulation of money.

1 WHAT IS MONEY? In its usual definition, money is anything that is accepted as a medium of exchange and a store of value because it exists in limited quantities and, above all, because people have
5 confidence in it. But at a market in Yemen, I found quite a few people who retained a more traditional view on what sort of money can be considered sound.

At Suq al Talh, a Saturday market close to the ancient city of Sadah, I found bearded money changers sitting
10 on concrete steps, curved daggers strapped around their waists, automatic rifles resting on their laps. In front of them were bundles of bank notes—Yemeni rials—and stacks of silver coins. The coins were all dated 1780, and the lady portrayed on them was
15 the Austrian empress Maria Theresa. A man had just bought a thousand of them for 75,000 rials; I asked him why.

"It is the main currency," he said. But isn't that what the rial is? He explained that in this area these coins
20 are *omla saaba*, meaning hard currency. He then walked off with 60 pounds (27 kilograms) of silver in a woven bag. "He bought them to make a profit,"
another man told me—they'd been going up in price; or, one might say, the rial had been
25 going down.

"The people you saw in Sadah may be illiterate, but they know economic affairs," said Mohamed Said Al-Attar, when I visited him at the Ministry of Trade in Yemen's capital, Sana'a. He told me that in the 18th
30 century, when French traders came to the port of Mocha to buy coffee, the Yemenis didn't want French money, but they liked the Austrian coin, called a taler, because of its high silver content. (From "taler," incidentally, comes the word "dollar.")

35 The reputation of the Austrian taler spread through much of the Arabian Peninsula and to Ethiopia, where the coin circulated until the 1950s. "We introduced the rial bank note," Dr. Al-Attar added, "after the 1962 revolution had ousted[1] the monarchy.
40 But for years we had difficulty getting people to trust paper money."

[1] When a ruler, leader, or government is **ousted** from power, they are ejected or removed, usually against their will.

▲ On the island of Yap, in Micronesia, *rai* stones once were a main form of currency. Some of these ancient "coins" are 3 meters (10 feet) in diameter, and weigh about 4 tons each.

The official Austrian mint in Vienna continues to turn out Maria Theresa talers, still dated 1780. So do foreign imitators, said a merchant in the Sana'a suq. 45 "They have agents in Yemen buy talers, which are 83 percent silver," Dr. Al-Attar told me. "They melt them down, strike new ones, and send them back to Yemen—less than 80 percent silver."

Alas,[2] debasing[3] coinage for a bit of profit is almost as 50 old as coinage itself.

COINS, NOTES, AND CLAMS

Many of today's currencies—the Italian lira, the British pound, the peso and peseta of Spanish-speaking countries—are named for units of weight 55 once used to measure amounts of metal. Silver, gold, and copper have functioned as money throughout most of recorded history. The earliest documented use of silver for payment appears around 2500 B.C. in Mesopotamian cuneiform tablets.

60 Some of the oldest known coins were made in the ancient kingdom of Lydia[4] in the seventh century B.C.—tiny, thumbnail-size lumps of electrum, a pale yellow alloy of gold and silver, washed down by streams from limestone mountains. The coins were 65 likely conceived as a convenience to the state, to be used as a standard medium for payments to officials and for public expenditures. They were also useful for the collection of taxes levied by ancient rulers. But merchants, long used to settling accounts in precious 70 metals, must have found them useful too; by using coins, they didn't have to do as much weighing for each transaction.

The idea of coinage spread from Asia Minor across the Mediterranean world. By the fourth century B.C. 75 a weight unit called the shekel lent its name to silver coins in the Middle East; gold was coined into the aureus of the Roman Empire, the dinar of Muslim lands, the florin of Florence, and the ducat of Venice.

The earliest paper currency issued by a government 80 appeared in China in the 11th century. A couple of centuries later in Persia, the Mongol ruler Geikhatu tried to enforce the use of paper money, but merchants refused to accept it. They closed their shops and hid their goods. Trade stopped. Facing 85 revolt, Geikhatu revised his decision (the official who had originally suggested it was torn to pieces in a bazaar).

Despite these initial setbacks, paper money would eventually become the norm. The first European bank 90 notes were printed in Sweden in 1661, when coins were in short supply. Soon after, paper notes were widespread across continents.

But money hasn't always been metal or paper. One of the oldest forms may have been a shiny white 95 or straw-colored mollusk[5] shell, just a couple of centimeters long, from the Indian Ocean. It's called the cowrie, and from it derives the Chinese character *cai* (財), representing wealth, or money. I once saw a display of other forms of money collected by 100 John Lenker of the International Primitive Money Society—a bronze drum from Malaysia, a block of salt from Ethiopia, a bowl with 11 legs from Fiji. And wampum, once prized by North American Indians—tiny clamshell pieces drilled and strung together like 105 beads. "All these tell stories just as coins do," said Mr. Lenker.

---

[2] The word "**Alas**" is used as to express sorrow, grief, pity, or concern.
[3] **Debasing** something means to lower its character, quality, or value.
[4] **Lydia** was an ancient kingdom in western Turkey.
[5] **Mollusks** are soft-bodied invertebrate animals, such as clams.

A MEANS OF EXCHANGE

The historian Fernand
110 Braudel has pointed out
how, in the Middle Ages,[6]
the role of money—and
hence trade and the entire
economy of Europe—
115 got a boost from Italian
ingenuity. A new scheme
was found to get around
the ban of the church
on the lending of money
120 at interest. Merchants
of Tuscany, especially
from Siena and Florence,
employed this new system
at the fairs of northeastern
125 France in the 13th
century. It was called the bill of exchange,
and it opened the door to modern banking.

▲ Coins from the 7th century B.C., made of electrum, a naturally occurring alloy of gold and silver.

I asked Michele Cassandro, professor of modern
economic history at the University of Siena, to clarify
130 for me how it worked: "It would say, for example,
'Signor A, having received so many Sienese scudi,
will pay to Signor B so many Florentine florins at
such and such a place on such and such a date.' That
looks like a currency exchange transaction, but in
135 fact it is a loan agreement, with the interest hidden in
the amount of florins Signor A will be paying." But
there's nothing that specifies it's a loan, and there's
no clause in the agreement that mentions interest—
so there's nothing illegal.

140 Outside the renaissance palace of the Monte dei
Paschi di Siena bank, I found another example of
Italian ingenuity: a foreign-exchange machine,
operating around the clock for the convenience
of tourists. Put in bank notes in any of a dozen
145 European currencies, or Japan's yen, or Canadian,
Australian, or U.S. dollars. In no more than 15
seconds a compartment opens, and there's the
equivalent in Italian lira, down to the last small coin.
An electronic display shows the exchange rates,
150 fluctuating daily.

For many years after World War II, foreign-exchange
rates were pretty much fixed. I remember seeing a
Washington, D.C. exhibit of bank notes from nearly
every country in the world, each with a notation of
155 its value in terms of the U.S. dollar; under the dollar

▲ Coins may have begun as a convenience, but some have taken
on great value today. In the countryside of southwestern Turkey,
treasure hunters with metal detectors hope to unearth ancient coins.

bill it said "equal to one thirty-fifth of a troy ounce[7]
of gold." During this time, foreign governments
were allowed to redeem[8] dollars for gold at the
U.S. treasury. But eventually the demand increased
160 so much that the "gold-exchange standard" was
suspended in 1971, and formally abandoned in 1978.

6 The **Middle Ages** (also called the medieval period) is a period of
European history from the fifth century to the 15th century, following
the fall of the Western Roman Empire in A.D. 476.
7 The **troy ounce** is the unit of weight traditionally used for precious
metals such as gold and platinum (1 troy ounce = 0.0311 kilograms).
8 If you **redeem** a debt or money that has been promised to you, it
means you receive that money.

▲ Walter Cavanagh, a financial planner from California, displays some of his 1,376 credit cards, which he began collecting in 1971. The credit card system as we know it today gained worldwide acceptance in the 1950s, ushering in the age of plastic money.

since the world's nations ceased relying on a direct link between currency and gold, 175 currencies have been "floating" against each other, at prices reflecting demand and supply. Governments try to keep such prices within certain limits but—as has often been the case in recent years—market forces can 180 bring about drastic fluctuations. In any case, today's worldwide foreign-exchange market is the biggest trading system ever, with an estimated daily turnover[11] of one trillion dollars.

185 THE VALUE OF MONEY

Back home I came across a formula that bankers and financial analysts know, that in fact everybody should know—the rule of 72. No one is certain who first discovered 190 the rule, but the principle is quite simple: Divide any number into 72 and the answer is the number of years it will take for a sum to double in financial terms.

For instance, imagine you are charged 18 195 percent interest on the unpaid balance of your credit-card account. Eighteen goes into 72 four times—so the debt will double in four years. The same will be true of any investment. Say your annual salary raise 200 is 6 percent; that number goes into 72 twelve times, so in twelve years your salary will double. And what if, at the same time, inflation runs at 6 percent a year? Then after a dozen years your money will be 205 worth half as much—so in a sense you'll be back where you started!

But look what can happen when inflation doesn't run at 6 percent, but rises at a much faster rate. That can occur when governments 210 issue more and more currency to cover increasing obligations as prices rise. When that happens, inflation can run wild.

Not that the world's governments have discarded[9] their gold bars—they keep lots of them as part of their reserves. In the world's largest gold depository, 165 the subterranean vaults of the Federal Reserve Bank of New York, some 60 countries store over nine million kilograms (10,000 tons) of gold bullion.[10] The U.S. treasury holds thousands of tons more, mainly in the famous vaults at Fort Knox, Kentucky, 170 at West Point, New York, and in Denver, Colorado.

The abandoning of the gold standard led to a paradigm shift in the way currencies are rated. Ever

---

[9] If something is **discarded**, it is thrown away, or gotten rid of.
[10] A **bullion** is a metal coin or bar struck from precious metal and kept as a store of value. The term also refers to a lot of precious metal being stored away.
[11] A **daily turnover** of a company is the amount of revenue it receives per day.

In 1986, Peru's currency—the sol, which is Spanish for sun—fell to 14,000 to the U. S. dollar. So the government cut off three zeroes and called it the inti, which means sun in Quechua, a language spoken by indigenous Peruvians. By mid-1991 a cup of coffee cost 500,000 intis. The government cut off six more zeroes and called it the sol again. Over five years, the inflation rate was 2,200,000 percent!

The most drastic inflation ever? Hungary 1946, after World War II, when Germany had taken away the national bank's gold reserves. By June the Hungarian pengo appeared in notes of a million million billion, which would look like this: 1,000,000,000,000,000,000,000. Then the gold came back, confidence returned, and in August, Hungary had a stable new currency, the forint.

TOWARD A CASHLESS SOCIETY?

Less than ten years after World War II, a new means for payment in place of currency began to spread from the U. S. to much of the world—the use of so-called plastic money, meaning charge cards and credit cards. ATM cards for use in automated teller machines have since proliferated[12] across much of the globe, while charge card payments are now commonplace everywhere from gas stations to supermarkets. In cities from London to Singapore, electronic scanners now allow road toll payments to be automatically deducted without drivers having to slow their car.

From metal to notes to plastic, money has come a long way since its early days in ancient Mesopotamia more than four millennia ago. Soon, perhaps, we will

▲ At the New York Stock Exchange, a securities trader observes the market data on the screen. Today, most NYSE stocks can be traded electronically.

all be living in a world where money is virtual, where notes, coins, and plastic cards are things of the past. In whatever form it takes, money will likely continue to play a central role in our lives, providing the fuel that keeps society moving.

[12] If something has **proliferated**, it has increased and spread at a rapid rate.

☐ Reading Comprehension

A. Multiple Choice. Choose the best answer for each question.

Gist **1.** The best alternative title for this reading would be _____.
a. Coins Now and in the Past
b. From China to the World
c. A Brief History of Money
d. Currency Questions in Yemen

Vocabulary **2.** The word *sound* in line 7 is closest in meaning to _____.
a. distinctive   c. old-fashioned
b. expensive   d. reliable

Detail **3.** To the Yemenis in this article, *omla saaba* (hard currency) is represented by _____.
a. Austrian talers
b. 18th century French coins
c. U.S. dollars
d. Yemeni rials

Detail **4.** Like many other forms of money, the *shekel* mentioned in paragraph 10 (from line 73) was _____.
a. made of both silver and gold
b. a type of paper money
c. named for a unit of weight
d. used throughout western Europe

Negative Detail **5.** Which of the following is NOT true about the first bills of exchange?
a. They provided a way for merchants to lend money despite a religious ban.
b. They involved an exchange of different forms of currency.
c. They represent an early stage in the development of modern banking.
d. They were based on a fixed interest rate set by the government.

Inference **6.** It can be inferred from paragraph 17 (from line 151) that, in the 1970s, U.S. officials _____.
a. wanted to increase the rate at which dollar bills could be exchanged for gold
b. were worried that too much gold was flowing out of the U.S. Treasury
c. decided to lower the rate at which the dollar was traded for other currencies
d. thought that the exchange rate should be fixed as it had been after World War II

Application **7.** According to the rule of 72, if you borrow $1,000 at an interest rate of 9% and do not pay any of it back, when will you owe $2,000?
a. in 4 years   c. in 12 years
b. in 8 years   d. in 18 years

Detail **8.** Which of these forms of currency suffered the worst inflation?
a. the sol   c. the pengo
b. the inti   d. the forint

Concept maps (or *mind maps*) are diagrams that can help you visualize the relationships of ideas in an article. In a typical mind map, the main topic of an article is placed in the center of the diagram. Important subtopics are clustered around the main topic; details are clustered around subtopics, and so on. Mind maps are useful not just for analyzing an article but also for planning your own writing. (See also Unit 3B.)

B. Scanning/Completion. Use information from the passage to complete the concept map. Write the letters of the key topics (**A–E**) and details (**a–n**) in the map, beginning with the earliest forms of money (1).

A. bills of exchange
B. coins
C. forms of money before coins
D. paper money
E. plastic money

a. can be used to get money from ATMs
b. earliest example used in Lydia
c. earliest example: cowrie shells
d. first became widespread in the USA
e. first introduced in China
f. first used at fairs in France
g. first use by a European bank was in Sweden
h. includes credit and charge cards
i. invented in Tuscany, Italy
j. opened the path to modern banking
k. other early examples: aureus, dinar
l. other examples: a drum, salt, clamshell pieces
m. replaced coins as most common form of currency
n. unsuccessfully introduced in Persia by the Mongols

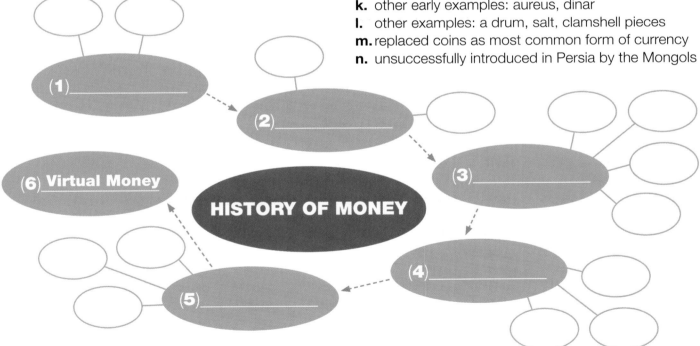

C. Critical Thinking. Discuss these questions with a partner.

1. Look through the article again and list five things you did not previously know about money, and five things you already knew. Compare your list with other students.

2. Do you agree with the author that the future of money is likely to be virtual? What do you think would be the pros and cons of a world without any physical money?

3. In what ways is the style and organization of this article similar to, and different from, the article on the history of writing in Unit 9B? Which do you think is more effective, and why?

Vocabulary Practice

A. Completion. Complete the information using the correct forms of the words in the box. Two words are extra.

affair	clarify	clause
formula	levy	obligated
paradigm	revise	specify
transaction		

▲ Horses adapted to life on the Tibetan Plateau were renowned for being tireless and sure-footed.

For centuries, porters carried heavy loads of tea from Southwest China to Lhasa in Tibet. For these porters, who were **1.** _____ to travel hundreds of kilometers on foot, every pound of tea was worth a pound of rice. But as records of taxes **2.** _____ in ancient China show, the true reward for exporting tea to Tibet was horses.

Tea was first brought to Tibet in about A.D. 641, and quickly became popular as a hot drink in a cold climate. Moreover, a simple **3.** _____ of tea, yak butter, and salt could be stored for days, providing meals for herders working in harsh weather. By the 11th century, it had become the main currency of China. In a typical **4.** _____, 130 pounds of tea were exchanged for a single Tibetan horse, based on a rate of exchange **5.** _____ by the Sichuan Tea and Horse Agency, established in 1074.

Soon, China was trading millions of pounds of tea for some 25,000 horses a year, a state of **6.** _____ that continued until the mid-nineteenth century. When China's need for horses faded, traders **7.** _____ their strategies, returning instead with hides, precious metals, and medicinal plants that thrive only in Tibet. Today, the **8.** _____ for trade here has shifted to a very different arrangement. The Tibetans who once traded horses now trade dried caterpillars, highly in demand as a cure-all for aging bodies, in exchange for motorbikes and modern luxuries.

B. Definitions. Use the correct form of words in the box in **A** to complete the definitions.

1. An act of buying or selling is a(n) _____ .
2. When you _____ something, you explain it to make the situation clearer.
3. If an organization or government _____ a sum of money, you have to pay it.
4. If you _____ something, you provide exact information about what is required.
5. When something is _____, it is changed to make it more appropriate for a particular purpose.
6. A legal document usually contains a number of _____.
7. The _____ for something is a list of the amounts of various substances which make up that thing.
8. When you are _____ to do something, it is your duty to do it.

Word Partnership

Use **obligation** with:
(adj.) **legal** obligation, **moral** obligation
(n.) **sense of** obligation
(v.) obligation **to pay, feel an** obligation, **fulfill an** obligation, **meet an** obligation

Precious Metal

What It's Worth

In coins and later backing for paper money, the price of gold has fluctuated with world crises and market forces. After 1971, when the dominant U.S. dollar was no longer tied to gold, the metal became a freely traded commodity. It reached US$1,000 per ounce for the first time in March 2008, but in real terms its actual value was still well below its peak in the early 1980s.

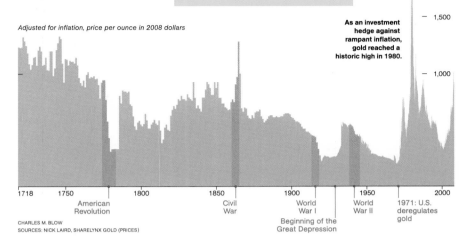

Adjusted for inflation, price per ounce in 2008 dollars

As an investment hedge against rampant inflation, gold reached a historic high in 1980.

1718 1750 1800 1850 1900 1950 2000

American Revolution   Civil War   World War I   World War II   1971: U.S. deregulates gold

Beginning of the Great Depression

CHARLES M. BLOW
SOURCES: NICK LAIRD, SHARELYNX GOLD (PRICES)

How It's Used

Jewelry dominates gold consumption. The metal is also widely used in electronics as an efficient and reliable conductor of electricity. Gold-backed investment funds (exchange-traded funds, or ETFs) became popular as a "safe option" during the financial crisis beginning in mid-2008.

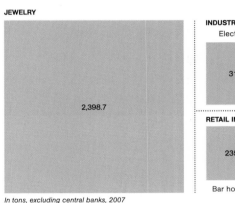

JEWELRY

2,398.7

In tons, excluding central banks, 2007

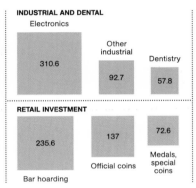

INDUSTRIAL AND DENTAL

Electronics 310.6

Other industrial 92.7

Dentistry 57.8

RETAIL INVESTMENT

Bar hoarding 235.6

Official coins 137

Medals, special coins 72.6

EXCHANGE-TRADED FUNDS 253.3

CHARLES M. BLOW
SOURCES: WORLD GOLD COUNSIL (USES)

☐ Before You Read

A. Understanding Charts. Read the information above and circle whether each statement below is true (**T**) or false (**F**).

1. Without adjustment for inflation, the first time gold reached US$1,000 per ounce was in 2008. **T F**
2. With adjustment for inflation, gold's highest ever value was during the American Civil War. **T F**
3. More gold is used for exchange-traded funds than for electronics. **T F**
4. More gold is used for jewelry than all other uses combined. **T F**

B. Skimming for Main Ideas. The author breaks the main part of the article (pages 230–233) into five sections, indicated by section breaks. Look quickly through the article and match each section with its topic. Then read through the passage to check your ideas.

Section **1** _____   **a.** how big mining companies are excavating the world's gold

Section **2** _____   **b.** the working life of a female truck driver at a gold mine

Section **3** _____   **c.** the attraction of gold from ancient to modern times

Section **4** _____   **d.** how a female truck driver feels about the pros and cons of her job

Section **5** _____   **e.** the influence of gold on India's economy and society

GOLD
A GLOBAL OBSESSION

From an open mine in an Indonesian rain forest to an elaborate wedding ceremony in southern India, writer Brook Larmer follows the path of humanity's most desired commodity.

▲ In the Democratic Republic of the Congo, a miner examines gold extracted from the rocks. Every piece counts when you are mining the world's most coveted metal.

1   As a girl growing up on the remote Indonesian island of Sumbawa, Nur Piah heard tales about vast quantities of gold buried beneath the mountain rain forests. They were legends—until geologists from an
5   American company, Newmont Mining Corporation, discovered a curious green rock near a dormant[1] volcano about 13 kilometers (eight miles) from her home. The rock's mossy color meant it contained copper, an occasional companion to gold, and it
10   wasn't long before Newmont began setting up a mine named Batu Hijau, meaning "green rock."

Nur Piah, then 24, replied to a Newmont ad seeking "operators," thinking that she might be able to get a job answering phones. When she arrived for training,
15   her boss showed her a different kind of operating booth—the cab of a Caterpillar 793, one of the world's largest trucks. Standing six meters (21 feet) tall and 13 meters (43 feet) long, the truck was bigger than her family home. Its wheels alone were double
20   her height. "The truck terrified me," Nur Piah recalls. Another shock soon followed when she saw the mine itself. "They had peeled the skin off the Earth!" she says. "I thought, whatever force can do that must be very powerful."

25   Ten years later, Nur Piah, the daughter of a Muslim cleric, is part of that force herself. Pulling a pink head scarf close around her face, she smiles demurely[2] as she starts up the Caterpillar's engine and heads into the pit at Batu Hijau. Her vehicle is part of a fleet of
30   more than a hundred trucks that removes close to a hundred million tons of rock from the ground every year.

For millions of years, a 550-meter (1,800-foot) volcano stood here, but now no hint of it remains.
35   Layers of rock have been removed, and the space the volcano once occupied has been turned into a 1.6-kilometer (one-mile) wide pit that reaches more than a hundred meters (345 feet) below sea level. By the time the gold supplies at Batu Hijau
40   have been depleted in 20 years or so, the pit will be about 450 meters (1,500 feet) below sea level. The environmental impact doesn't concern Nur Piah anymore. "I only think about getting my salary," she says.

[1] When a volcano is **dormant**, it is inactive but may become active in the future.
[2] If an action is done **demurely**, it is done in a modest and reserved manner. The term is most often used with reference to young women.

THERE IS ONE THING, however, that Nur Piah finds curious: In a decade at Batu Hijau, she has never seen a speck of the gold she has helped mine. The engineers monitoring the process track its presence in the copper compounds that are extracted. And since the gold is shipped out to smelters[3] overseas, nobody on Sumbawa ever sees the hidden treasure that has transformed their island.

Newmont is one of several giant mining corporations that are pursuing gold to the ends of the Earth, from the lowlands of Ghana to the mountaintops of Peru. Part of the challenge of mining for gold is that there is so little of it. In all of history, only about 160,000 tons (145 million kilograms) of gold have been mined, barely enough to fill two Olympic-size swimming pools. More than half of that has been extracted in the past 50 years. Now the world's richest deposits—particularly those in the U.S., South Africa, and Australia—are fast being depleted, and new discoveries are rare.

In recent years, attracted by the benefits of operating in the developing world—lower costs, higher yields, fewer regulations—Newmont has generated tens of thousands of jobs in poorer regions of the world. But it has also come under attack from conservationists, who have filed complaints about unrestrained ecological destruction and the forced relocation of villagers. At Batu Hijau, where Newmont is responsible for the mine's operation, the company has responded by spending more on its community development and environmental programs—and dismissing its critics.

"Why is it that activists thousands of miles away are yelling, but nobody around the mine complains?" asks Malik Salim, Batu Hijau's senior external relations manager. "Gold is what drives everybody crazy."

GOLD HAS BEEN DRIVING people crazy for millennia. The desire to possess gold has driven people to extremes, fueling wars and conquests, boosting empires and currencies, leveling mountains and forests. Gold is not vital to human existence; it has, in fact, relatively few practical uses. Yet its chief attractions—its unusual density and malleability[4] along with its imperishable[5] shine—have made it one of the world's most desired commodities, a symbol of beauty, wealth, and immortality. From pharaohs (who chose to be buried in what they called the "flesh of the gods") to financiers (who, following Sir Isaac

▲ Trucks haul waste rock out of the mine area at Batu Hijau, a copper and gold mine in Indonesia. Where a volcanic mountain once stood, there is now only a vast pit.

Newton's advice, made it the foundation of the global economy), nearly every society has invested gold with an almost mythological status.

Humankind's feverish attachment to gold shouldn't have survived the modern world. Few cultures still believe that gold can give eternal life, and every country in the world—the United States was last, in 1971—has done away with the gold standard, which the economist John Maynard Keynes[6] famously called "a barbarous[7] relic." But gold's appeal not only endures; fueled by global uncertainty, it grows stronger.

[3] **Smelters** are people or companies who melt ores in order to extract the metals they contain.

[4] **Malleability** refers to the ease with which an object or a person can be altered and changed.
[5] If something is **imperishable**, it never dies out or disappears.
[6] **John Maynard Keynes** (1883–1946) was a British economist whose ideas led to what is known as Keynesian economics.
[7] If something is described as **barbarous**, it is considered primitive and uncivilized.

110 Aside from extravagance,[8] gold is also reprising its role as a safe haven in financially unstable times. Gold's recent surges have been amplified by concerns over a looming global recession. In 2007, demand exceeded mine production by 59 percent. "Gold
115 has always had this kind of magic," says Peter L. Bernstein, author of *The Power of Gold*. "But it's never been clear if we have gold—or gold has us."

While investors flock to gold-backed funds, jewelry still accounts for two-thirds of the demand,
120 generating a record $53.5 billion in worldwide sales in 2007. In the U.S. an activist-driven "No Dirty Gold" campaign has persuaded many top jewelry
125 retailers to stop selling gold from mines that cause severe social or environmental damage. But such concerns have little impact on the biggest consumer nations,
130 namely China—which surpassed the U.S. in 2007 to become the world's second largest buyer of gold jewelry—and, above all, India.

135 NOWHERE IS THE GOLD OBSESSION more culturally entrenched[9] than in India. Per capita income in this country of a billion people is $2,700, but it has been
140 the world's runaway leader in gold demand for several decades. In 2007, India consumed 773.6 tons of gold, about 20 percent of the world gold market and more than double
145 that purchased by either of its closest followers, China (363.3 tons) and the U.S. (278.1 tons). India produces very little gold of its own, but its citizens have hoarded[10] up to 18,000 tons of the yellow metal—more than 40 times the amount held in the
150 country's central bank.

India's obsession stems not simply from a love of extravagance, or the rising prosperity of an emerging middle class. For Muslims, Hindus, Sikhs, and Christians alike, gold plays a central role at nearly
155 every turning point in life—most of all when a couple marries. There are some ten million weddings in India every year, and in all but a few, gold is crucial both to the spectacular event itself and to the transaction

between families and generations. "It's written into
160 our DNA," says K. A. Babu, a manager at the Alapatt jewelry store in the southwestern city of Cochin (Kochi). "Gold equals good fortune."

The importance of gold is most obvious during the springtime festival of Akshaya Tritiya, considered the
165 most auspicious day to buy gold according to the Hindu calendar. The quantity of gold jewelry Indians purchase on this day—49 tons in 2008—so exceeds the amount bought on any other day of the year

▲ The gold vault at the Federal Reserve Bank of New York lies 80 feet below street level. It is reputedly the largest gold repository in the world, currently holding approximately 5,000 metric tons of gold bullion.

throughout the world that it often pushes gold
170 prices higher.

"We grow up in an atmosphere of gold," says Renjith Leen, a magazine editor based in Kerala, a relatively prosperous state on India's southern tip that claims just 3 percent of the country's population but 7 to
175 8 percent of its gold market. When a baby is born, a grandmother rubs a gold coin in honey and places a drop of the liquid on the child's tongue for good luck. When the child is three years old, a learned family member takes a gold coin and traces words on
180 the child's tongue to give the gift of eloquence.[11]

---

[8] **Extravagance** is the spending of more money than is reasonable or than you can afford.
[9] If something such as a custom or an idea is **entrenched**, it is firmly established and difficult to change.
[10] When something is **hoarded**, it is accumulated and kept hidden away for future use.
[11] Someone who has the gift of **eloquence** can write and speak very well.

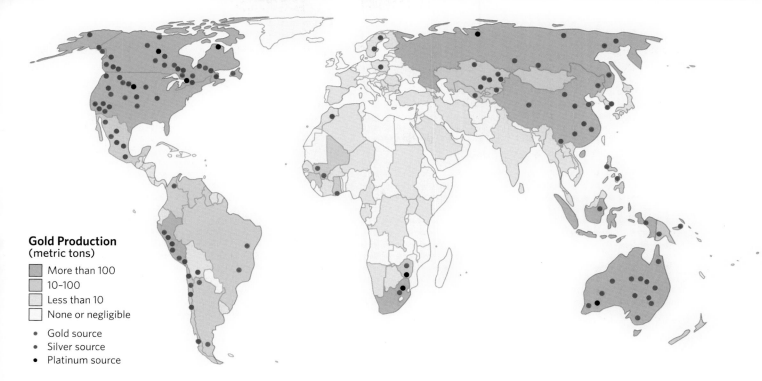

Gold Production
(metric tons)

- More than 100
- 10–100
- Less than 10
- None or negligible

- Gold source
- Silver source
- Platinum source

In all of history, only about 160,000 tons of gold have been mined, barely enough to fill two Olympic-size swimming pools.

Aside from its cultural significance, gold is also the bedrock of the Indian economy. "Gold is the basis of our financial system," says K.A. Babu. "People see it as the best form of security, and nothing else
185 lets you get cash as quickly." Hoarding gold as an intergenerational family nest egg[12] is an ancient tradition in India. So, too, is pawning[13] gold jewelry for emergency loans—and then buying it back.

As the price of the metal goes up, however, poor
190 Indian families are having a harder time raising the gold they need for dowries.[14] Rajam Chidambaram, a 59-year-old widow living in a slum on the outskirts of Cochin, recently found a young man to marry her only daughter, age 27. The groom's family,
195 however, demanded a dowry far out of her reach: 25 sovereigns, or 200 grams (seven ounces), of gold (worth more than $5,000 today). Chidambaram, a cleaning woman, has only the two earrings she wears; the gold necklace she once owned went to pay off
200 her deceased husband's hospital bills. "I had to agree to the groom's demand," Chidambaram says, wiping away tears. "If I refuse, my daughter will stay home forever."

In the end, local financiers advanced a loan for her
205 daughter's dowry. Her daughter may now be married, but Chidambaram is now faced with a debt that she may spend the rest of her life trying to repay.

FOUR THOUSAND KILOMETERS (2,500 miles) away, in her new house in the village of Jereweh, Nur Piah
210 is focused more on the present than the future. "So many people depend on me," she says. Her husband makes some money as a timber trader, but Nur Piah's salary—about $650 a month—paid for their two-story concrete home. As if in tribute, she has hung a
215 large painting of the yellow Caterpillar 793 on her wall.

Nur Piah's job is not without its hardships. Maneuvering the enormous truck over a 12-hour shift is especially stressful, she says, when the pit's graded
220 roads are slicked by torrential rains. But now, after a long day, she smiles contentedly as her child, age six, falls asleep on her lap. The girl's middle name? Higrid, the Indonesian approximation of "high-grade," the best ore in the mine.

---

[12] Someone's **nest egg** refers to their monetary savings, which have been put aside for later use.

[13] **Pawning** something is the act of giving or depositing items of personal property (with a pawnbroker) as security for the payment of money borrowed.

[14] **Dowries** are portions of money or property given by a bride's family to her husband at marriage.

A GOLDEN WEDDING

225 The gold ornaments come out of the velvet boxes one by one, family treasures that Nagavi, a 23-year-old Indian bride, always knew she would wear on her wedding day. The eldest daughter of a coffee plantation owner in the southern Indian state of

230 Karnataka, Nagavi grew up marveling at the weddings that mark the merger of two wealthy Indian families. But not until the morning of her own arranged wedding to the only son of another coffee plantation family does she understand just how beautiful the

235 golden tradition can be.

By the time Nagavi is ready for her wedding, the university graduate has been transformed into an Indian princess, covered in gold. An elaborately crafted hairpiece is so heavy—two and a half

240 kilograms (5.5 lb)—that it pulls her head back. Three gold necklaces and a dozen other pieces of jewelry act as effective counterweights. As the family members convene, Nagavi walks slowly out of her home, trying to keep her balance as she tosses rice over her head in

245 a traditional gesture of farewell.

The gold treasures Nagavi wears are not a traditional dowry. In this circle of coffee growers around the town of Chikmagalur—unlike in many poorer parts of the country—it is considered inappropriate for a

250 groom's family to make explicit demands. "This is seen as my 'share' of the family wealth," says Nagavi, gazing at the millions of dollars of gold jewelry. As with any Indian wedding, the gold also serves to display the value she brings to the union. "With

255 daughters, you have to start saving gold from the day they are born," says Nagavi's father, C. P. Ravi Shankar. "It's important to marry them off well."

▲ Wearing her fortune, from gold threads in her sari to a priceless ▶ golden headpiece, bride Nagavi prepares for her elaborate wedding day.

Reading Comprehension

A. Multiple Choice. Choose the best answer for each question.

Detail

1. Before Newmont began mining operations, the area in Sumbawa that is now a gold mine was _____.
a. an inactive volcano
b. a deep pit
c. a copper mine
d. a remote village

Rhetorical Purpose

2. What is the main purpose of paragraph 6 (from line 52)?
a. to show how gold production has decreased in the past 50 years
b. to emphasize that gold is actually a very rare commodity
c. to point out how successful giant mining companies have been
d. to indicate that some rich new gold deposits have been found

Cohesion

3. Where would be the best place to insert this sentence in paragraph 7 (from line 68)?
For example, it stresses its efforts to reclaim the heaps of discarded rock, by covering them with soil and allowing the jungle to grow again.
a. before the first sentence
b. after the first sentence
c. after the second sentence
d. after the third sentence

Inference

4. The quote from John Maynard Keynes in line 107 shows that Keynes thought that _____.
a. the U.S. should have maintained the gold standard
b. gold's appeal was about to end
c. the gold standard was out of date
d. no one still believed that gold gives eternal life

Detail

5. Today the country that consumes the second-largest amount of gold jewelry is _____.
a. China
b. India
d. Indonesia
c. the United States

Application

6. Given the information in paragraph 13 (from line 135), approximately how many tons of gold is held in the central bank of India?
a. 450
b. 775
c. 18,000
d. 720,000

Detail

7. Which of the following causes Nur Piah the most job-related stress?
a. the difficulty of finding gold
b. the low wages she receives
c. driving her truck in bad weather
d. spending long hours at work

Detail

8. Which of the following is true about Nagavi?
a. her husband used to work on her father's coffee plantation
b. she got married after she had graduated from university
c. her family is from a very poor part of India
d. she is her father's only daughter

Strategy Focus: Identifying Coherence Devices

Authors use a number of devices to achieve *coherence*. These expressions join together paragraphs, sentences, and parts of a sentence. Coherence makes an article feel unified and whole. Examples include:

Pronouns and Similar Words

Personal pronouns: Newmont is an American mining company. It is based in Denver, Colorado. (The word *It* links the second sentence to Newmont in the first sentence.)

Demonstratives (This/That): Only about 160,000 tons of gold have ever been mined. And about half of that (or that gold) has been extracted. (*That* or *that gold* joins the second sentence to the first by referring to about 160,000 tons of gold in the first sentence.)

Forms of other (another, other, others): One place mining companies have looked for gold is in in the lowlands of Ghana. Another (or Another place) is in the mountains of Peru. (The phrase *One place* is linked to the phrase *Another* or *Another place* in the second sentence.)

Connecting Words

Conjunctions (and, but, or, yet, etc.): Gold is not vital to human existence. Yet it is one of the world's most valued commodities. (The conjunction *Yet* joins the two sentences and shows the contrast between the ideas.)

Signal Words (therefore, however, in addition, for example, etc.): The gold ore that is found on Sumbawa is all shipped overseas. Therefore, no one on the island sees any pure gold. (The word *therefore* joins the two sentences by showing the relationship of cause/effect.)

Synonyms and Repetition

Synonyms: Aside from its cultural significance, gold is also the bedrock of the Indian economy. "Gold is the basis of our financial system." (The words *bedrock* and *basis* are synonyms; so are *economy* and *financial system*. The use of these synonyms links the two sentences.)

Repetition: When a baby is born, a grandmother rubs a gold coin in honey and places a drop of the liquid on the child's tongue for good luck. When the child is three years old, a learned family member takes a gold coin and traces words on the child's tongue to give the gift of eloquence. (The repetition of the word *child* joins the first sentence to the two parts of the second sentence; it also acts as a synonym in the first sentence for baby)

B. Scanning/Classification. Look again at the first page of the article (page 230). Scan for examples of coherence devices and note them in the chart.

Coherence device	Type of device (pronoun, connecting word, etc.)	What is joined? (parts of a sentence, two sentences, two paragraphs)

C. Critical Thinking. Discuss these questions with a partner.

1. Why do you think the author focuses on the personal stories of Nur Piah and Nagavi? Do the stories effectively support the main focus of the article?

2. The author presents some positive and negative aspects of mining and buying gold. List the pro-gold and anti-gold ideas he mentions. Can you think of other aspects not mentioned?

3. Imagine that a mining company has found a rich deposit of gold near your hometown. The company has promised to bring 4,000 well-paying jobs to your town if it is allowed to mine the gold. Would you favor the company's plan or oppose it? Why?

Vocabulary Practice

A. Definitions. Read the information below and match each word in red with its definition.

▲ On top of a mountain, a Mongolian shaman conducts rituals worshiping the spirits of the land.

Mongolia has some of the Earth's largest high-grade gold, copper, and uranium reserves. At present, the mining industry makes up two-thirds of Mongolia's export transactions. For many, such a mining boom marks an auspicious time in the growth of the country's economy.

But as mining companies rush to extract Mongolia's vast deposits of gold and other minerals, government regulations—including laws that explicitly state that mining may not be done near rivers—are being violated or ignored. Many rivers now run dry, or are polluted, making it difficult for nomadic herders to find water for their animals.

In addition, many of the mining sites abandoned by larger companies due to protests filed by local activists, or because their resources have been depleted, have been taken over by illegal miners known as "ninjas." Such ninja miners convene in remote settlements, where their unofficial status has allowed for the unrestrained use of mercury in the mines, which pollute and poison nearby rivers. Environmentalists are concerned that the situation is grim for the survival of nomadic herders, who depend on the Mongolian land and its waters for their way of life.

1. clearly and directly _____
2. likely to be successful _____
3. reduced in quantity _____
4. level of quality _____
5. made an official complaint, or request _____
6. social, professional, or legal position _____
7. uncontrolled _____
8. come together _____

Word Partnership

Use **status** with:
(*v.*) **achieve** status, **maintain one's** status
(*n.*) **celebrity** status, **wealth and** status, **change of** status, **tax** status
(*adj.*) **current** status, **economic** status, **marital** status, **financial** status, **legal** status

B. Completion. Complete the information by circling the most appropriate word in each pair.

In India, gold is an important element in the **1.** merger / reprise of two families through marriage. In the wedding transaction, it is usual for the groom's family to make **2.** auspicious / explicit requests for the bride to bring gold jewelry into the family. The higher the couple's **3.** status / grade in society, the more gold is expected. Even relatively poor Indian families are required to provide gold for a daughter's wedding, sometimes **4.** reprising / depleting their limited financial resources. When the families finally **5.** convene / deplete for the wedding, the gold is worn by the bride to publicly display the value she has brought to the marriage.

The Art Smuggler

▲ A team of police search a street market in Rome for stolen art.

A. Preview. You will hear these phrases in the video. What do you think they mean? Match each phrase to its meaning.

1. . . . [He] does not deny he has bent the rules . . .

2. . . . knowing you have a stolen object. You have laundered it and you can sell it . . .

3. . . . give hope that something can be done to stem the trade . . .

4. . . . but justice does sometimes prevail . . .

a. _____ to stop or hold back

b. _____ to win out over, or against, someone or something

c. _____ to do something that is not usually allowed

d. _____ to disguise the source or nature of something, for example, illegal funds, by channeling them through an intermediate agent

B. Summarize. Watch the video, *The Art Smuggler*. Then complete the summary below using the correct form of words in the box. Two words are extra.

auspicious	context	convene	deny	fake
paradigm	participate	status	transaction	valid

Michel Van Rijn was once an infamous art smuggler. He does not
1. _____ his colorful past, nor that he has bent the rules. Today, Van Rijn works as a consultant, helping the police to expose art crimes. So far, he has **2.** _____ in the recovery of several valuable artworks around the world.

Van Rijn explains that it is often quite easy for smugglers to give stolen art and artifacts the illusion of legal **3.** _____, before shipping them elsewhere to be sold. These pieces are usually sold in major cities, such as New York and London, where art smugglers and buyers often
4. _____. One way to make a piece of stolen art seem legal is to create a **5.** _____ paper trail. For example, if only the smugglers know a piece of art exists, they can send a photo of the object to the Art Loss Register. They may then receive a **6.** _____ letter certifying that it does not match any record of known stolen art. From then on, the
7. _____ involved in selling the piece will seem to be perfectly legal.

Sadly, the profitability of the illegal art trade continues to motivate people to steal art and artifacts. By completely removing items from their original
8. _____, art theft often prevents historians from discovering their true histories, and with it, their true value as artifacts of the past.

C. Think About It.

1. Do you think former criminals, such as Michel Van Rijn, should be allowed to help with police investigations? Should it depend on the nature of the crime?

2. Think of some art works and historical pieces that are extremely valuable. Why are they worth so much money? Is it due mainly to their beauty, rarity, fame, or another reason?

 To learn more about wealth and finance, visit elt.heinle.com/explorer

☐ Reading Extension 4

A. World Heritage Spotlight. Read the information about Robben Island on pages 240–241 and answer the questions (**1–3**).

1. Sequencing. Number the events in the order they occurred (**1–8**).

_____ Dutch colonialists start moving prisoners to Robben Island.

_____ Early humans cross to Robben Island via a land bridge.

_____ Nelson Mandela becomes President.

_____ Nelson Mandela gives a speech on poverty in London.

__6__ Nelson Mandela is released from prison.

_____ Nelson Mandela's autobiography is published.

_____ Robben Island becomes a World Heritage Site.

_____ Robben Island is used to house people with leprosy.

_____ The first apartheid prisoners are moved to Robben Island.

_____ The first Europeans arrive on Robben Island.

_____ The UN establishes Nelson Mandela International Day.

2. Vocabulary from Context. Find words or phrases on page 240 that are closest in meaning to the following (**a–f**).

a. _____ given a legal punishment by a court

b. _____ imagine that you are experiencing (something) again

c. _____ official practice of keeping certain people apart, e.g., different sexes or races

d. _____ serious or sad

e. _____ people who campaign for social or political changes

f. _____ people who have been sent away from a place against their will

3. Discussion. Do you think Nelson Mandela was an appropriate choice as the first individual to be awarded a UN International Day? If you could declare an "International Day" in recognition of someone, who would it be, and why?

B. A Global View. Read the text and graphics on pages 242–243 and discuss the following questions with a partner.

1. What are three ways in which the UN hopes to develop a global partnership for development?

2. In which parts of the world are people most, and least, connected to the Internet?

3. What does FrontlineSMS enable people to do? What kinds of people might benefit?

4. How does a debt-for-nature deal work? What benefits does this type of arrangement offer? Can you think of any potential problems?

5. What does the GINI Index represent? Is there any correlation between GINI and levels of debt?

6. What kind of gap exists between rich and poor people in your country? Do you think it is widening or getting narrower? Why?

Island of Exiles

Site: **Robben Island**

Location: **South Africa**

Category: **Cultural**

Status: **World Heritage Site since 1999**

Cape Town

The summit of a submerged mountain, Robben Island (foreground) was once linked to the mainland and may have been occupied by early humans.

Just seven kilometers (4.5 miles) from the beaches of Cape Town, at the southernmost point of the African continent, is Robben Island, a low-lying rocky island also known as the Isle of Exiles. Despite its dramatic setting and Mediterranean climate, this is no pleasure resort. Instead, it has been a place of imprisonment, exile, and isolation for four centuries—most notably serving as a prison for South Africa's anti-apartheid leaders, including the country's first democratically elected president, Nelson Mandela.

The first Europeans to arrive there were probably members of Vasco de Gama's fleet, who stopped in search of supplies during their pioneering voyage from Europe to India in 1498. In later centuries the island was used by Dutch colonialists as a place to send slaves and prisoners of war, including Muslim activists fighting Dutch colonization in the Far East. They were succeeded by the British who continued to use it as a prison, as well as a settlement for people suffering from leprosy (a disease characterized by a severe skin condition).

In 1959, the South African authorities converted the island into a maximum security prison for those sentenced by the apartheid regime (a system of legal racial discrimination and segregation enforced by the National Party government between 1948 and 1994). The most celebrated prisoner, Nelson Mandela, spent some 20 years on the island before his eventual release in 1990. Following its closure in 1996, the prison was developed as a museum where visitors can relive some of the island's somber history. It is recognized by UNESCO as a symbol "of the triumph of the human spirit" and was made a World Heritage Site in 1999.

▲ *I was assigned a cell at the head of the corridor. It overlooked the courtyard and had a small eye-level window. I could walk the length of my cell in three paces. When I lay down, I could feel the wall with my feet and my head grazed the concrete at the other side. The width was about six feet, and the walls were at least two feet thick . . . I was forty-six years old, a political prisoner with a life sentence, and that small cramped space was to be my home for I knew not how long.*

– from Nelson Mandela's autobiography, *Long Walk to Freedom* (1995)

A Global Ambassador

Following his release from prison in 1990, and subsequent period as South African President (1994–1999), Nelson Mandela traveled widely as an ambassador of peace, negotiating an end to conflicts, promoting gender equality and the rights of children, and raising awareness of the poorest and most vulnerable communities.

"[I]n this new century, millions of people in the world's poorest countries remain imprisoned, enslaved, and in chains," he said in a speech in London in 2005. "They are trapped in the prison of poverty . . . Overcoming poverty is not a gesture of charity. It is an act of justice."

In November 2009, the UN General Assembly declared 18 July "Nelson Mandela International Day" in recognition of his contribution to the culture of peace and freedom. It was the first time that the UN had dedicated an International Day to an individual.

Prison Islands

Islands are often chosen as prison locations due to their remoteness. Five of the most famous:

Alcatraz, USA

Known as The Rock, this island in San Francisco Bay housed several of America's most notorious criminals, including Al Capone. The prison closed in 1963 and is now a popular tourist site.

Devil's Island, French Guiana

This tiny island off the coast of South America was used as a French prison until 1952. It became world famous with the publication in 1970 of the book *Papillon*. The author, Henri Charriere, claimed the events in the book were true. Others accused him of making up details of his supposed escape attempts.

Tarutao, Thailand

At the end of World War II, supplies from the mainland to this Thai prison island were cut off. Consequently, the island's guards and prisoners decided to join forces and launch pirate raids on ships sailing near the island. The pirates were eventually defeated and the prison shut down.

Sado Island, Japan

A remote Japanese island off the coast of Niigata, Sado was used as a place of exile for nearly one thousand years, from the 8th century until 1700. Among its prisoners were the former Emperor Juntoku and the Buddhist monk Nichiren Daishonin.

St. Helena

One of the most isolated islands in the world, this rocky British colony in the Atlantic Ocean is best known as the place where Napoleon I was exiled following his defeat at the Battle of Waterloo in 1815. He died on the island in 1821, although the exact cause of his death remains controversial.

Global Development

A Global View

Goal 8 of the UN MDGs is to develop a global partnership for development. Specifically, this requires developing a more open trading and financial system, addressing the special needs of least developed countries—for example, by increasing development aid from richer donor countries, and reducing the poorest countries' debt—and increasing global access to new technologies, especially information and communication technologies (ICTs).

Despite the recent financial crisis, overall levels of official development assistance (ODA) have continued to rise, reaching almost $120 billion in 2009. In that year, the largest donors in terms of volume of development aid were the United States, France, Germany, the United Kingdom, and Japan, although none of these achieved the UN target of donating 0.7 percent of gross national income.

Developing countries are also more connected to the rest of the world than ever before, primarily through trade and technology. Over 40 percent of global trade involves developing economies, compared to 35 percent in 2000. In addition, access to ICTs is expanding fast. By the end of 2008, 1.6 billion people—nearly a quarter of the world's population—were using the Internet. Nevertheless, in some parts of the developing world, access is still limited; in Southern Asia, Oceania, and sub-Saharan Africa, fewer than one in 15 people are online.

▲ A group of boys sits atop the sand at a beach near the Angolan capital of Luanda. Angola has experienced a steady improvement in its economy since the end of its civil war in 2002. However, like many other sub-Saharan countries, it is still heavily dependent on foreign assistance and trade to meet its domestic needs.

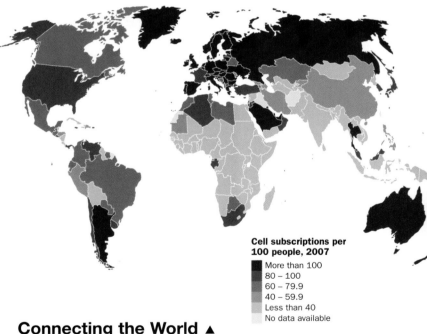

Cell subscriptions per 100 people, 2007

- More than 100
- 80 – 100
- 60 – 79.9
- 40 – 59.9
- Less than 40
- No data available

Connecting the World ▲

While the number of traditional telephone lines continues to grow steadily, cell phone subscriptions are booming, particularly in the developing world. In sub-Saharan Africa, where only 1 percent of people have access to fixed telephone lines, more than 30 percent now have mobile phones.

According to innovator Ken Banks, there is huge potential for using cell phones to link people in remote areas who have no Internet access. Banks created a system called FrontlineSMS, which enables people in more than 50 nations to send and receive information using a laptop connected to a cell phone. Now farmers in Indonesia, Cambodia, Niger, and El Salvador can receive up-to-date market prices for crops and fish via text message, allowing them to be more economically competitive. "FrontlineSMS gives [people] tools to create their own projects and make a difference," says Banks.

Swapping Debt for Nature

The map below shows each nation's outstanding foreign debt in relation to the size of its economy (Gross Domestic Product, or GDP). In recent years, overall debt burdens have eased for developing countries. However, the external debt ratio is still high among some nations in Africa, South America, and central Asia, many of which rely on foreign money to finance investment and consumption.

In 2010, the United States and Brazilian governments approved a deal converting $21 million of Brazilian debt into a fund to protect tropical ecosystems. Instead of paying back the debt, Brazil will use the money to conserve its Atlantic coastal rainforest and other ecosystems. Another debt-for-nature deal was initiated in 2006 between France and Cameroon. In return for debt relief, Cameroon committed to invest at least $25 million in protecting parts of the Congo River basin, the world's second largest tropical rainforest.

▲ Debt-for-nature swaps involving Central African countries, such as the France-Cameroon partnership, could help preserve many of the Congo Basin's most threatened species, including the lowland gorilla.

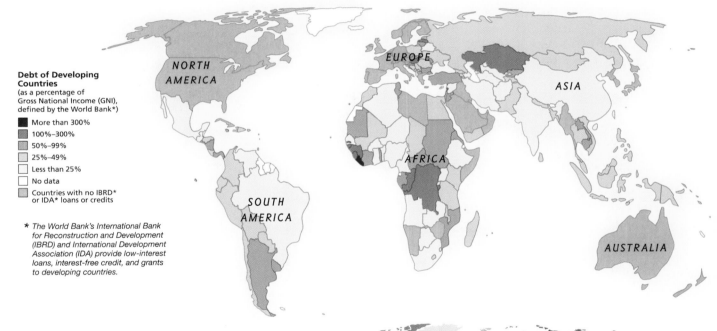

Debt of Developing Countries
(as a percentage of Gross National Income (GNI), defined by the World Bank*)

- ■ More than 300%
- ■ 100%–300%
- ■ 50%–99%
- ■ 25%–49%
- □ Less than 25%
- □ No data
- ■ Countries with no IBRD* or IDA* loans or credits

* *The World Bank's International Bank for Reconstruction and Development (IBRD) and International Development Association (IDA) provide low-interest loans, interest-free credit, and grants to developing countries.*

Rich and Poor

The GINI index is used as a measure of inequality of income and wealth within countries. Scandinavian countries have the lowest values, meaning there is very little difference between their richest and poorest citizens. Some sub-Saharan and Latin American countries rank the highest, with Bolivia, the Central African Republic, and Botswana having the widest gap between their poorest and wealthiest.

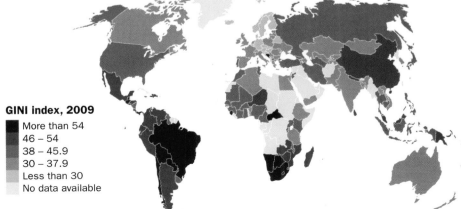

GINI index, 2009

- ■ More than 54
- ■ 46 – 54
- ■ 38 – 45.9
- ■ 30 – 37.9
- □ Less than 30
- □ No data available

A Global View **243**

□ Vocabulary Building 4

A. Word Link. Each of the words in the box contains **inter**, meaning *between*. Match each word with its meaning. One word is extra. Use your dictionary to help you.

interchange	interfere	intermediate	intermingle	intermission
intermittent	international	interpersonal	intersection	

1. _____ (to) mix together (e.g., two or more groups of people) (*v.*)

2. _____ between beginning and advanced (*adj.*)

3. _____ relating to relationships between people (*adj.*)

4. _____ exchange of ideas or thoughts (*n.*)

5. _____ a short break in a concert or play (*n.*)

6. _____ happening occasionally rather than continuously (*adj.*)

7. _____ (to) deliberately get involved in something that does not concern you (*v.*)

8. _____ place where roads meet or cross (*n.*)

B. Word Forms. Complete the chart with the missing noun forms. Then complete the sentences below, using the correct words from the chart. Two words are extra.

1. The _____ for success is hard work plus a certain amount of luck.

2. In some countries, women are _____ to men in certain aspects of society.

3. Talented employees may be able to work their way up through a corporate _____ until they became company president.

Adjective	Noun
demonstrative	
discriminatory	
ethical	
formulaic	
hierarchical	
investigative	
justifiable	
obligatory	
statistical	
subordinate	

4. Some people believe that violence in war is never _____.

5. In some professions, it is _____ for workers to retire at the age of sixty-five.

6. There is still widespread _____ against people with minority status.

7. Governments impose laws and regulations to ensure companies conduct their business in a(n) _____ way.

8. Official crime _____ show how many robberies and other crimes occur each year.

C. Word Partnership. In each space below, write the word from the box that can follow all three words to form common word partnerships. Then match a word partnership with each definition below.

affairs hierarchy	discrimination status	evaluation transaction	formula violation

1. simple, mathematical, chemical   _____
2. current, foreign, love   _____
3. gender, religious, age   _____
4. marital, legal, social   _____
5. traffic, ethical, rights   _____
6. financial, bank, cash   _____
7. social, corporate, organizational   _____
8. product, student, health   _____

a. _____ married, single, divorced, widowed
b. _____ incident involving a vehicle that breaks the law
c. _____ payment with notes and coins
d. _____ levels of importance in a business
e. _____ political relationships between countries
f. _____ series of numbers or letters that represent a rule
g. _____ negative bias based on sex
h. _____ report on academic performance

D. Choosing the Right Definition. Study the numbered definitions for *liberal*. Then write the number of the definition (**1–5**) that relates to each sentence below. One definition is extra.

liberal /lɪbərəl/ (liberals) **1** ADJ Someone who has **liberal** views believes people should have a lot of freedom in deciding how to behave and think. N-COUNT *Liberal* is also a noun. **2** ADJ A **liberal** system allows people or organizations a lot of political or economic freedom. **3** ADJ A **liberal** politician or voter is a member of or voter for a **liberal** party. **4** ADJ **Liberal** means giving, using, or taking a lot of something, or existing in large quantities. ADV **liberally** **5** N-PLU At a university or college, **liberal arts** courses are on subjects such as history or literature.

_____ **a.** The **Liberal** Democratic Party (LDP) is one of the largest political parties in Japan.
_____ **b.** Guests at the wedding party are often provided with **liberal** amounts of food and drink.
_____ **c.** **Liberal** laws on economic and social reform have led to prosperity in some countries.
_____ **d.** The politician was well known for his **liberal** views on social issues.

Target Vocabulary

Target Vocabulary

Academic Word List Index

The Academic Word List (AWL) was developed by researcher Averil Coxhead and contains the 570 word families in English that are most needed to study at tertiary institutions. The list does not include words that are in the most frequent 2,000 words of English. Each word appears in context at least once in *Reading Explorer 5*. The reading passage in which each word first appears is listed below. For more information on the AWL, see http://www.victoria.ac.nz/lals/resources/academicwordlist/.

1 Temples in the Jungle

Narrator:

In Southeast Asia, an abandoned city lies at the heart of Cambodia. Its hundreds of monuments contain more stone than the Egyptian Pyramids, and cover more ground than modern Paris.

This is Angkor, the capital of a sophisticated civilization that once controlled most of Southeast Asia. Its people were called the Khmer. And more than five hundred years ago, they fled this grand city.

In 1860, Henri Mouhot, a French naturalist, travelled to these ruins hidden by the jungle. In his writings, he described the wonders of Angkor and drew pictures of it, attracting the world's attention. But the questions had only just begun. Who were Angkor's builders? And why was it abandoned?

Today, Angkor is a World Heritage Site, prized for both its history and its intrinsic beauty. Its story has been pieced together by archaeologists and historians, who tell us Angkor's greatest marvel, Angkor Wat, served as a shrine, an observatory, and a funerary temple, and suspect it took almost thirty years to build.

Soon after, disaster struck the city. Drawn by its wealth and beauty, the Chams, from what is now Vietnam, attacked and burned the city.

But the Khmer civilization persisted. The capital was rebuilt, and the king built a walled city, Angkor Thom, to protect them in time of war. Nevertheless, the Khmer's story came to an end not long afterward.

Twenty two kings over 500 years worked the land, developing ingenious irrigation systems to channel water to the fields. But eventually, the rice harvest failed.

Early in the 15th century, the kingdom of Siam made raids into Khmer territory. Angkor was more vulnerable than ever. A huge battle around 1431 almost destroyed the Khmer. What remained of the people began to disperse, and the city was consumed by the jungle.

2 Comet Watchers

Narrator:

The Islands of Hawaii. Ancient Polynesians had to use the stars to find them, and it is the stars that bring a new breed of explorers here now.

Here lies the earth's highest volcano, Mauna Kea—the highest point on these tropical islands. It stands above city lights and industrial pollution, a freezing mountaintop which may be the best astronomical site in the world. This month's star attraction is Comet Halley, a cloud of ice and dust making its way across the night sky.

Dale Cruikshank, University of Hawaii comet specialist:

"I think the amateur astronomers and professional astronomers share a lot of the same enthusiasm over something as exciting as a comet and in particular a comet as famous as this one. We all enjoy looking at it, taking pictures of it, trying to understand more about it and enjoying the whole nighttime sky that we'll soon have available to us here in a few minutes."

Narrator:

Minutes are nothing in the context of the comet's four billion year past—or even the 76 year wait since Halley's last appearance. As a once-in-a-lifetime experience, Halley creates a special excitement.

Comet Watcher 1:

"It's something that you want to be able to experience. Even for those of us who don't do much in comet watching or star gazing. I have trouble finding the Big Dipper in the sky. But I just love the idea of being able to see something that I . . . you know, once."

Ron, Infrared Specialist:

"I think that people do expect to be able to walk out and see this big bright object in the sky and without searching very hard. I think people expect to see the comet in the sky and see it moving. The pictures that you see published show a big long tail which makes it look like it's flying through the atmosphere and spewing off this tail. And although that's what it looks like, the object is really millions of miles away. The tail is being caused by the solar wind."

Narrator:

Renowned astronomers come here for what they call "the best seeing in the world." The top of Mauna Kea reaches halfway to outer space, and giant telescopes take astronomers the rest of the way. These telescopes require intensive care. Refrigerated domes keep temperatures constant. Any variation can affect the telescope's mechanisms and distort the images. This 61-centimeter telescope is less sophisticated than its more advanced neighbors, but it compensates with a special camera, which makes an important contribution.

Dale Cruikshank:

"We have to ensure that the telescope tracks very accurately on the comet during this half hour exposure. It's hard to imagine anything much more exciting than a comet that makes a quick pass through the solar system. What this camera, with its photographic film, does is take a very wide angle picture of the sky. We have electronic detectors that make excellent images of small spots in the sky but when you want to study something that's very large, such as the comet tail, then photography is still really the best way to do it."

Narrator:

Making several half hour exposures a night, Cruikshank charts the changes in the comet's tail, which stretches 16 million kilometers from the core—the equivalent of a toy marble leaving a 16 kilometer trail. At two of Mauna Kea's telescopes, observations continue 24 hours a day. At NASA's infrared facility, astronomers can survey data from wavelengths unseen by the human eye. In the infrared, it's possible to tell the temperatures of distant objects and to identify their composition. Aimed at Halley, this telescope's data suggest that the comet is made of many things which make up our own atmosphere, including water, methane, carbon, and oxygen.

Persistent analysis from earth-bound telescopes has given scientists a great deal of information about what they call the "cosmic refrigerator." To confirm their thesis, astronomers have taken their vision to space. Two Japanese spacecraft took pictures of the glowing hydrogen atoms surrounding the comet and measured solar winds. Both traveled to within about 140,000 kilometers of the core. Russia then sent two spacecraft much closer, to within almost 8,000 kilometers of Halley. Both were damaged by clouds of dust smashing into them at 240,000 kilometers an hour. But the outcome was the closest view of the comet ever recorded, confirming what scientists had suspected—that Halley has a solid core, one that is about 14 kilometers across. To the untrained eye, Halley's journey may be rather inconspicuous. But scientists are beginning to see Halley very clearly. The probe Giotto, for instance, reached within almost 560 kilometers of the nucleus, revealing jets of dust bursting from conical vents on the comet's surface. It is certain that we will learn more from this appearance of the comet, than in all previous observations combined.

Dale Cruikshank:

"There's a lot of romance and even drama standing here in the cold looking at the stars. Either through a telescope like I'm doing now or just whenever there are a few extra moments—just looking at the stars field outside the dome. The stars that most people never get to see because they're glued to their TV sets and their nice well-lit rooms and in their well-lit cities are a constant source of beauty. A source of beauty that most of us miss these days. It's a kind of communion with nature. And I think that always helps us understand more about ourselves as well as the world we live in."

3 Fighting Malaria

Narrator:

Against the stunning view of the flamingos on Kenya's Lake Nakuru begins the search for the world's most dangerous animal. Among the country's more famous predators thrives a less conspicuous killer.

The Anopheles mosquito may be tiny but it is deadly. For it's responsible for spreading the killer disease, malaria. The insects on this man's arm have been bred solely for research.

At this institute just outside the Kenyan capital Nairobi, researchers are working hard to learn more about this killer disease.

Dr. Mary Wambui-Ndungu, International Center of Insect Physiology and Ecology (ICIPE):

"Malaria is still the most important parasitic disease in the wild and according to W.H.O. estimates 1983, 40% of the world population are at risk of malaria in one year. That accounts to about three to four hundred million cases. In Africa we lose between one to two million children in one year."

Narrator:

Children are among those most susceptible to malaria, which is why a large proportion of those who die from the disease are less than five years old. However help is on the way, in the form of a flower—pyrethrum, a type of chrysanthemum. Seventy percent of the world's pyrethrum comes from Kenya.

This is ideal pyrethrum country, as the plant grows best on elevated grounds in a semi-arid climate. Once harvested the flowers are sun-dried until their moisture content reduces to about ten percent. The pyrethrum is then used to create an insecticide that has a fast knockdown effect on mosquitoes. Once released, it works in two ways. First it paralyses the insect's nervous system, leaving it completely vulnerable; then it kills the creature almost instantaneously.

The benefits of pyrethrum over a synthetic insecticide are that it's environmentally friendly, and the mosquitoes have no time to build up any resistance to this compound.

This is a small farm in the Molo district of Kenya's Rift Valley. This section is given over to pyrethrum. Throughout the course of the year, this farmer is able to harvest as much as four hundred kilograms of dried flowers from this area.

Once dried, the plant is weighed and graded for pyrethrum content. The flower heads are then transported to large scale processing plants.

Joshua Kiptoon, Pyrethrum Board of Kenya:

"Flowers are grown, flowers are delivered here and once they are received in our factory we process those flowers into saleable by-products. The first process involves the extraction of the actives from the flowers. The second process is really refining those products ready for sale locally and for export. Our major export market includes the U.S., Europe, Asia, South America, and Africa."

Narrator:

The pyrethrum extract is a principal component in a wide range of environmentally-friendly insecticides. As mosquitoes become increasingly tolerant of synthetic defenses and anti-malarial drugs then the need for pyrethrum is sure to increase on a global scale.

Joshua Kiptoon:

"Pyrethrum is one of the most important plants in the world because it's used to kill insects that carry diseases that harm man. It fights his enemies."

Narrator:

Who would have thought that, with all the sophisticated products available today, the best mosquito repellent would come from a chrysanthemum flower—a flower that can improve the lives of millions of people?

4 High Road to Shangri-La

Narrator:

In the 1930s, author James Hilton wrote a novel called "Lost Horizon." It became a best-seller, and added a word to our vocabulary: Shangri-La, a mythic lost paradise of perfect serenity. But this paradise has its roots in reality, here in a far corner of western China—a mysterious land visited by explorer Joseph Rock in the 1920s. Today, a team of explorers has come to retrace Rock's journey.

Peter Klika, Expedition Leader:

"I knew that this was a place that I absolutely had to go, no matter how much energy it took and how long it took me to get there."

Pete Athans, Mountain Climber:

"In addition to having the most beautiful mountains on earth, this is a perfect place for an explorer like me to come."

Narrator:

Throughout history, humans have always searched for paradise on Earth. Few ever find it. But one man did. In 1928, Joseph Rock discovered his very own Shangri-La, the Duron Valley, hidden deep in mountains near the border of China and Tibet.

Joseph Rock Re-enactor:

"I've finally made it—the land of my dreams. Unless I can work in the unexplored regions, I would have no incentive to live."

Narrator:

Rock revealed the secrets of this world in the pages of *National Geographic Magazine*, intriguing more than a million readers with his descriptions of obscure villages hidden amidst mountain peaks. This modern expedition wants to take Rock's journey one step further . . . to explore parts of the mountain range where not even Rock had managed to survey. After five days on the road, they sight the mountains made famous by Rock's photographs. The team has come hundreds of kilometers and is now approaching the Konkaling region deep in the Tibetan borderlands.

Peter Klika:

"It's quite possible that we're the first Westerners to ever travel this road and those peaks are definitely unclimbed."

Narrator:

As Rock traveled this way, he encountered situations far more threatening than a desolate land, for instance, a gang of bandits determined to rob him. Rock commented that:

Joseph Rock Re-enactor:

"We encountered the bandit chief. His entourage was composed of the scum of outlaws, their solemn faces hinting at loot and murder. These outlaws are no respecters of person and would just as likely kill us as they would a sheep or yak."

Narrator:

Even faced with such a crisis, Rock's connections saved him. He sought out the king of Muli himself, a local monarch he befriended and photographed four years earlier. Rock brought his majesty a gift—a copy of *National Geographic Magazine* complete with the king's photo. Pleased with his gift, the king intervened, ordering the bandits not to attack Rock, but to protect him. Hence, they became his bodyguards for the moment. After more than a week, the team reaches its destination, the end of the road to Shangri-La.

Peter Klika:

"This is it. Do you like your view of the mountains?"

Team Member:

"Doesn't get much better."

Peter Klika:

"Yeah, it doesn't get much better."

Narrator:

The team stands in awe of the eternal peaks that frame the scenery, the same mountains that overwhelmed Rock and generations of Buddhists who still worship them as the home of the gods. At a high plateau they make camp in the same place Rock slept. If they can get to the top of the mountain range, they'll be able to view the whole region, a view that Rock himself never had the chance to see.

Pete Athens:

"Without Rock ever having stepped foot into this area and taken such incredible photographs of it, we might not even be here, so this is an amazing privilege."

Bill Crouse, Mountain Climber:

"His base camp, you know, coming to life is fabulous."

Narrator:

Exerting all their strength, the expedition members reach a high mountain ridge. It's then a slow climb to the top, more than 5,700 meters high. The summit is close. But a blizzard of wind-driven snow continues to impede their progress. Finally, the team is forced to submit. They will not get their ultimate view of Shangri-La.

Joseph Rock eventually lost the paradise he had discovered. On his last expedition to the region, Rock's old friend, the King of Muli, said he could no longer protect him. The bandits who once served as his bodyguards told him they'd rob and kill him if he ever returned.

Joseph Rock Re-enactor:

"Knowing their cruelty and determination, we took the hint, and thus the land of the Konkaling outlaws is again closed and their mountains remain guarded as of yore."

Narrator:

Rock stayed on in China for another 20 years—collecting plants, writing stories, and taking photos. In his words and pictures, Rock left an extraordinary legacy, a dramatic portrait of a people, a place, and a time, now largely lost forever.

5 Our Stormy Star

Narrator:

At the center of our solar system, there is a huge hydrogen bomb exploding with mega-ton eruptions every second . . . It's our closest star, the sun.

The sun has burned bright for at least four and a half billion years. Virtually all life on Earth depends on the energy that it yields. Over the years, we have admired it, feared it, and even elevated it to the status of a god.

While it may look like a giant ball of fire, the sun is actually a sphere of super-heated hydrogen and helium gas, powered by a process called nuclear fusion. In a fusion reaction, two atomic nuclei join together, creating a new nucleus, releasing enormous amounts of energy.

The sun is so large it could accommodate more than one million Earths. But in a wider context, the sun is pretty average. Stars that are much larger and smaller are commonplace, even in our own Milky Way galaxy.

While the sun may be ordinary compared to other stars, for life on Earth it's of primary importance. The sun's gravity keeps Earth in a stable orbit, preventing us from heading out into outer space. Its energy circulates within our atmosphere, creating our weather and climate. Its light is absorbed by plants, which, through photosynthesis, manufacture the food and oxygen that all animals need to eat and breathe.

It takes 8 minutes for the light and heat of the sun to be seen and felt here on Earth, about 150 million kilometers away . . . But even from that distance, the sun has dramatic effects on Earth. Take the seasons, for instance. A 23-and-a-half degree tilt in the Earth's axis toward or away from the sun means the difference between steamy summers and freezing winters, so even the slightest change in the sun could inflict great harm on the Earth.

Earth's magnetic fields usually protect us from most of the sun's particles. But they can still have a rather spectacular effect on Earth. When strong solar winds strike our magnetic field, they release particles which crash into the atmosphere over the poles. These particles create magnificent light shows called auroras. Powerful as they are, the sun's nuclear reactions will not go on forever. Approximately five billion years from now, the sun will burn up its fuel source and swell to what's called a red giant. At this point, the sun may destroy the Earth.

But that's a long time away, and the sun continues as a seemingly ever-renewable source of energy to power life on our planet.

6 Lighting the Dark

Narrator:

In the deepest, darkest water of Suruga Bay, just over a hundred kilometers southwest of Tokyo, off the coast of Mount Fuji, scientists encounter a mysterious world that few have seen.

One of the bay's somewhat unusual inhabitants, for instance, is the anglerfish, which can walk across the sand with fins that have "elbows."

These depths would impose huge challenges for human camera crews, so scientists use an ROV—a remotely-operated vehicle—to send pictures of the ocean floor to the surface.

The technology allows us to catch a glimpse of exotic eels . . .

And a giant spider crab—the largest crab in the world, found only in Japan. Up to three meters across, they're also known as the "Dead Man's Crab" because they've been found feeding on the bodies of drowning victims.

This submarine can descend more than two kilometers, charting the sea floor and revealing facets of life never seen before.

These are the first known moving images of the Abyssal Cusk eel, a species of fish that can live deeper in the sea than any other known fish.

Also found here are "Lantern Sharks." the tiniest sharks in existence. They're so small they can fit in the palm of a man's hand.

And finally, in a rarely-seen occurrence, a female Chimera is seen in the process of releasing her eggs.

With advances in technology, scientists are able to shine light on even the most discrete regions of the sea floor—a mysterious and unseen world far beneath the waves.

7 Bionic Mountaineer

Hugh Herr:

"I started climbing when I was, I think, 7 years old. Very quickly I loved the sport. I did everything possible to do some climbing every day. I sometimes think if the accident never occurred, what would have happened to my life? Where would I have gone?"

Narrator:

In 1982, Hugh Herr and a friend set out to climb Mount Washington, in New Hampshire. When they started the hike it was lightly snowing. But the shower turned into a storm. The boys got disoriented and wandered through the storm for three days and nights. Hugh fell three times through the fragile ice into a river. Exposed to the elements, they grew sick and weak. Suffering from frostbite they started to lose sensation in their limbs. Hugh was near death. Eventually, a woman out snow shoeing came across a set of footprints. Within hours, Jeff and Hugh were rescued and taken to safety. Doctors tried to salvage what they could of Hugh's legs, but in the end he lost both his legs below the knee to gangrene. It took many intricate surgeries before he could even walk again. But Hugh still wanted to climb.

Hugh Herr:

"It occurred to me that the legs that were given to me were designed for the horizontal world, for walking. And what I needed to do was to redesign the legs for the vertical world.
So I set out on this mission. I decided that I didn't need a heel for climbing. So I cut off the heel. I decided that, the optimal climbing foot should be very short, should be like a baby's foot in length."

Narrator:

Hugh constructed a number of prosthetic legs. Instead of compromising his ability to climb, Hugh's new legs were in some ways more versatile than before.

Hugh Herr:

"I began actually ascending rock faces that I could not have ascended before the accident with biological legs. Some of my colleagues in the climbing world accused me of cheating, which was music to my ears, because to me that meant that they fully accepted my physical difference."

Narrator:

Hugh discovered a new passion. He earned his PhD in bio-physics and now designs advanced prosthetics at the Massachusetts Institute of Technology. He's now working on getting muscle tissue to survive outside the body, perhaps to power an artificial limb. He's developing ways to allow the brain to manipulate a prosthesis. He's even looking to the animal world for design ideas.

Hugh Herr:

"The problem of developing an artificial leg, it's very difficult. So, we came up with the idea of, well, let's look to nature. One could use the muscle activity at the hip, to control the energetics of the ankle. And this is the example of the camel."

Narrator:

A camel's leg is thin, with the bulk of its muscle on its hip—much like an amputee.

Hugh Herr:

"So instead of putting a motor at the ankle the idea in my head is to build an above-knee prosthesis where the energetics of the hip muscles can be harnessed to power the ankle. And that could be done by a series of springs that not only span a single joint, but span multiple joints, the knee and the ankle."

Narrator:

Hugh's camel leg takes its first steps across a computer screen. The implications of Hugh's ideas are astounding. If his ideas are implemented successfully, they could represent a revolution in the field of prosthetics.

Hugh Herr:

"It works . . . We're at, at the brink of a new age. I can imagine in the coming years a prosthesis that will enable an amputee to run faster than is possible with a biological leg. I could imagine that people with biological legs will choose to get their legs amputated so they can achieve the same performance advantage. I can imagine that."

8 | Monarch Migration

Narrator:

Each year, up to 300 million monarch butterflies travel more than 3,000 kilometers from northern America and Canada to a remote forest two hundred miles west of Mexico City. The annual migration of these butterflies is one of the great spectacles of nature. But these vibrant creatures are as fragile as they are beautiful. Sudden changes in their environment can mean disaster. A January 2002 rainstorm followed with freezing temperatures proved fatal for as many as 250 million monarchs, almost 80 percent of the population in the El Rosario butterfly sanctuary. Their bodies covered the forest floor.

Mike Quinn is a Texas biologist with the organization Monarch Watch. He suspects logging may have contributed to the kill off, by destroying much of what had been secure wintering grounds for the monarchs.

Mike Quinn, Biologist:

"Logging is right up to the edge of the colony and logging opens up the forest and lets in the cold air and freezes penetrate into the forest whereas an intact forest acts as both an umbrella and as a blanket and that will severely protect the monarchs."

Narrator:

In the last few decades, nearly half of the woods the monarchs depend on in this region have been destroyed . . . primarily by illegal logging. The Mexican government, along with the World Wildlife Fund, has launched efforts to preserve what is left . . . offering payments to landowners to persuade them not to cut down trees. The 2002 storm wasn't the first to strike the delicate monarch population, nor will it likely be the last. But for the moment, millions still take flight each year, setting the skies ablaze with their stunning beauty and their inspiring will to survive.

9 The Birthplace of Writing

Narrator:

It is known as the cradle of civilization. Beneath the desert of modern Iraq . . . in the greatest depths of history . . . the civilizations of Mesopotamia developed between the Tigris and Euphrates rivers. Much of what we know of that chapter in the region's history has come from excavations of ruined cities, supplemented by translations of ancient clay tablets.

Archeologists have found traces of early agriculture in the north that date back 9,000 years . . . but recorded history begins further south with a group known as the Sumerians. Around 5000 B.C., people settled into an agricultural lifestyle in the fertile plain fed by the Tigris and Euphrates.

In a land of little rainfall, Mesopotamians built a system of canals to channel the flood waters that flowed for a short duration each year. These irrigation systems ensured rich harvests, and this stability enabled the Mesopotamians to build the world's first cities, such as Ur and Nineveh.

Towns of brick were built with temples at their center. Incorporated into the temple complex were grain stores, a treasury, and sections for priests, officials, entertainers, and craftsmen.

Above it all, rose the ziggurat . . . a holy tower with a spiraling ramp. Over the years, towns evolved into city-states, eventually integrated as an empire.

As society became more complex, people needed tools for recording the trade of animals and food. Using clay tablets, early Mesopotamians developed cuneiform, the first written language, and the first format in which history could be reliably recorded. By carving symbols into the soft clay, they could keep transaction records of commodities like sheep and grain.

The new written code proved versatile and quickly spread to other uses. Sumerian scribes used it to write the first major literary work known to Western civilization . . . the epic of Gilgamesh . . . the story of a king who wanted to live forever.

Perhaps the best known of Mesopotamia's civilizations was Babylon. During the second millennia B.C., it rose from a regional capital to become the center of a kingdom that stretched across southern Iraq and beyond. Its hanging gardens were famous as an ancient wonder, and its king, Hammurabi, left his mark with a remarkable collection of laws. Hammurabi's code defined the constraints of private property, as well as legal decisions for crimes, and family disputes.

Although it was eventually lost to the sands of time, Mesopotamia left a legacy of law, literature, and engineering, for modern civilizations to build on.

10 Sigmund Freud

Narrator:

On May 6th, 1856, Sigmund Freud was born in what is today the Czech Republic. And 150 years later . . . the man known as "the founding father of psychotherapy" is still generating controversy.

As a young child, Sigmund Freud moved with his family to the city of Vienna. He received his medical degree there in 1881, and began studying the human brain. But over time, Freud's interests began to deviate from the work of his contemporaries. He became fascinated by something he couldn't see or touch—the human mind.

In the 1890s, Freud began developing the theories behind the practice he named "psychoanalysis." He believed that all human beings have an unconscious portion of the mind. In the unconscious, according to Freud's thesis, strong sexual and aggressive drives struggle against the mind's attempts to suppress them.

Freud believed that analysis of dreams could give us insights into our mental state, including our deepest desires and fears. The publication of *The Interpretation of Dreams*, based on Freud's analysis of his own dreams and those of his research participants, made psychology one of the most controversial sciences of the new century.

Not everyone approved of Freud's ideas. In 1938, when Freud was 81, the Nazis annexed Austria. They had already burned his books in Germany. Freud fled to England that same year, and died the next autumn, on September 23rd, 1939.

Recent statistics suggest fewer than 5,000 patients in the U.S. are treated with Freud's method of psychoanalysis, a type of therapy where patients explore their unconscious over the course of five to six years. His methods as a doctor may be in decline, but as a theorist, Sigmund Freud had a major influence on how people think about the human mind.

11 Cultural Crossroads

Narrator:

Spain. Lying at the crossroads between Europe and Africa, its history has been shaped by both continents. This combination of cultures can still be seen in many facets of Spanish life.

Madrid is Europe's highest capital, and home to the royal palace, built on the site of a ninth-century Moorish fortress. Its gardens are known as the "Field of the Moor," invoking the history of the place where Muslim forces camped in the 12th century, during an attempt to recapture Madrid from the Christians.

Northeast of Madrid is Barcelona, the second largest city in Spain. Here, visitors are surrounded by the work of artists like Miró, Picasso, and Gaudí. Antoni Gaudí's buildings can be seen throughout the city. His last and most important commission, Sagrada Familia, is said to unify Modernist, Gothic, and Eastern architectural elements. The massive church has been under construction since 1882.

One of the best ways to get a sense of Spain is in its restaurants. Here folks gather to talk and enjoy small traditional appetizers called "tapas."

In some restaurants you may be able to accompany your meal with a performance of flamenco. Composed of three disciplines—voice, guitar, and dance—it originates in Andalucía, a region in southern Spain.

In flamenco, one can see and hear Arab, Jewish, Christian, and Gitano (or Gypsy) musical traditions, blended together to produce this world renowned sound. Experts believe flamenco began between the 9th and 14th century when gypsies arrived from north India, via Egypt, and Eastern Europe and fused their music with immigrants from North Africa.

In addition to influencing its music, the North African Moorish presence in Spain can be seen incorporated in many of its most spectacular buildings. In Granada, the Alhambra, derived from the Arabic word for "red," is a palace and fortress built by Moorish rulers of the past.

Similarly, once a Roman city, Córdoba was captured in A.D. 711 by a Muslim army, and became subordinate to the rule of the Umayyad Moors. The Great Mosque, since converted to a Catholic cathedral, once stood as the second largest mosque in the world.

Wherever your travels may take you in Spain, most likely at every turn, you'll encounter that Spanish spirit, a unique mix of ideologies, cultures, and peoples, located at the crossroads of continents.

12 The Art Smuggler

Narrator:
In the world of art and antiquities, the rarer a piece, the higher its value in the eyes of art collectors around the world. Michel Van Rijn has smuggled art and antiquities in the past. He does not deny that he has bent the rules. By his own admission, he's had a very colorful past.

Michel van Rijn, Art Theft Consultant:
"I smuggled from Libya. I stole at the time from Qaddafi."

Narrator:
As Van Rijn found, the art world has plenty of opportunity for crime and profit. Richard Ellis is the former head of the U.K. police force's art squad.

Richard Ellis, Art Theft Consultant:
"It's estimated somewhere between three and six billion pounds a year is what is represented in stolen art, antiques, and cultural property."

Narrator:
And when Van Rijn decided to switch sides, he called Ellis.

Michel van Rijn:
"We met because he was chasing me for ten years all over the world. So one day, I was in the Dorchester Hotel . . . and I called him, we had never spoken. And I said, well, you're very welcome for a drink, you know. Handcuffs are optional. What do you think? He said, well, that might be difficult if we have a drink together. So let's . . . so we met in the bar."

Narrator:
And so they negotiated a partnership. Michel Van Rijn now works as a consultant, helping the police to expose the world's art crimes. Recently, he participated in the recovery of this priceless Mayan headdress. Despite these recoveries, experts suspect many treasures still slip through borders undetected.

Richard Ellis:
"You'll find whole container loads of antiquities . . . the hazards should we say of trafficking in antiquities are pretty low."

Michel van Rijn:
"You know, things which are stolen are found fresh in the ground in Iraq, Iran and Pakistan, Afghanistan."

Narrator:
Once in transit, antiquities can be sold anywhere, but Ellis says the primary destinations are New York and London, where art collectors often convene. Moving stolen artifacts is only part of the operation. The object needs to be given the illusion of legal status. It has to be laundered. One way is to create fake paper trails documenting its history, or provenance.

Richard Ellis:
"Provenance of an object is literally its history, who made it, when it was made, where it was made, who owned it . . . "

Narrator:
Another way is to misuse legitimate tools. The art loss register is a database of known stolen art. If an art piece is obscure, and only the smuggler knows it exists, the database can be used to hide the object's tracks. As Van Rijn explains, a gallery owner can send a photo of the object to the register. He may then receive a valid letter saying it doesn't match the archives.

Michel van Rijn:
"From that moment on, you can turn around as a dealer, knowing you have a stolen object. You have laundered it and you can sell it to any museum in the world, or you can sell it to any collector, or via any auction in the world."

Narrator:
Furthermore, while some collectors justify their illegal transactions saying they are saving endangered antiquities, frequently the opposite is true. These pictures are taken from one of Richard Ellis' investigations in Egypt. Hieroglyphs that once decorated the tomb of Hatepka were sold on the foreign market. Today, the tomb walls have been stripped bare.

Richard Ellis:
"The value of the object placed on it by the marketplace can be vastly different to that placed on it by the archeologist and science. And when an object is illegally excavated, it loses its context."

Narrator:
The struggle to catch smugglers may be difficult, but justice does sometimes prevail. In 2006, Italian authorities were able to reclaim a set of ancient Greek vessels that had been looted decades earlier. The vessels had been on display at New York's Metropolitan Museum since 1972. After investigations revealed a faked provenance for the items, the museum agreed to return the artifacts to Italy. Examples like this give hope that something can be done to stem the trade. But the challenges facing investigators are considerable.

Richard Ellis:
"There isn't a country in the world that doesn't suffer from cultural property theft. Not one."

Photo Credits

1 Michael Nichols/NGIC, 3 Joe Scherschel/NGIC, 4 (t to b) Mark Thiessen/NGIC, Robert Clark/NGIC, Pascal Martinez/NGIC, 5 (t, l) Sarah Leen/NGIC, (c) Kenneth Garrett/National Geographic Stock, (t, r) Joe McNally/NGIC, (b) Fritz Hoffmann/NGIC, 6, 7 (t, l to r) Heather Perry/NGIC, Mitsuhiko Imamori/Minden Pictures/ Tyrone Turner/NGIC, Maggie Steber/NGIC, Victor R. Boswell Jr./NGIC, James Snyder/National Geographic My Shot/ NGIC, 6, 7 (b, l to r) Robert Clark/NGIC, David Evans/NGIC, Kenneth Garrett/National Geographic Stock, Tyrone Turner/ NGIC, Mark Thiessen/NGIC, Jim Richardson/NGIC, Michael S. Yamashita/NGIC, 6 (t to b) Joe Petersburger/NGIC, Robert Clark/ NGIC, Jeremiah Cunningham/NGIC, 7 (t to b) Fritz Hoffmann/ NGIC, Charles O'Rear/NGIC, 8 (l) Steve McCurry/NGIC, (r) Richard Nowitz/NGIC, (b) Wes C. Skiles/NGIC, 9 Steve McCurry/ NGIC, 10, 11, 12 (t, l) Robert Clark/NGIC, 12 (t, r) Jon Foster/ NGIC, 13 (t to b) Robert Clark/NGIC, 16 Simon Norfolk/NGIC, 17–18 Robert Clark/NGIC, 19 (b) Steve McCurry/NGIC, 20 (t) Robert Clark/NGIC, 22 Jeremiah Cunningham/NGIC, 23 (t) Nicholas Metiver Gallery, Toranto/NGIC, (b) Joe Petersburger/ NGIC, 24 Kris Leboutillier/NGIC, 26 (t) NASA Images, (b, l to r) SSPL/Getty Images, Joe McNally/NGIC, Steven Wynn/ iStockphoto, 27 Jim Richardson/NGIC, 28 (t, l) Roger Ressmeyer/ NGIC, (t, r) NASA, ESA, and M. Livio and the Hubble 20th Anniversary Team (STSCI), 29 (inset) Pascal Martinez/NGIC, 31 NASA, ESA, and M. Livio and the Hubble 20th Anniversary Team (STSCI), 32 NASA Images, 34 Joe McNally/NGIC, 35 NASA/ESA/NGIC, 36 (t) NASA/JPL-Caltech, (b) Stephen St. John/NGIC, 38 Roger Ressmeyer/NGIC, 39 NASA Images, 40 HultonArchive/iStockphoto, 41 Tino Soriano/NGIC, 42–44 Robert Clark/NGIC, 49 Martin Oeggerli/NGIC, 50 David McLain/NGIC, 52 David McLain/NGIC, 55 David McLain/NGIC, 56 (t) NGIC, 57 Kenneth Garrett/NGIC, 58, 59 (b/g) Kenneth Garrett/National Geographic Stock, 59 (t, l) Kenneth Garrett/National Geographic Stock, (t, r) Kenneth Garrett/NGIC, 60, 61 (t, l to r) Heather Perry/NGIC, Jim Richardson/NGIC, Jim Richardson/NGIC, Jim Richardson/NGIC, Karen Kasmauski/NGIC, Elke Dennis/ Shutterstock, Joe McNally/NGIC, Japanese_photo/iStockphoto, 60 (c) John Stanmeyer LLC/NGIC, (b) Kevin Cole/Flickr, 63 Bruno Barbey/Magnum/NGIC, 64 (t) Michael S. Yamashita/ NGIC, (b), 65 Jodi Cobb/NGIC, 66 Michael S. Yamashita/NGIC, 67 Jodi Cobb/NGIC, 69 Michael S. Yamashita/NGIC, 70 Melissa Farlow/NGIC, 71 (t and b, r) Dr. Joseph F. Rock/NGIC, 72 Fritz Hoffmann/NGIC, 73 George Steinmetz/NGIC, 74 (t, l and r) Michael S. Yamashita/NGIC, 74 (b), 76 Fritz Hoffmann/NGIC, 77 Pascal Maitre/NGIC, 78 Dr. Joseph F. Rock/NGIC, 79 Michael Melford/NGIC, 81–85 Tyrone Turner/NGIC, 86 Joel Sartore/ NGIC, 88–99 Michael Melford/NGIC, 90 Joe McNally/NGIC, 92 Michael Melford/NGIC, 93 Sarah Leen/NGIC, 95 Indian State Railways/NGIC, 97 Joe McNally/NGIC, 98 James Snyder/ National Geographic My Shot/NGIC, 99–104 Joe McNally/NGIC, 105 (t) Ira Block/NGIC, 105 (b) Westinghouse Electric Corp/ NGIC, 106–109 (all) Joe McNally/NGIC, 110 (t) Emory Kristof/ NGIC, 111 James Balog/NGIC, 112, 113 (b/g) Michael Melford/ NGIC, 112(c, r) Joel Sartore/NGIC, 113 (l) Michael Melford/ NGIC, (r) James Balog/NGIC, 114–115 (t, l to r) Michael Melford/ NGIC, Michael S. Yamashita/NGIC, Robert Clark/NGIC, Stephen Alvarez/NGIC, Jim Richardson/NGIC, 114 (b) Robert Clark/ NGIC, 115 (c, b) Joel Sartore/NGIC, 119 Mark Thiessen/NGIC, 120 Frans Lanting/NGIC, 121, 122 Cary Wolinsky/NGIC, 124 Ottomano Vito/NGIC, 126, 127 Cary Wolinsky/NGIC, 129–134 (all) Mark Thiessen/NGIC, 135 Cary Wolinsky/NGIC, 136 Jerod Harris/Wireimage/Getty Images, 137 Michael Nichols/NGIC, 138 Bobby Haas/NGIC, 139 Peter Essick/NGIC, 140 (t) Mark W. Moffett/NGIC, (b) Peter Essick/NGIC, 141–142 (all) Peter Essick/ NGIC, 144 (l) Mark W. Moffett/NGIC, (r) Peter Essick/NGIC, 145 Martin Vavra/NGIC, 146 Roy Toft/NGIC, 147 Bob Sacha/ NGIC, 148 (t) Mark Moffett/NGIC, 148 (b) Mitsuhiko Imamori/ Minden Pictures/NGIC, 149 Robert Clark/NGIC, 150 Martin Lukasiewicz/National Geographic My Shot/NGIC, 152 Mitsuhiko Imamori/Minden Pictures/NGIC, 154 (l) Joel Sartore/NGIC, 155 The Print Collector/Alamy, 156 Classic Image/Alamy, 157 Rex A. Stucky/NGIC, 158 (t) James L. Amos/NGIC, (b) Dennis Hallinan/Alamy, 159 (t) James L. Amos/NGIC, (b) Bruce Dale/ NGIC, 160 James L. Amos/NGIC, 163 (t) Janaka Dharmasena/ Shutterstock, (b) Drmadra/Shutterstock, 165 Randy Olson/NGIC, 166 Cary Wolinsky/NGIC, 167 Dewitt Jones/NGIC, 168 (t) AJ Wilhelm/NGIC, (b) Richard Nowitz/NGIC, 171 Michael S. Lewis/ NGIC, 172 (t, r) Steve McCurry/NGIC, 173 Randy Olson/NGIC, 174, 175 (b/g) Randy Olson/NGIC, 174 (b) Steve McCurry/NGIC, 176–177 (t, l to r) Robert Clark/NGIC, Randy Olson/NGIC, AJ Wilhelm/NGIC, Michael S. Yamashita/NGIC, Peter Essick/NGIC, 177 (b) Chris Rainer/NGIC, 182 Lynn Johnson/NGIC, 183–186 (all) Peter Essick/NGIC, 189 Paul Nicklen/NGIC, 191 Jose Azel/ NGIC, 192–193 (all) Maggie Steber/NGIC, 194 (t) W.E. Garrett/ NGIC, (b) University of Louisville Photographic Archives, 197 Eric A. Nofzinger/NGIC, 198 Anthony Baggett/iStockphoto, 199 Joe Scherschel/NGIC, 201–205 (all) James L. Stanfield/NGIC, 208 Duncan1890/iStockphoto, 209 Reuters/NGIC, 210 Bruno Barbey/Magnum/NGIC, 212 Victor R. Boswell Jr./NGIC, 213 Tino Soriano/NGIC, 214 (t) Bruno Barbey/Magnum/NGIC, (b) Gervais Courtellemont/NGIC, 216 Joe Scherschel/NGIC, 217 M. Flynn/Alamy, 218 Annie Griffiths/NGIC, 219 Robert Clark/ NGIC, 220 William Albert Allard/NGIC, 221 David Evans/NGIC, 222–224 (all) Charles O'Rear/NGIC, 225 Justin Guariglia/NGIC, 228 Santisiri Thor/NGIC, 230–234 (all) Randy Olson/NGIC, 237 David Edwards/NGIC, 238 O. Louis Mazzatenta/NGIC, 239 Steve McCurry/NGIC, 240, 241 (b/g) Steve McCurry/NGIC, 240 (b, r) Steve McCurry/NGIC, 241 Chris Johns/NGIC, 242–243 (t, l to r) William Albert Allard/NGIC, Randy Olson/NGIC, Randy Olson/ NGIC, Charles O'Rear/NGIC, David Evans/NGIC, Justin Guariglia/ NGIC, 242 (r) Miguel Costa/NGIC, 242 (b, l) Charles O'Rear/ NGIC, 243 (t) Ian Nichols/NGIC, 253 Joel Sartore/NGIC

Illustration Credits

4, 5 (b/g), 17 (t, r), 33, 42 (t), 60 (b, r), 61 (c, b), 80, 87, 112 (t, r), 114 (r, b), 115 (c), 153, 154 (r), 162, 164, 174 (t), 176 (b), 177 (c), 190, 200, 211, 229, 233, 242 (b, r), 243 (b) National Geographic Maps, 7 (3rd from r) Dana Berry/NGIC, 10 (inset) Fernando G. Baptista/ NGIC, 17 (t) Bruce Morser/NGIC, 19 (t, r) Bruce Morser/NGIC, 20 (b, r) Bruce Morser/NGIC, 25 Dana Berry/NGIC, 29 (t) Herbert Zodet/NGIC, 45 Bryan Christie/NGIC, 48 Davis Meltzer/NGIC, 51 (t) Ned M. Seidler/NGIC, 51 (b, r) NGM Art/NGIC, 58 (b) Christopher Klein/NGIC, 59 (b) H. Tom Hall/NGIC, 94 SOHO/EIT/NGIC, 96 Christos Magganas/NGIC, 102 Moonrunner Design Ltd/NGIC, 123 Jon Foster/NGIC, 128 Bryan Christie Design, 175 David Blossom/ NGIC, 181 Anne Keiser/NGIC

Text Credits

11–13 Adapted from "Spirits in the Sand," by Stephen S. Hall: NGM March 2010, 18–20 Adapted from "Diving Angkor," by Richard Stone: NGM July 2009, 27–29 Adapted from "Cosmic Vision," by Timothy Ferris: NGM July 2009, 34–36 Adapted from "Worlds Apart," by Timothy Ferris: NGM Dec 2009, 43–45 Adapted from "Mending Broken Hearts," by Jennifer Kahn: NGM Feb 2007, 50–52 Adapted from "Misery for All Seasons," by Judith Newman: NGM May 2006, 65–67 Adapted from "Vanishing Venice," by Cathy Newman: NGM Aug 2009, 72–74 Adapted from "Searching for Shangri-La," by Mark Jenkins: NGM May 2009, 81–83 Adapted from "It Starts at Home," by Peter Miller: NGM March 2009, 88–90 Adapted from "Plugging into the Sun," by George Johnson: NGM Sep 2009, 97–99, 104–106 Adapted from "The Power of Light," by Joel Achenbach: NGM Oct 2001, 121–124 Adapted from "The Downside of Upright," by Jennifer Ackerman: NGM Jul 2006, 129–132 Adapted from "bi-on-ics," by Josh Fischman: NGM Jan 2010, 139–142 Adapted from "The Genius of Swarms," by Peter Miller: NGM Jul 2007, 147–150 Adapted from "Edward O. Wilson: From Ants, Onward," Interview by Tim Appenzeller: NGM Apr 2006, 157–160 Adapted from "A Man For All Ages," by Kenneth MacLeish: NGM Sept 1977, 165–168 Adapted from "The Power of Writing," by Joel L. Swerdlow: NGM Aug 1999, 183–186 Adapted from "The Pollution Within," by David Ewing Duncan: NGM Oct 2006, 191–194 Adapted from "The Secrets of Sleep," by D. T. Max: NGM May 2010, 201–205 Adapted from "The World of Suleyman the Magnificent," by Merle Severy: NGM Nov 1987, 210–214 Adapted from "When the Moors Ruled Spain," by Thomas J. Abercrombie: NGM Jul 1988, 221–225 Adapted from "The Power of Money," by Peter T. White: NGM Jan 1993, 230–234 Adapted from "The Real Price of Gold," by Brook Larmer: NGM Jan 2009

National Geographic Image Collection = NGIC
National Geographic Magazine = NGM